THE RIDDLE OF BIRDHURST RISE

The Croydon Poisoning Mystery

by
RICHARD WHITTINGTON-EGAN

PENGUIN BOOKS

For
Molly Whittington-Egan
wife and helpmate,
every step of the way

PENGUIN BOOKS

Published by the Penguin Group
27 Wrights Lane, London W8 5TZ, England
Viking Penguin Inc., 40 West 23rd Street, New York, New York 10010, USA
Penguin Books Australia Ltd, Ringwood, Victoria, Australia
Penguin Books Canada Ltd, 2801 John Street, Markham, Ontario, Canada L3R 1B4
Penguin Books (NZ) Ltd, 182–190 Wairau Road, Auckland 10, New Zealand

Penguin Books Ltd, Registered Offices: Harmondsworth, Middlesex, England

First published in Great Britain by Harrap 1975
Published in Penguin Books 1988
10 9 8 7 6 5 4 3 2 1

Made and printed in Great Britain by
Richard Clay Ltd,
Bungay, Suffolk

ACKNOWLEDGMENTS

First of all I owe a debt of gratitude to Mr Thomas Sidney, who helped to clear up many points which would otherwise have remained obscure, and who has contributed a personal note.

I am also deeply grateful to the late Dr John Archibald Binning, who decided to trust me.

To those who played active parts in the case, Mrs Kathleen Noakes; the late Dr Robert Graham Elwell; the late Sir William Bentley Purchase and Mr John Henry Baker, I am thankful for the opportunities they gave me to discuss the affair with them.

I wish to acknowledge, too, the assistance given to me by the coroner's widow, the late Mrs Hilda Jackson; Mr William Arthur Fearnley-Whittingstall's widow, Mrs Margaret Nancy Fearnley-Whittingstall, and his brother, Mr Robert Fearnley-Whittingstall; the late Divisional Detective-Inspector Frederick Hedges' daughter, Miss Muriel Hedges; Mrs Lilian Smith; Mr Douglas Cator; Miss Beatrice Bainbridge; Mr Eric S. Rose, M.P.S.; Mrs Clifford N. Hunt; Mr James E. Shakespeare and Mr Douglas James Shakespeare.

Without the generous help of Mr Stanley G. Pryor, I should have found myself in considerable difficulties.

I would like to express my thanks to Beaverbrook Newspapers, for kind permission to quote from Hannen Swaffer's article in the *Daily Express*, and Edgar Wallace's article in the *Sunday Express*.

I am grateful, too, to *The Times*, the *Daily Telegraph*, the *Daily Mail*, the *Evening News* and the *Croydon Advertiser*.

The Law Society gave me a great deal of willing assistance.

I am indebted to the late Professor Francis E. Camps and to Professor Keith Simpson for medical advice, and to Mr H. Montgomery Hyde and Mr Edgar Lustgarten.

I am particularly happy to acknowledge my gratitude to Grace Duff's son, Mr Alastair Duff, and to her daughter, Miss Grace Mary Duff, both of whom treated me with a courtesy and kindness which, in the circumstances, I had small right to expect, and in deference to their wishes I have suppressed the name of the town in which their mother spent the last years of her life. I was pleased to be able to extend to Miss Duff an invitation to write her own afterword to this book, and am even more pleased that she accepted that invitation.

I realize, only too well, that what I have found it necessary to write about the newly-dead may seem cruel to the living. It is not my intention or desire to hurt anyone. The simple truth is that the Croydon murders occupy a very important place in criminological history. So important that they were bound to be written about. So important that, justifiably *sub specie aeternitatis*, their reporting had to transcend individual considerations.

Finally, I thank Mr Jonathan Goodman who made himself unfailingly available whenever his services were most needed, and Mr Joseph Hatchell Hogarth Gaute, whose continual interest and many acts of kindness contributed more than any other single factor to making this book possible.

RICHARD WHITTINGTON-EGAN

CONTENTS

ILLUSTRATIONS

THE RIDDLE OF BIRDHURST RISE
Prologue

Birdhurst Rise is a straggling crescent of haphazardly assorted
Victorian houses, which curves, gracefully bizarre as its name,
between the dagger thrust of Croham and the slender rapier
length of Coombe Roads, South Croydon. It is well styled. For,
from its southern end, it rises like a flock of motley-architected
birds, and then, seeming to exhaust itself, gently descends to
peter out sparsely into the flatlands of its northern extremity.

About half-way along, close to the pinnacle of this upward-
soaring flight of stoutly-built and once-desirable residences, is
Number 29 — tall, gabled, and of naked, liver-coloured brick.To-
day, the house is fragmented into a clustered rookery of ten
flatlets, but here, in the late twenties, lived only two people — 68-
year-old Mrs Violet Emilia Sidney, comfortably situated widow
of a successful barrister, and her 40-year-old, unmarried
daughter, Vera.

A few minutes' walk away, and running approximately parallel to Birdhurst Rise, is South Park Hill Road. There, at number
6, christened in a moment of unfortunate aberration Pauliva,
lived Mrs Sidney's 38-year-old son, Thomas, his young American
wife, Margaret, and their two children, Cedric, aged four, and
Virginia, aged two. He, too, was quite comfortably off, earning
an adequate living as a professional entertainer, playing the piano,
singing, reciting monologues, and performing character sketches
at smokers, masonics and private concerts.

Five doors up South Park Hill Road, at Hurst View, number
16, lived old Mrs Sidney's married daughter, Grace. She was
forty-one and her husband, Edmund Creighton Duff, nearly
eighteen years her senior. They had three children — John
Edmund Sidney, aged fourteen, Grace Mary, aged twelve, and
a year old baby, Alastair Michael.

The Sidneys and the Duffs. These then were the personalities
about whom, at the beginning of 1928, the shadows of impend-
ing tragedy were massing. Their background, a sedate residen-
tial district whose green-hazed roads yet bore a residual ethos of
the Victorian age when most of the property thereabouts had
been built.

South Croydon was then — and still is — a place of foursquare respectability, laurel-girt carriage-drives and abundant stucco, hiding more, it would seem, than proletarian red bricks. An incongruous setting for one of the most remarkable murder mysteries of the twentieth century, this genteel paradise of the prosperously retired, whose rare excitements amounted to little more spectacular than the perennial church bazaar or sale of work, the mild rivalry of golf matches and games of bridge, the occasional expedition out to afternoon tea.

Soon all that was to be altered. The quiet surface of the surburban backwater was to be shattered. It would never be quite the same again. Within the eleven months compassed between April 1928 and March 1929, three members of that close and apparently happy little family group would be dead, poisoned with arsenic. There was to be no hint of motive: no clue as to the killer. Of course there were inquests, and there was gossip, discreet and muted. But when the whole thing came to nothing, when the corpses had been neatly tidied away beneath the ground and the juries dismissed, respectable Croydon was glad to put the unseemly episode behind it.

And so the mystery has remained all these years, undiscussed as well as unsolved.

There is something singularly disquieting about the stealthy crimes of the secret poisoner. They do not assault the sensibilities crudely, as the butcheries of a Jack the Ripper; they do not have the traumatic impact of sudden blood-lettings with knife or pistol; but the lethally precise dispensing of slow death to the unsuspecting victim provokes a peculiarly individual *frisson* of horror. It is murder at its meanest, often motivated, conceived and carried out in defiance of the trust that sits about the family hearth. Yet it is also murder at its most fascinating, for the domestic murder by poison frequently brings to public light emotional realities hitherto decently concealed behind the drawing-room charades.

It may be that all murder is intrinsically sordid, but there is another point of view. In the chronicling of a crime one is, after all, recording a kind of history, perpetuating a species of historical material only recently rescued by the sociologist from the neglect of the professional historians. For them, history is a matter of politics, of the affairs of kings and queens and windy statesmen. Such sociological data as recorded by conventional history are of a narrow relevance, dealing as they do with the highly specialised circumstances cocooning the lives of eminent and, *ipso facto*, untypically situated personages.

On the other hand, certain crimes uniquely mirror the age, atmosphere and wider social climate of their commission. In the bloody annals of the deeds of Burke and Hare, for instance, is embalmed a significant slice of the early history of anatomy. In the visceral sequence of the Ripper slayings is reflected not only the gas-lit London of the eighties, but the very reek of those mean East End streets which were the hypocritically masked reverse of the glittering West End London of the old Queen's reign. In the Crippen case vibrates the authentic pioneering excitement of the new era that was to catch its first murderer by wireless. And John Reginald Halliday Christie's essays into mass murder epitomise all the unrest, sick-mindedness and neurotic turpitude of a morally out-at-elbows society whose values had been blighted by the brutalising legacy of the Second World War.

The Croydon affair is surely cast in the major tradition of such classic cases. Certainly it fulfils the primary condition of supplying a distinct and recognisable aspect of a vanished phase of social climate. The atmosphere that it evokes is one of solid bourgeois crime: the assassin's hand gloved in good quality kid. It is a mystery flavoured with an Edwardian essence that Sherlock Holmes and the readers of the old *Strand Magazine* would have found exactly to their tastes. Its archetypal milieu a London suburb at the tail-end of its respectable heyday, Hurst View securely takes its place beside Pondicherry Lodge, and in the geography of the imagination Birdhurst Rise is forever linked with those other leafy suburban roads where Holmes and Watson forayed in pursuit of their prey. Indeed, Croydon *did* figure in the Baker Street saga, as readers of the curious adventure of *The Cardboard Box* will recollect. The mysterious death of Major Edmund Creighton Duff, retired British Resident in Northern Nigeria, and the sequel of two further inexplicable deaths, provides a most absorbing and provocative problem which fits precisely in the Holmesian genre.

When I first determined to reinvestigate the circumstances surrounding the deaths of the three victims of the Croydon poisoner, I realised that the great difference between undertaking a reassessment of this enigma, as compared with such a case as, say, the Bravo poisoning mystery, which was enacted only a few miles away at Balham in 1876, lay in the fact that at the time when I began my inquiries many of the persons who had been actually concerned in the Croydon affair were still alive. That meant that I was able to put those people in the witness-box for a second time as it were, and submit them to a direct personal cross-examination. Thus, not only was it possible for me to meet Mrs Grace Duff, Mr Thomas Sidney, Mrs Kathleen Noakes, Dr Elwell and Dr Binning, all of whom were chief protagonists, but there was also a sufficient number of old Croydon residents surviving, friends and neighbours of the Sidney and Duff families, from whom I was able to gather a body of day-to-day details regarding the lives and personalities of those principally involved.

The reconstruction of the events of the twenty-six sittings of the three inquests had to be done slowly, with the aid of mountains of flaking papers, but, as month succeeded month, the drama of those inquests came vividly to life. I grew to know the finically precise tones of the coroner, Dr Jackson, and the rotund oratory of counsel, Mr Fearnley-Whittingstall, as he pinned a faltering witness down on some point that told in favour of his clients, Thomas Sidney and Grace Duff, or tried to shake the uncompromising medical evidence of Sir Bernard Spilsbury. I became familiar, too, with the hesitations of Inspector Hedges, the apprehensive stammerings of Mrs Noakes and other timid servants, and the blustering outbursts of indignation which rose every so often from poor, slightly bewildered Tom Sidney.

But it was not, I felt, enough merely to pore, however diligently, over a mass of documents nearly half-a-century old. From those I could learn no more than was known when, at the last of the three inquests, the coroner accepted and recorded a verdict 'of wilful murder by some person or persons unknown'. If I wanted to discover by whose hand were administered those fatal doses of arsenic for three, I would have to do some practical research. I would need to lift and poke and peer, rummage in dusty corners, draw up a few suburban blinds, let light into musty places where secrets might lie hidden. And that is what I did. What I found, and how I found it, forms the third part of this book.

It might seem that a murder hunt at close on fifty years' remove must have only the most tenuous chance of uncovering anything in the nature of fresh evidence, but I have been able to unearth facts which, to my mind, point in a very decisive direction. Perhaps most important of all, I was able to persuade Dr Binning, the doctor who was called in to all three victims, and saw each of them die, to break the silence of more than a quarter of a century. He has contributed an invaluable personal report. In it he has some startling things to say: things which throw a novel and extremely significant light upon the mystery and, incidentally, provide strong confirmation of certain conclusions which I myself had reached by independent analysis.

Mr Thomas Sidney, too, proved unexpectedly frank and co-operative, and the revelations which he made to me buttressed the edifice of suspicion whose first footings I had already dug.

The plan which I have adopted in the arrangement of this book is simple.

I begin, in Part One, as a storyteller, recounting in detail the exact circumstances of the three deaths by arsenic.

The second part concerns itself with the proceedings at the three inquests, and here, acting as court reporter, I record their unsuccessful attempt to explicate how the bodies of Edmund Duff, and Vera and Violet Emilia Sidney, came to be permeated with arsenic. The reader may feel a shade daunted by the three chapters in which the inquests are dealt with. They are long. So were the three inquests — 26 sittings, covering five months, in which more than 150,000 words of evidence were recorded. But all that ever came out in public, came out at those inquests. There were never any further proceedings at a magistrate's court. There was no trial. So, it is essential to go carefully over the ground and take stock of the vital evidence which they elicited.

When the reader has completed these first two parts, he will be in possession of all the facts that were known on that August day in 1929 when the case was officially closed.

Part Three begins where the inquests ended. After a backward look at the painstaking series of investigations carried out by Divisional Detective-Inspector Frederick Hedges, I turn detective myself, retail the course of my own reinvestigation and, from the vantage point of a considerable body of newly acquired information, critically re-examine the entire affair against the factual and psychological background.

Finally, I assume the role of counsel, and present to you, the jury, the argument wherein, as I believe, lies the true answer to the riddle of Birdhurst Rise.

'Sooner or later the whole truth must come out'.

Grace Duff

PART ONE

ARSENIC FOR THREE

THE CRIMES

1

EDMUND'S BEER

I

Edmund Creighton Duff died suddenly and in great pain one April night in 1928. At that time he was fifty-nine years old, a seemingly robust, healthy man, eight years retired from the active out-door life of a British Resident in the civil service of Northern Nigeria. He lived with his wife, Grace, and their three surviving children at Hurst View, a pleasant suburban house which they rented at 16 South Park Hill Road, South Croydon.

The Duffs were not rich. Edmund had a Colonial Office pension of £30 8s. a month, which he supplemented to the extent of a further £182 a year by taking a rather inferior job as a clerk at Spicer Brothers, a City firm of paper manufacturers with offices in New Bridge Street. This, together with small sums which he earned by the writing of occasional articles and stories, based for the most part on his life and experiences in Africa, constituted his entire income, and, even in those days when the pound was worth considerably more in terms of purchasing power than it is now, an income of between £500 and £600 fell inconveniently short of adequacy for a man with Edmund Duff's commitments and social pretensions. Indeed, there were times when he found it hard to preserve those standards which he thought befitting to a gentleman of his position and background, but he nevertheless managed to present to the genteel neighbourhood in which he lived an aspect of, perhaps not prosperous, but at any rate of dignified and comfortable living. There might be dry-rot in the rafters, but at least the stucco of his house was in outward order. The furniture might be shabby, but, as many who knew the Duffs were afterwards to testify, their home was made pleasing by the atmosphere of affectionate contentment which suffused it.

II

On Monday, April 23rd, 1928, Edmund Duff left home for Fordingbridge in Hampshire. He was off to spend a short fishing holiday with an old Colonial Service friend of his, Harold Stanley Whitfield Edwardes, who, since his retirement in 1925, had settled in a delightful villa named Armsley, situated at an isolated spot on the verge of the New Forest, a mile or so beyond the village of Undercastle.

The fishing expedition had been postponed twice previously. The first time because Edmund's 14-year-old son, John, who was to go with him, had trodden on a needle, which had to be cut out of his foot: the second time because John was again indisposed. Finally Edmund decided to go alone.

His wife, Grace, and daughter, Mary, saw him off from South Croydon station. He seemed to be very well indeed that morning — 'In absolutely bounding good health,' was how his wife was subsequently to describe him — and at the station he was particularly jolly, saying, 'I feel like a schoolboy going off on a holiday.'

The first couple of days of that holiday passed happily. An enthusiastic angler, Edmund enjoyed himself thoroughly, sitting quietly beside the Avon, which lapped the lower reaches of the Edwardes' garden, smoking his pipe and waiting for the trout to bite. It was a welcome change from the confining daily routine of a City office and, no doubt, brought back memories of the freer and more spacious life he had known in Africa.

On the evening of Tuesday, April 24th, — his fifty-ninth birthday — Edmund telephoned his wife. He told her that he had been fishing all day and had had a glorious time. The weather had been perfect, hot and sunny, and he was especially jubilant because he had just caught a fine chub. He sounded fit and well and, according to his wife, did not mention his health, but he did say that he thought he would come home on the Thursday. And on Thursday morning Grace received a postcard from him telling her the train that he would be coming by. Once again, nothing was said to indicate that he was in anything but the best of health.

III

His shivering body wrapped in a blanket of self-pity, Edmund Duff sat wretchedly in the train bearing him on the last lap of his journey home from Fordingbridge. He looked at his watch. Just coming up to 6.40 p.m. God! the journey seemed endless. The train had positively crawled these last few miles between Clapham and Croydon. The dreary grey length of East Croydon station slipped away behind the carriage window. Only a few more minutes now . . . The next station would be his.

With an effort he picked up his case, fishing-rod and tackle, braced himself, disciplined his slack body into the rigid mould of the retired military gentleman, which rôle he always affected, and . . . *Major* Edmund Creighton Duff stepped smartly down from the carriage.

Bronzed and rosy-cheeked, he did not look like a sick man. Indeed, his wife's first words of greeting as he marched briskly to where she and baby Alastair were waiting to meet him at the corner of South Park Hill Road, were, 'How awfully well you look.'

'It's not wellness, it's fever,' he replied dolefully, adding that he would not kiss the baby because he thought that he might have something infectious.

A porter had taken his bag, rod and tackle. The back garden of Hurst View ran right down to the far platform of South Croydon station, and Edmund's son, John, was waiting there to help to lift the luggage over when, later, the porter handed it up across the fence. Meanwhile, gratefully unencumbered, Major and Mrs Duff walked with Alastair the few score yards up South Park Hill Road to the front-gate of Hurst View.

It was 6.50 p.m. when they reached the house, and the first thing Edmund did was to go down to the bottom of the garden to retrieve his belongings. But by the time he joined John at the fence his hands were trembling so violently that the boy insisted on taking the luggage from the porter and carrying it up to the house for his father.

Edmund, Grace and the children then went into the drawing-room. Edmund seemed very worried about himself, but Grace was not inclined to take his indisposition particularly seriously. She thought that, like most people who normally enjoy rude good health, he was tending to magnify a minor ailment into a major disorder, but when he said that he thought she ought to call in the doctor, just in case it was something catching, she agreed. So, at about seven o'clock, Grace telephoned their family doctor, Dr Robert Graham Elwell, of Eastmead, 14 Addiscombe Road, East Croydon.

'Edmund has come home and is not feeling well,' she told him, 'and he wants you to come round and see him.'

At ten minutes past seven the maid, Amy Clarke, brought some supper into the drawing-room for Edmund. It was a simple meal — a plate of hot roast chicken, a tureen of potatoes, some cheese and a bottle of beer — and the tray was set down on a small table beside Edmund's armchair. While her husband was having his meal, Grace took the baby up to bed and, shortly afterwards, John and Mary also left the drawing-room. Edmund ate very little, a mouthful or two of chicken and a morsel of potato. He left the cheese untouched, but drank the beer. When Grace came back into the room he told her that he was feeling rather sickly, and said that the journey home seemed to have shaken him up.

Dr Elwell arrived at Hurst View at about eight o'clock. He found Major and Mrs Duff in the drawing-room. Edmund was sitting in an armchair, an unlit pipe in his hand, and he told the doctor that he was feeling rotten. He said that his throat was stiff and dry, that he had a slight headache, and thought that he must be in for a bout of malaria. Elwell took his temperature. It was just over 99° F, and after making a brief examination, in the course of which he discovered nothing abnormal, told him to keep to a light diet, and prescribed aspirin, quinine and bed. He did not seem to think that there was any cause for alarm and left the house at about 8.20 p.m.

After the doctor had gone Edmund and Grace remained chatting together in the drawing-room. Edmund said that he had started to feel off-colour on the Wednesday while he was away, sort of 'all-overish', as though he had something coming on. He had not wanted to be taken ill in someone else's house, and that was why he had returned rather earlier than he had originally planned. As they sat talking about his holiday, he kept mentioning how weird he was feeling. He said that he was aching all over, complained of feeling shivery and added that he felt the same as he did once, many years before, when he was out in India and had had an inoculation against bubonic plague, which had made him very ill.

They went up to bed between ten and eleven o'clock, which was the time for the baby's last feed. As they were going upstairs Edmund suddenly had a very nasty attack.

'Oh my God, I'm dizzy. I feel as sick as a dog,' he said, and Grace was startled to see that his face, which had previously been very red and flushed, had turned a greenish colour. When they reached the landing Edmund hurried into the bathroom, where Grace thought she heard him being sick. He remained in there for quite a while.

Grace fed the baby and was in bed when, some time afterwards, her husband came in to say good-night. He then told her that he was feeling better. Nevertheless, a few minutes later, she got out of bed and took a bottle of quinine tablets to him in his bedroom, which was next-door to hers.

During the night Grace heard Edmund go into the bathroom again and begin retching. Later, about two o'clock in the morning, she heard him walking restlessly about the house and groaning. Once, after he gave an especially loud groan, she got up, lit a candle, and went into his bedroom and asked him if he was feeling very bad.

'Don't disturb me, I'm just trying to get to sleep,' he said irritably, and sent her back to her own room.

IV

About seven o'clock next morning — Friday, April 27th — Grace went downstairs and made a pot of tea. She poured out cups for herself and Mary, and then sent her daughter up with one for Edmund. A minute or two later she heard him being violently sick and rushed into his bedroom to see what was the matter. He told her that he had taken some of the tea, but had brought it up again immediately. He was very distressed and said that he had no idea what could be wrong with him. He had had a 'hell of a night,' wandering up and down, and not knowing what he was doing.

'My throat is simply awful,' he said. 'I must have something to soothe it.'

Grace went and fetched some cough-mixture from her son, John's, room. But Edmund spat it out as soon as he took it, and was violently sick again.

Around 9.30 a.m. Grace telephoned Dr Elwell and asked him to call.

Edmund continued very ill all that morning, complaining a great deal about his throat, vomiting and plagued by diarrhoea. He remained in bed, but Grace, who had seen him sick and liverish before and knew his tendency to become unduly alarmed about himself, was still not seriously worried, although she was by now pretty sure that he was sickening for something.

By eleven o'clock he seemed to have grown much worse. He had several exceptionally severe spasms of vomiting in rapid succession, and it was then that Grace decided to telephone again to Dr Elwell, who had not yet called.

Elwell himself was out on his rounds, but his partner, Dr John Archibald Binning, came instead. He arrived at Hurst View somewhere about midday. Edmund greeted him quite cheerfully, saying that he was better than he had been. Binning did not think that he looked like a really sick man and, after a cursory examination, decided that he was making more fuss than his condition warranted. He diagnosed an ordinary form of colic, caused by some indiscretion in diet, and suggested to Grace that her husband might have small doses of calomel. The entire visit lasted only five or ten minutes.

As the day wore on, Edmund's condition steadily deteriorated. He perspired profusely, at the same time shivering with cold. The retching and vomiting continued at intervals, as did the diarrhoea, and at about three o'clock he started to complain of pain in his feet, in particular, cramp in his big toe. Later, he complained, too, of cramp in his stomach, saying, 'Oh, these cramps. I can't bear them.' And later still he had severe cramps in his back. He was unable to eat anything, but Grace sent for a bottle of whisky for him, and he had several whisky-and-sodas and a glass of neat whisky, which seemed to relieve him for a short while.

Somewhere between three and five o'clock that afternoon, Dr Elwell looked in. He found Edmund considerably worse than when he had last seen him. He was now rather collapsed and said that he had been 'beastly sick.' He also had a certain amount of abdominal pain. Elwell left, puzzled as to the cause of the persistent vomiting, but still quite optimistic regarding the patient's prospects of recovery.

Dr Binning called for the second time between six and eight o'clock that evening, following a message that had been left at his home by Grace. He saw at once a radical change in Edmund's condition. He was still complaining of abdominal pain, pain in the legs and of feeling cold and shivery. His colour was greyish, and when the doctor examined him, he found his pulse fast, his hands and feet icy cold and his body clammy. Binning now thought he was suffering from some form of acute poisoning, probably ptomaine poisoning. The doctor found marked tenderness in Duff's abdomen and, with the help of Grace, applied some hot turpentine stupes to the stomach to relieve the pain.

While Dr Binning was in the drawing-room and Grace was in the kitchen preparing the baby's feed, they heard a groan, followed by a loud crash. Binning rushed upstairs and found Edmund lying on the floor, where he had had a large motion.

'Don't come in. Your husband has fallen,' he shouted.

But Grace came into the room, and, between them, she and Dr Binning got Edmund back into bed. Duff, who was still quite sensible and able to talk, explained that he had been trying to get to the lavatory when the room seemed to go round and round and he fell. After making him as comfortable as possible, Binning left, returned to his home and telephoned Elwell, telling him that Duff had been very sick, that he did not like the look of things and that he thought that the patient might be dying.

Shortly after eight o'clock Edmund said to Grace, 'I believe my number's up.'

'Nonsense,' she replied.

Some time later he asked for a sleeping-cachet which Elwell had left for him. He had been retching for about twenty minutes, but had not actually been sick. He managed to swallow the cachet without any difficulty, and then said that he would like a cup of tea.

'But you'd better ring the doctor first and ask him if it will be all right for me to have one,' he told Grace.

Binning had scarcely put the receiver down after speaking to Elwell, when his telephone rang. It was Grace Duff. She asked

if she might give her husband a drink of tea. Binning said that
she could.

A couple of minutes later the telephone rang once more. It
was Mrs Duff again. She sounded very agitated and said that
Edmund seemed much worse. While she was making the tea he
had called out to her, and when she went in to him he said,
'Something has gone wrong with my throat. I can't breathe. I
can't speak.'

He never spoke again.

Alarmed, Grace had run downstairs in a panic and telephoned
Dr Binning. He did his best to reassure her, and said that he
would come round at once.

Elwell was already there when, at about 10.30 p.m., Binning
reached Hurst View. He had arrived a few minutes before in
response to a frantic telephone call from Mrs Duff. Elwell had
found the patient collapsed and practically pulseless. The
doctors gave him digitalis and strychnine hypodermically and,
a little later, 1 cc of pituitrin. Gradually Edmund's breathing
grew a little easier, but they both saw that he was not really
reacting.

It was by now just after eleven o'clock, and Grace brought in
some tea. Lying propped up on pillows, hovering between consciousness and unconsciousness, Edmund tried to swallow a
mouthful from the cup which Elwell held to his lips, but it
ran out of his mouth again and dribbled down his chin. He gave
three or four convulsive gasps and fell back on the pillow.

Edmund Duff was dead.

V

The end had come with unexpected suddenness and the two
doctors told the tearful widow that, as they had frankly no idea
from what her husband had died, they could not, in the circumstances, give a death certificate. Dr Elwell added that he was
bound to report the death to the coroner, and said that there
would have to be an inquest.

The following morning — Saturday, April 28th — at Elwell's
request, Grace telephoned Mr Edwardes at Armsley, and asked
him whether anyone else in the house had been taken ill.
No-one had. Elwell then wrote to the Croydon Borough Coroner,
Dr Henry Beecher Jackson, informing him of Duff's death.
He said that in his opinion it was a case of ptomaine poisoning,
but he felt unable to issue a certificate of death without further
examination.

The coroner decided that an inquest was necessary and asked
Dr Robert Matthew Brontë, a well-known pathologist, to make

a post-mortem examination and set aside the requisite organs for bacteriological investigation and chemical analysis. He also went with his officer, Mr Samuel John Clarke, to see Mrs Duff that Saturday. She told him the circumstances of her husband's illness and death and, on the coroner's order, the body was removed to the Croydon Public Mortuary at the Mayday Hospital.

There, on Sunday, April 29th, Dr Brontë carried out his autopsy. He found the wall of Duff's stomach normal and showing no evidence of any irritation such as might be caused by poison. He removed the stomach, liver, spleen, heart, kidneys and portions of the brain, intestines and lungs and placed them in a large stone jar, which he tied up, labelled and sealed. These organs were collected by Clarke on May 3rd and delivered by him to Mr Hugh Charles Herbert Candy, lecturer in chemistry at the London Hospital Medical College, for analysis. Other portions of organs, set aside in a smaller glass jar, were also examined by Dr William McDonald Scott, of the Ministry of Health Pathological Laboratory, at Dudley House, Endell Street, London, W.C.2.

Dr Jackson opened the inquest on Edmund Creighton Duff on Wednesday, May 2nd, 1928. Mrs Grace Duff, who at times appeared much distressed, said that her husband had resided in Northern Nigeria for eighteen years, holding a government post and also acting as a magistrate there. He had had malaria and black-water fever out in Africa, but had recently enjoyed very good health. Generally he was of a cheerful disposition, but on the rare occasions when he felt ill he became gloomy and depressed. She recounted the events of his home-coming from Fordingbridge, and those of that nightmare night of April 26th. When she came to the bit about how he had sent her back to her room, she broke down and sobbed, 'I wish I'd never gone now.'

'You could not have done anything for him, I'm afraid,' the coroner pointed out sympathetically.

'No', replied Grace, 'but I did not realise then how bad he was. Later during the night I heard him wandering about and I didn't like to go in to him.'

Dr Scott reported that no food-poisoning organisms or other abnormal bacteria had been found to account for the death, and, in view of the fact that the other medical investigations had not yet been completed, the coroner adjourned the inquest for a month.

Later on May 2nd, the coroner's officer visited Hurst View again. After searching the house and taking possession of a number of bottles and other articles, he asked Mrs Duff if she had any poisonous substances on the premises. She said that she had, and took him down to the cellar where she pointed to a gallon tin of Noble's liquid weed-killer. The tin was full and there was a cork in it which was difficult to remove, but it was not sealed and, with the aid of a tin funnel, Mr Clarke managed to take a sample. He said afterwards that Mrs Duff was most co-operative and gave him every facility.

The adjourned inquest was resumed on Friday, June 1st. Dr Elwell then gave evidence. He said that he was present at Duff's death, and that acute heart failure preceded it. Mr Candy reported that analysis of the tissues had yielded no toxic substance other than quinine and mercury, and said that there was no evidence that either of these had been taken in anything more than medicinal quantities.

Dr Brontë deposed that the general condition of the body showed no evidence of poisoning and that in his opinion death was due to chronic myocarditis — degeneration of the heart muscle. He thought that the cause of the vomiting was a heart attack, very possibly brought on by sitting fishing in the sun with no head covering. He said that he would expect the symptoms to set in within forty-eight hours, adding that those who have lived in hot countries are most susceptible to sunstroke. The continual vomiting and diarrhoea were, in his view, contributory factors, if they did not actually cause death.

'Are you satisfied that it was a perfectly natural death?' asked the coroner.

'I am, sir,' answered Brontë. 'One can quite exclude the possibility of poisoning.'

After so categorical a statement as that, it is hardly surprising that the jury returned a verdict of 'Death from natural causes.'

Myocarditis. Somebody somewhere gave a sigh of relief, and the family were glad to know at last the answer to a problem which had been vexing them for weeks. Indeed, there had been a positive turmoil of speculation, opinion and controversy among them as to the cause of Edmund's death. One thought that he had been poisoned through eating freshwater fish while he was in Hampshire; another put it down to sunstroke, which had affected him in some unknown way; a third, that he had died from the delayed results of a disease, picked up in the tropics, which the doctors could not diagnose. The one thing that none of them suggested was that he had died of a dose of arsenic slipped into a bottle of beer. Thirteen months were to elapse before that possibility was suggested, and by then two more of them would have joined him in Croydon's Queen's Road Cemetery.

Meanwhile, Edmund Duff lay in peace. It was not until one May morning in 1929 that his rest was disturbed by the spades of the grave-diggers who had orders to exhume his corpse.

2

VERA'S SOUP

I

February 1929 was a bitterly cold month. A perpetual wintry twilight drained the short dull days of any colour. The earth of Edmund Duff's grave was frozen iron-hard. For some weeks his sister-in-law, Vera Sidney, had not been feeling her normal healthy self. Generally something of a Spartan, a believer in the virtues of fresh air and brisk exercise, now, for practically the first time in her life, Vera was suffering from the cold, feeling run-down and vulnerable.

The small diary which for twenty years she had been in the habit of keeping, and whose entries usually related to such matters as her prowess as a golfer and her progress as a bridge-player, began during those first weeks of 1929 to contain jottings of an alien kind:

Tuesday, January 1st — *Very* tired tonight.

Wednesday, January 2nd — Feeling very tired after a very bad night.

Saturday, January 5th — Had a bad night after a dance, so did not have breakfast till 10. Got home 11.20 and slept badly again.

Sunday, January 13th — Feeling extraordinarily tired still. I seem always tired now.

Friday, January 25th — Some people came for bridge and stayed till 6.45. Had a rotten night. Feeling very sick for ages and was very sick at 4.15 a.m.

Monday, February 11th — . . . Feeling rotten. After dinner I was feeling sick again, and then later in the evening, as late as 11.30.

February 11th, 1929. That is a crucial date in the story of Vera Sidney, for that was the day on which someone who had decided to destroy her gave her her first dose of arsenic.

II

Unmarried, forty years of age, Vera lived with her widowed mother, Mrs Violet Emilia Sidney, at number 29 Birdhurst Rise,

South Croydon. The sole other occupant of the large detached
house which they shared was Mrs Kathleen Noakes — otherwise
Kate — their 40-year-old cook-general.

Vera was the only one of Mrs Sidney's three children who
had remained at home all her life, and the pair were devoted to
each other. The two women formed the axis about which the
Sidney family wheel revolved — its other spokes, Vera's elder
sister, Grace Duff, and her younger brother, Tom Sidney. These
two were both married, but had settled, with their respective
families, only a few minutes away from their mother's house,
and were forever in and out of one another's homes. On Sundays
the entire Sidney clan invariably forgathered at old Mrs Sidney's
as a sort of familial ritual, and throughout the week scarcely a day
passed without Grace's calling in at some time or other to see
her mother and sister. As the coroner was later to point out,
'The one outstanding fact with regard to the Sidney family is the
mutual affection of the various members.'

Apart from the rigid doctrine of personal hardiness to which
she subscribed, and a consequent tendency to impatience with
those who fussed about their health, Vera seems to have been a
kindly, generous and affectionate person. A God-fearing woman.
A dutiful daughter. A loving sister. If she had no particularly
close friends outside the family, neither does she appear to have
had any recognisable enemies. Sexually she had never developed.
Such twinges of sensuality as she may have felt were sublimated,
her energies worked healthily off in sport. She was not so
much frigid as disinterested. Active and, on the whole, of a
cheerful temperament, Vera divided her time between keeping
house for her mother, supervising Kate Noakes, playing a
good deal of golf at the nearby Croham Hurst Golf Club, bridge,
and driving about in her $7\frac{1}{2}$ h.p. Citroën motor-car. Financially
well placed, with an adequate inherited income of her own,
she had no need to earn a living — although she was a trained
masseuse and did in fact see occasional patients — and had nothing to worry her. Certainly nothing that would suggest the likelihood of her taking her own life. For the last couple of years she
had, it is true, suffered from slight attacks of rheumatism in her
shoulder, but she took them in her sensible, flat-heeled stride,
dismissing them as firmly as she dismissed the minor ills of
others. But now, in these first weeks of 1929, she began to be
plagued by a persistent malaise which she found impossible to
ignore.

This vague feeling of ill-health, which throughout January
alternately rose to peaks of biliousness and extreme fatigue, and
receded to a plateau of nagging debility and sleeplessness, reached
a climacteric on Sunday, February 10th. That morning Vera
came down to breakfast as usual, but complained of a bad cold

in the head. She stayed in all day, which in itself was unusual for her, and remarked to Kate how bitterly cold it was, advising her to wrap up well before she went out. Grace came in before supper and stayed until about eight o'clock, but Tom Sidney was absent from the family gathering that evening as he himself was not feeling too well, having returned late on the Saturday night from a visit to Scotland, in the throes of an attack of influenza. Vera told Grace that she felt very seedy, and Grace thought that her sister was off-colour as a result of overdoing things.

Next day, however, Vera determined to try to shake off her indisposition.

'I went for a brisk walk up to the woods by the golf club, and then over the tenth hole across the links,' she notes in her diary.

Then, at three o'clock, she visited some friends to play a rubber or two of what proved to be very dull bridge.

'Got home about seven, feeling rotten,' continues the diary. 'After dinner I was feeling sick again, and then later in the evening, as late as 11.30.'

Let us look a little more closely at the events of that Monday evening.

III

Shortly after seven o'clock, Vera and her mother sat down to supper as usual. The meal consisted of soup, fish, fried potatoes, pudding and fruit. The soup, a vegetable one, had been made by Mrs Noakes the previous day. Its ingredients were carrots, turnips, onions, Symington's soup powder and ordinary tap-water. It was Mrs Sidney's practice to order two or three packets of the soup powder at a time. These she would store in her bedroom upstairs, and dole out to Mrs Noakes as she required them.

As a rule, Vera was the only person in the house who took soup. Her mother never touched it, and neither did Mrs Noakes, who generally had just fish and pudding for her evening meal. On this particular night, however, Mrs Noakes happened to fancy a little soup. She had a cold and thought that it might be good for it. So she poured herself out half a breakfast-cupful and, as there was a small quantity left over in the saucepan, she gave it to Bingo, the cat.

Mrs Noakes drank her soup while she was waiting to serve Mrs and Miss Sidney with their fish. She did not notice anything unusual about the flavour, but almost immediately after drinking some of it she 'felt funny inside.' While she was standing at the sink starting to wash up the supper things, she suddenly felt very sick and went upstairs to get herself an orange. On the way she passed Vera, who put her hand to her mouth and said, 'I do feel so sick.'

'So do I, Miss Vera,' replied Mrs Noakes.

And indeed, during the course of the evening they were both violently sick.

Meeting again, later, on the stairs, Mrs Noakes asked Vera, 'I wonder what made you sick like that?' adding, 'I think I can account for myself as I had some rich cake on Sunday.' She was referring to a slice of iced cake which she had had on her afternoon off the previous day, when she went to her friend Mr Ernest Carey's house, at 44 Scarbrook Road, Croydon, where his son was celebrating his twenty-first birthday.

Vera did not say what she thought was the cause of her sickness, but told Mrs Noakes that she had a very nasty flavour in her mouth and seemed to have lost her sense of taste.

At midnight Mrs Noakes was sick again, and Vera continued to vomit at intervals throughout the night.

The next morning Mrs Noakes found that the cat had been sick too, a discovery which, in her queasy condition, promptly induced her to vomit again. Upstairs, Vera was in an extremely low state, and Grace, who looked in to see how she was that Tuesday, February 12th, found her very ill. She said that she had been sick all night and that her eyes could scarcely bear the light.

The diary entry for that day read:

'Did not go out all day. Felt rough. Stayed in bed. Grace came. I made an effort and went down to tea. Felt bad. Grace came in about seven; had a chat. . . . I did not do any eating during the day, only tea and Oxo.'

It was the last time that Vera Sidney was to write in her diary.

On the Wednesday morning (February 13th) Vera seemed better. She got up, came down to breakfast, ate a boiled egg and telephoned her garage in Bensham Lane. The mechanic there told her that the radiator of her car was frozen and after a hot bath, she decided to go along and have a look at it. Before she went, she left a message with Mrs Noakes that if Mrs Duff were to call she was to be told that she would not be long. A few minutes after Vera's departure, Grace telephoned and asked, 'How is the invalid?' When Mrs Noakes told her that Miss Vera had gone out to look after her car, Grace exclaimed, 'However could she do it when she has been so ill all night?'

While she was out Vera called briefly at her brother, Tom's, house. He knew that she had been ill and was surprised to see her. He said that he thought that she must be suffering from gastric 'flu, which was very prevalent at the time.

Mrs Noakes met Vera in the hall on her return just before lunch. She was looking very ill and said, 'I feel so cold I feel that I shall never get warm again.'

That Wednesday there was a guest for lunch at Birdhurst Rise, old Mrs Sidney's sister-in-law, Mrs Gwendoline Greenwell, who was on a short visit to London from her home in Newcastle. She was met at South Croydon station by Grace, who escorted her round to Number 29, where they arrived just before one o'clock, Mrs Greenwell clutching a large, fresh pineapple which she had brought as a gift for her sister-in-law. Grace said afterwards that when she met her, her aunt told her that she had had 'flu and a nasty cough, and had been feeling very poorly. Grace thought she looked rather pale, but not really ill. Because she had to prepare her children's midday meal, Grace was unable to stay to lunch at her mother's, but, before leaving, she invited Auntie Gwen and Vera to come to tea with her at her home later in the afternoon. Then Mrs Noakes sounded the gong, and Mrs Greenwell, Mrs Sidney and Vera left the drawing-room and went into the dining-room.

Lunch was cooked and served by Mrs Noakes — soup, boiled chicken, parsley sauce, Brussels sprouts, boiled potatoes, stewed pears and a baked custard pudding. The soup had been prepared on the Tuesday. It was a thick brown one, made from carrots, turnips, a knuckle of veal — left over from the previous Friday or Saturday — and the customary soup powder. When it was put on the table Vera said, 'Here's this wretched soup that made me ill on Monday,' a remark which drew a rapid silencing frown from her mother. As usual, Mrs Sidney did not have any soup and, after the first few spoonfuls, Mrs Greenwell said that she had had sufficient. Vera, who had already had rather more of it than her aunt, also pushed her plate aside saying, 'You know, Mother, this soup made me sick on Monday.'

'Oh, nonsense, Vera,' snapped Mrs Sidney. 'That couldn't have done you any harm.'

Vera did not reply, but she took no more soup.

After lunch the party went into the drawing-room, but before Mrs Noakes had had time to clear away the lunch things both Vera and Mrs Greenwell were taken ill with vomiting and diarrhoea. Vera went out to the kitchen. She said that she thought their sickness might be due to the old saucepans, and examined the big one in which the soup had been made. She asked Mrs Noakes if it had been clean when she put the soup in, and Mrs Noakes said that it most definitely was.

Later, left alone in the drawing-room with her aunt for a little while, Vera said, 'I hope I haven't given you a germ, Auntie.'

'That's quite impossible,' replied Mrs Greenwell, 'I haven't been in the house long enough.'

Then Vera told her how she, the cook and the cat had all been sick the previous Monday night after taking the soup. 'But I'm quite sure I've not had 'flu,' she added. 'You've been sick, I've been sick and Mrs Noakes has been sick, and we're the only people who've had the soup. Do you think it could be the soup?'

Just then Mrs Greenwell heard Mrs Sidney coming back along the hall and begged Vera not to say anything more about it, as she feared that it might upset her sister-in-law.

Between half-past two and a quarter to three Vera telephoned Grace and explained that she and Auntie Gwen had been sick several times and were both feeling too ill to come round. So, at about three o'clock, Grace went along to her mother's instead. When Mrs Noakes opened the door to her she said, 'Kate, whatever's the matter with the family?' And on being told that both Miss Vera and Mrs Greenwell had been sick, Grace asked, 'What do you think it is?'

'I think it's the veal,' said Mrs Noakes.

Grace found Vera and her aunt sitting in the drawing-room looking cold and miserable. She thought that they must both have bad chills. Mrs Greenwell continued to have bouts of sickness. Around tea-time Tom Sidney's wife, Margaret, arrived at Number 29 and, just after four o'clock, Mrs Greenwell told old Mrs Sidney that she was afraid she would have to go home. Turning to Vera she said, 'The only thing you can do is to have a good dose of castor-oil, and I shall do the same.'

Grace offered to go and fetch some for Vera. She left the drawing-room, dashed up the road to Number 59,[1] and was back in a few minutes with a bottle of castor-oil and a bottle of brandy. Vera took some of the castor-oil in orange juice, but said that it made her feel sick and she thought that she would go up to bed. She was holding her hand in front of her mouth — half in fun and half in earnest. She was obviously feeling very sick, but trying to bear up and treat it as a joke.

'As soon as you lot have gone I'm going to bed,' she said.

Auntie Gwen kissed Vera goodbye, and then, accompanied by Grace, made her way to the station.

Mrs Greenwell was ill in bed at her hotel for six days before she eventually recovered.

Vera was not to be so lucky.

IV

Having seen Auntie Gwen safely off from South Croydon

[1] Grace Duff had left Hurst View after the death of her husband and moved to 59 Birdhurst Rise in August 1928.

station, Grace returned to Birdhurst Rise and telephoned Dr Elwell. He was out, but she left a message asking him to call at Number 29. Then she made her way back to her own home. At this stage Grace was not really anxious about her sister. She thought that Vera was suffering from a bad gastric attack, the worst of which was probably already over, and that the next day would see her more like her old self.

But Thursday, February 14th, was to be cast in an unexpectedly tragic mould, and when, soon after breakfast that morning, Grace saw Vera, she at once realised that her optimism of the afternoon before had been without justification. Vera was in bed, clearly very ill, complaining of 'awful weakness,' and saying that she had no strength in her. Mrs Sidney was very distressed. She said that Dr Elwell had come round at nine o' clock the previous evening, and remained until midnight. He had returned just over an hour later, and Vera was then in such pain that he had given her an injection of morphine. He had not left until half-past two in the morning and Mrs Sidney had been up all night looking after Vera.

Disturbed by this bad news, Grace went off to see if she could get the address of a hospital nurse who could come in and take some of the burden off her mother, but she subsequently ran into Dr Elwell, who told her that he had been in touch with a nurse himself and was actually on his way to fetch her. Dr Elwell seemed very worried over Vera's condition, and Grace thought that she had better go along to see her brother, Tom, and let him know the serious turn that their sister's illness had taken. She told him that Vera was terribly ill, her face so worn with suffering that she had hardly been able to recognise her.

Meanwhile, Dr Elwell was back with his patient. Vera was suffering from very marked collapse. She was a grey colour and her pulse was absent. She had told the doctor that she thought she had a chill, but made no suggestion that her illness might be due to anything that she had eaten. Indeed, the only reference that she made to food was when she said that she had come in from the garage on the Wednesday feeling very bad, and had had some soup, after which she had had to retire, and that she was sick when she got upstairs. Elwell told Mrs Sidney that in his opinion her daughter was very critically ill, but that she had youth on her side.

Dr Elwell remained with Vera practically all that Thursday. He called Dr Binning in for a consultation, and Binning said that he, too, considered Vera to be an acutely sick woman.

Between four and five o'clock in the afternoon, they decided to summon a London specialist, Dr Charles Bolton, an authority on gastro-intestinal disease. After examining the patient, Bolton said that in his view it was a case of gastro-intestinal influenza, aggravated by dilation of the heart, brought on by the violent exercise of turning the starter handle of her car on the Wednesday morning. He confirmed the gravity of Vera's condition.

Grace had looked in to see her sister in the afternoon, shortly before Dr Bolton arrived. Vera was then complaining of pains in her feet. She said that they had gone dead, and she thought that gangrene would set in if they were not bathed in very warm water. The nurse, Miss Mary Keetley, who had arrived at about 11.20 that morning, said she was afraid that the patient was wandering a little.

When Grace came in again during the evening she found Vera only half conscious, in a strange, restless state and in great pain. Dr Elwell, who was by now exceedingly anxious about her, said that sleep was her only hope. Nurse Keetley was going off to bed because she was very tired, having been up with a patient all the previous night, and Elwell said that he would go to fetch another nurse.

Dr Binning, who was also there, thought that Vera was too seriously ill to be left without a professional medical attendant, and said that he would remain with her. Mrs Sidney wanted to stay in the sickroom, but Binning said it would be better if she did not. He did not want anyone there to disturb Vera, who by this time was delirious.

Just before midnight, Elwell came back with a second nurse, Miss Daisy Geer. They went upstairs. Vera had now reached a crisis, and was fighting hard. It was a harrowing scene in that quiet, suburban bedroom, the young woman tossing and turning in a prolonged agony on her stained and rumpled bed. But the end was very near.

At 12.20 a.m. on Friday, February 15th, 1929, Vera Sidney's body arched into a last convulsive jerk. Then, slowly, it subsided. The suffering drained from her features as they relaxed into the bland serenity of death. Dr Binning closed the glazing eyes and gently pulled the sheet over the face.

Mrs Sidney asked Dr Elwell if there would have to be an inquest.

'No,' he told her. 'There is no question about that.'

Why should there be? Neither doctor suspected that it was anything other than death as a result of natural disease.

The death certificate was issued.

On Tuesday, February 19th, Vera was laid to rest in the same cemetery as Edmund.

After the funeral, red-eyed with weeping, old Mrs Sidney sat forlornly alone in the empty house in Birdhurst Rise. Without her dearly-loved Vera the future stretched bleak before her. Staring out at the black trees and dull greens of the stark winter landscape, she wondered how she would endure the loneliness.

Spring would come, and the green wave of summer would flow with its bright froth of flowers into the garden where she and Vera used to sit. But still she would be alone. Waking to solitude. Sitting with solitude. Retiring to bed in solitude.

But it was not going to be like that.

As she sat there, alone in the gathering dusk, she did not know it, but that future amounted to precisely fourteen days.

3

VIOLET'S MEDICINE

I

Old Mrs Sidney uncorked the medicine-bottle, measured out two teaspoonfuls of the dark red fluid into a wine glass of water and swallowed it.

Then she began to pull faces.

At that moment Kate Noakes came into the dining room to lay the table for lunch. She saw her mistress grimacing.

'Whatever's the matter, mum?' she asked.

'It's my medicine. It tasted so nasty and gritty,' replied Mrs Sidney, still twisting her face.

'Did you shake it up?'

'No, I don't think I have been doing so, Kate.'

The two women agreed that the reason why it tasted so disagreeable was probably because it was the last dose at the bottom of the bottle.

It was the last dose all right.

The fatal dose.

The date was Tuesday, March 5th, 1929, the day that Mrs Violet Emilia Sidney was to be reunited with Vera.

II

For nearly three weeks now, Mrs Sidney had been grieving deeply over the tragically sudden death of her favourite child. So terrible had been her anguish that, at first, her son, Tom, had feared that his mother, who had a weak heart and high blood pressure, would not survive the shock. He did not think that she would live more than three days, but that she would succumb to a heart attack or a stroke. His unease was intensified by the fits of giddiness which she had recently developed. Holding her head in her hands, the grief-stricken old lady would ask pathetically over and over again, 'How am I going to go on living?'

Her two surviving children did their best. Every day since Vera's death, and sometimes twice a day, Tom looked in at Number 29 to try to cheer his mother up. And every day, too, Grace called at the house in Birdhurst Rise.

Gradually, Mrs Sidney's will to live reasserted itself. It was not that she missed Vera any the less, but, as time passed and she had no more tears left to weep, she came to accept the bitter truism that life must go on. She began to improve in health. She seemed to recover her spirits, too, and was even talking vaguely of leaving Birdhurst Rise and taking a house by the sea.

On February 25th, Dr Elwell, who had been keeping an eye on her, prescribed Phyllosan tablets, and a tonic called Metatone. He paid a routine visit to his patient on the morning of March 5th. Mrs Sidney then seemed to him to be fairly well — in fact rather better than she had been for some weeks. A cold, which had started a few days after Vera died, had much improved, and she remarked that she was pleased because she had got her sense of taste back.

That morning of March 5th, Mrs Sidney came downstairs at nine o'clock. She made some coffee and boiled an egg for breakfast on the gas-ring in the dining-room. When she had finished her meal, she cleared the table and left the dirty dishes on the butler's tray in the hall outside the dining-room door, for Mrs Noakes to collect. And while Mrs Noakes was washing up the breakfast things, her mistress came into the kitchen and gave her her orders for the day. That would be at about half-past nine.

Mrs Sidney then telephoned orders to several tradespeople — Sainsbury's and Cashman's, the fishmongers — before going upstairs and tidying her bedroom in preparation for Mrs Noakes to turn it out later.

After that, she sat down and wrote a letter to her sister-in-law, Miss Gertrude Amy Stafford Sidney, who lived at St Leonards-on-Sea:[1]

My Dear Amy,

It is very kind of you to ask me to pay you a little visit. I thank you so much for your kind thought — but it is really impossible for me to leave home at present. I have been *very* unwell, and have not been out of the house for three weeks, and could not take the shortest journey now. The doctor tells me to keep very quiet and is giving me a tonic. My cold is better but I feel very weak and even speaking to anyone for a little while brings on neuralgia.

The worst is that my maid, who was to have gone at Xmas, is leaving me in ten days, and I have not found another yet. The pipes have been a great worry, four burst, and there was other trouble, but I hope nothing more will happen, and

[1] Gertrude Amy Stafford Sidney, born 1868, died 1956, spinster, lived at 16 Dane Road, St Leonards-on-Sea.

that the men finished up the repairs this morning.

I am sorry you have had pipe trouble too, and that cook is still unwell, it has been a terrible winter. Thank you for your previous letter and the comfort you tried to give me. My faith in God is there and I know that life is not put out by death, and that the earthly body is only laid aside as an outworn garment, but grief is very selfish and oh, how I miss my darling Vera, and how heart-broken I feel without her. All joy is gone out of life for me.

Thanking you very much for your kind invitation and sympathy.

Yours with love,
Violet E. Sidney

There is a terrible poignancy about that letter — the touching mixture of trivia and tragedy, anguish and acceptance — written as it was by an old and sorrowing woman, towards whom the shadow of death was, even as she sat penning it, rapidly and remorselessly moving.

Between 10.30 and 10.40 a.m. Grace called to see her mother, and stayed talking with her in the dining-room for about twenty minutes. During that time Mrs Noakes heard Mrs Sidney come upstairs. She came into the bedroom where Mrs Noakes was cleaning, opened her chest of drawers and took something out — Mrs Noakes thought that it was her purse or handbag — and then went downstairs again and rejoined Grace in the dining-room. Soon after, Grace left, saying that she would fetch some butter, milk and a reel of cotton back from the shops for her mother, and also promising to call in at the registry office and put Mrs Sidney's name down for someone to take Mrs Noakes' place, as she was leaving service to go and live at her friend, Mr Carey's.

Later that morning Dr Elwell called. He stayed for about five or ten minutes and, after he had gone, a little before one o'clock, Mrs Noakes brought Mrs Sidney's lunch into the dining-room — some chicken, which had been cooked the previous week, brown bread and butter, a pudding of rolled oats with brown sugar and milk, and water to drink.

Mrs Noakes had just finished her own midday meal in the kitchen, when her mistress rang for her to come to the dining-room to clear her lunch dishes away. Mrs Sidney was sitting there eating half an apple, and said, 'I feel so sick, and I can't be sick.'

'Have you eaten that apple too quickly, mum?' asked Kate.

'I don't think so.'

Then Mrs Sidney went into the scullery and fetched an enamel bowl. As she was sitting there with the bowl on her lap trying to vomit, there was a knock at the front-door, and Mrs

Noakes went to open it. It was Grace.

'I suppose Mother is having lunch,' she said.

'She's had lunch,' replied Mrs Noakes.

Grace went into the dining-room. Her mother was sitting all huddled up, her head hanging on one side — 'I thought she was dead. Her face was absolutely deathly white, just as if she were dead. I thought she had had a stroke.'

Mrs Sidney looked up as her daughter came in. 'I think I have had some poison,' she told her.

Grace turned to Mrs Noakes and asked in some alarm, 'What's the matter with Mother?'

'It's that nasty medicine,' said Kate.

'It gave me a nasty turn, but I enjoyed my chicken. I couldn't eat my rolled oats, and now I feel I want to be sick, but I can't be,' explained Mrs Sidney feebly. 'I took the last dose of medicine, and it tasted very strong and had a nasty gritty sediment in it. I wish I'd shaken it.'

'Where is the medicine?' asked Grace.

Mrs Noakes picked the bottle up from the sideboard and handed it to her. Grace took the cork out and smelt it. 'It doesn't smell very nice,' she commented. Then, at her mother's suggestion, she went out to the kitchen and mixed a cupful of hot water and salt. 'Perhaps that will make Mother sick, and then she'll feel better,' she told Mrs Noakes.

Mrs Sidney drank it and it seemed to revive her a little. Mrs Noakes stayed with her mistress while Grace went out into the hall to telephone Dr Elwell.

'I don't want a doctor,' Mrs Sidney called out petulantly.

Dr Elwell was out, so Grace hurried down the road to ask Dr Binning to come round.

Mrs Sidney was sick twice before Binning arrived. As soon as she had got her breath back after vomiting for the first time, she said, 'I believe I've been poisoned, Kate.' And she then had a sudden and exceedingly violent attack of diarrhoea where she sat. Mrs Noakes valiantly coped with the cleaning up of the mess and had just finished when the doctor arrived.

Dr Binning found the patient sitting in a chair in the dining-room. She was in a very collapsed condition, her colour was ashy grey and she looked like a stricken woman. He asked her how she was and she immediately replied that she had been poisoned. She went on to tell him that her last dose of medicine had had a very peculiar taste.

'I had my lunch,' she said. 'The chicken was quite nice and I had a good appetite for it. Then, gradually, I felt ill, and when I was halfway through my pudding I felt so sick that I couldn't eat any more.'

'It must have been something in the medicine,' said Grace.

'I think it must,' Dr Binning agreed.

Grace then helped her mother upstairs and put her to bed, while Kate got hot water bottles for her.

Left alone in the dining-room, Dr Binning took the medicine-bottle from the sideboard, where it was standing beside a wine glass. He noticed a sediment which looked like sago grains clinging to the inside of it. He uncorked it and sniffed it, but did not notice any peculiar smell. On the bottle was a label bearing the name of the chemist who had dispensed it — F.S. Rose, George Street, Croydon. Binning promptly telephoned him and, after ordering another medicine for Mrs Sidney, asked what had been in the one previously supplied. After consulting his books, Rose said that it was Metatone, a patent tonic prescription, that it had been prescribed by Dr Elwell, and that the only poisonous substance in it was strychnine, to the extent of one ninety-sixth part of a grain to the dose, which is less than the ordinary safe minimum dosage. Binning then gave the patient some brandy and water, followed by a dose of bicarbonate and water.

About two o'clock, Tom Sidney arrived at Number 29 on his usual daily visit and was surprised to find Dr Binning there. Binning told him that his mother had been taken suddenly ill and that he was rather worried about her condition. Tom went straight up to his mother's bedroom. Almost the moment she saw him, Mrs Sidney repeated that she had been poisoned, that her medicine had had a nasty flavour, that it had tasted gritty and that it was the last dose in the bottle. Then she began to vomit again. She seemed very cold and shivery and had three or four more attacks of vomiting in rapid succession. She complained, too, of a pain in her stomach and of persistent diarrhoea.

As soon as Tom heard about the medicine he asked, 'Where is the medicine?' adding, 'That must be looked after.'

He subsequently suggested to Dr Binning that someone should take care of the bottle and implied that he wanted the police to have it before anybody else touched it. He later explained that it was in his mind that poison might have got into the medicine accidentally, due to carelessness.

Some time later, about four o'clock, Tom saw the medicine-bottle standing in the middle of the dining-room table. He, too, observed a thick sediment round the inside of it. He did not touch the bottle, but was very surprised to find it left unguarded, as Dr Binning had told him that he had taken charge of it and that its contents would be analysed. Almost immediately, two or three people came into the room and Binning removed the bottle.

When Dr Elwell arrived, Binning showed him the bottle, and

Elwell said that there was nothing in the medicine that would be too strong for Mrs Sidney. Questioned by Tom, Elwell affirmed that there was nothing in it 'sufficient to kill a baby.' And when Mrs Sidney herself told him that she thought she had been poisoned, and that it must have been the medicine, Elwell emphatically repeated that there was nothing strong in the tonic that could possibly have harmed her. Finally reassured, Mrs Sidney then began to wonder if it might have been the chicken, and Dr Binning started to think in terms of ptomaine poisoning from some item of food.

Mrs Sidney seemed somewhat better then. She had two cups of tea and appeared quite perky. Dr Binning left, but Dr Elwell said that he would stay and keep an eye on her, and Grace, who thought the corner was turned, went home to attend to her baby.

Between 4 and 4.30 p.m. Mrs Sidney fainted on the bedpan, and then collapsed completely. Dr Elwell telephoned Grace, who returned at once to Number 29, and a nurse, Maggie Eveline Gillman, and a specialist were summoned.

The specialist, Dr Frederic John Poynton, was unable to reach any definite diagnosis. He thought that it might be either a mineral poison — copper was specifically suggested — or a ptomaine poison that was the cause of the illness. But when, shortly after 6.45 p.m., Poynton had left, the doctors made it clear to Tom and Grace that their mother might die. And, some forty minutes later, at about 7.25 p.m., in the presence of Grace, Tom, and the two doctors, Violet Emilia Sidney did die.

Helped by Tom, Dr Binning collected samples of the remaining portions of the food which the dead woman had had for lunch — half a loaf of bread, two apples, some chicken bones, the remainder of a bottle of milk and a portion of pudding — and placed them, together with the medicine-bottle, in his car.

Mrs Noakes packed a few necessities and went off to stay the night with the Careys.

After a last, sad, lingering look at the still figure on the bed, Tom Sidney extinguished the lights. The bang as he closed the front-door echoed through the now lifeless house in Birdhurst Rise.

III

The circumstances surrounding the death of Violet Emilia Sidney were such that neither Dr Elwell nor Dr Binning felt that it would be possible for them to issue a death certificate, for the very good reason that they had been unable to reach any firm conclusion as to the cause of death. Therefore, in accordance with the law, the Croydon coroner, Dr Henry Beecher Jackson, directed that a post-mortem examination should be made, and, on March 6th, that same Dr Brontë who, eleven months before, had performed the autopsy on Edmund Duff, examined the corpse of his mother-in-law at the Mayday Road Mortuary.

Dr Brontë found that the lining of Mrs Sidney's stomach showed a slight reddening, and that the large intestine displayed signs of irritation, but could discover no gross pathological indications to account for death. He removed certain organs, however, and placed them in jars, one of which was handed over to Dr Herbert William Southgate, the Croydon Borough Pathologist, to be examined for bacteriological evidence of food poisoning. The others were sent to Dr John Henry Ryffel, one of the Home Office analysts, at Guy's Hospital.

That same day — Wednesday, March 6th — Divisional Detective-Inspector Frederick Hedges, the Scotland Yard CID officer in charge of Z Division, Croydon, accompanied by Detective-Inspector Reginald Morrish, and Mr Samuel John Clarke, the Croydon coroner's officer, went with Tom Sidney to 29 Birdhurst Rise.

They searched the house from top to bottom and the coroner's officer took possession of a number of bottles. They left Number 29 at 6 p.m., Tom locking the place up after them, and, at 9.30 p.m. that evening, Hedges, Morrish and Clarke called at number 1 Birdhurst Road, the house of Dr Binning, where the doctor handed over the medicine-bottle, and also another bottle, and a jar containing fluid.

The following morning — March 7th — Hedges, Morrish and Clarke paid a second visit to Number 29. This time they removed the wine glass from the dining-room sideboard.

The inquest on Violet Emilia Sidney opened at Croydon Coroner's Court at 4 p.m. on Friday, March 8th, but after formal evidence of identification had been given it was adjourned until April 4th. No explanation was offered for this unusually long adjournment, nor did the coroner place before the jury any medical evidence concerning the cause of death.

A susurration of excited gossip swept Croydon. It was obvious that something strange was afoot. Rumour, speculation and conjecture wild-fired from lip to eager ear. The whispers intensified into an audible rumble. In the cafés, the shops, the drawing-rooms and the kitchens, tongues rose in a perceptible spate of suspicion. 'Three of them dying like that in a year. Stretching coincidence a bit wasn't it?' To paraphrase Lady Bracknell: To lose a husband is tragic. To lose a sister is sad. To lose a mother is disastrous. To lose all three savours of criminal carelessness. Thus and thus, the tenor of their prejudice and ill-informed *niaiserie.*

The first hint of official confirmation of all this speculative suspicion came in the morning papers of March 11th —.

'Certain investigations are now being made by the police in connection with the death of Mrs Violet Emilia Sidney.'

Under the supervision of Inspector Hedges, those investigations were indeed proceeding apace. On March 9th he and Clarke had been once more to Dr Binning's and collected from him the samples of foodstuffs that he had secured on the evening of Mrs Sidney's death. They had also returned to Number 29 and taken possession of a further selection of bottles, some apples and a package of soup powder.

On the morning of March 10th, Arthur Henry Lane, a jobbing gardener who had worked for both Mrs Sidney and Mrs Grace Duff, handed a large tin of Noble's liquid weed-killer to Detective Constable Carl Louis William Hagen. Lane said that he had had the tin in his possession for about six months. He had received it from Mrs Duff. It had been lying in her garden, and she had told him to take it away in case her children touched it.

On March 11th, Violet Emilia Sidney took her place beside her beloved Vera in grave 35879, Plot A1, in Queen's Road Cemetery.

On March 11th, too, Inspector Hedges visited the George Street premises of Mr Frederick Sandford Rose, pharmacist, and took from him a large 80 oz bottle labelled 'Metatone'. There was only a small quantity of liquid remaining in it when he received it. Hedges handed the bottle and its contents to the coroner's officer.

A week later, on March 18th, the following announcement in the *Daily News* provided something for the gossip-mongers to get their teeth into at last:

THE DEATH OF VIOLET SIDNEY

'Inquest records in the Croydon district were examined by Scotland Yard officers last night, following an adjournment at Croydon Coroner's Court on March 8th.

Divisional Detective-Inspector Hedges, in conjunction with Superintendent Brown and other Scotland Yard officers have for some days past been engaged on inquiries in connection with the deaths of three persons and the utmost secrecy is maintained as to the nature of the inquiries.

Should the inquiries develop on a certain line application may be made to the Home Office for the issue of exhumation orders in two cases of relatives who have died.

Verdicts of 'Death from natural causes' were returned at the inquests in these two cases.

Certain papers will in all probability be sent to the Public Prosecutor for examination.

In the other case the inquest was adjourned for a month to enable a detailed medical examination to be made as three doctors were unable to agree as to the actual cause of death.[1] '

Events were gathering momentum now. Statements were taken by the police from members of the Sidney family, their relatives and employees and on March 19th, detectives paid a surprise visit to the family grave in Queen's Road Cemetery.

The indefatigable Inspector Hedges, accompanied by Morrish, called at Grace Duff's home on the evening of March 20th. They searched the house and took a number of bottles away with them. Later that evening they visited Tom Sidney's house. From there they removed a tin, labelled 'Eureka Weed-Killer' and containing a lavender-coloured powder, which they found on a shelf in the garden tool-shed, and a cardboard box containing Rodine rat-poison. The bottles, tin of weed-killer and the rat-poison were all handed over to Dr Ryffel on March 23rd, and three days later he also received Lane's tin of Noble's liquid weed-killer from Inspector Hedges.

But what the public did not know was that Dr Ryffel had already recovered a significant quantity of arsenic from the dregs in Mrs Sidney's medicine-bottle and wine glass, and that tests had also established the presence of arsenic in the organs which Dr Brontë had removed from Mrs Sidney's body.

It was these discoveries which led to the dramatic events that took place under cover of darkness on the night of March 21st—22nd.

IV

Queen's Road Cemetery closed its gates at the usual time as twilight fell on March 21st, but later that night two grave-diggers were unexpectedly recalled to duty. They were met at the entrance to the cemetery by police-officers and led through the darkness to the grave, in the shadow of the cemetery chapel, where Violet and Vera Sidney lay buried. Canvas screens were erected round it and, by the flickering light of muffled hurricane-lamps, the men began to dig. The Home Office had

[1] This was not quite accurate. There had been an inquest in the case of Edmund Duff, but in the case of Vera Sidney there had been no inquest, Dr Elwell having issued a certificate of death from natural causes.

that evening issued an order for the exhumation of the bodies of Violet and Vera Sidney.

At 2 a.m. Sir Bernard Spilsbury, the Home Office patholo- gist, arrived at the cemetery. He joined Hedges, Morrish and the group of police-officers and other officials who were standing with Tom Sidney by the open graveside. He was just in time to see the first coffin reached. Straps were passed under it and it was raised to the surface. He watched as it was lifted on to a hand-cart and trundled off to a small building beside the chapel. Then the digging began again. Presently, a second coffin was uncovered, and heaved on the taut straps to the surface. It, too, was wheeled to the building by the chapel, before, along with the first coffin, it was slid into a hearse and driven off to the Mayday Hospital Mortuary, where Dr Brontë was waiting.

There, at 3.30 a.m., Violet Emilia Sidney's coffin was un- screwed, and Tom Sidney identified the body which it con- tained as that of his mother.

Sir Bernard, watched by Brontë, proceeded to make a detail- ed examination of the corpse, removing a number of parts and sealing them in carefully labelled jars.

He then turned his attention to the second coffin, in which lay a body which Tom Sidney duly identified as that of his sister, Vera. Considering that it had been buried for nearly five weeks, the body was in a remarkable state of preservation, and a bunch of hyacinths which Vera held in her hand looked strangely fresh.

Slowly, systematically, Sir Bernard carried out his dissection, removing and placing in jars all the main organs, together with various fluids and tissue specimens.

The time ticked silently on in that stark, white-tiled room, with its twin autopsy tables, its mingled reek of death and dis- infectant, and its harsh yellow light.

The sky outside was rimmed with dawn when, just after 6 a.m., he had at last completed his work.

Of course he would have to wait for the analyst's report, but, in his own mind, Sir Bernard was already convinced that the police had not one, but two cases of murder on their hands.

PART TWO

INQUISITION ON THREE

TRIAL BY CORONER

4

INQUEST ON VIOLET

I

Despite all the elaborate precautions, the news of the exhumations soon leaked out. The morning papers of March 22nd informed their readers that members of the 'Big Five' of Scotland Yard, cemetery officials, and doctors had been at Queen's Road Cemetery in the early hours of that day, when two bodies were exhumed with great secrecy.

The *Sunday Express* of March 24th contained an interview with Grace Duff —

'A slender, dark-haired woman, with wide-open, slate-blue eyes, is waiting anxiously in the silence of her home today for news of the laboratory tests which are being made by the Home Office chemical and medical experts on the exhumed bodies of her mother and sister. . . . '

A representative of the *Daily News* called to see her later on the day that the *Sunday Express* story appeared.

'It has naturally been a terrible time for us all,' she is reported as saying. 'If there has been anything wrong we shall know at the inquest, when I hope everything will be cleared up. My little girl takes (up) a lot of my time, and my baby has been very ill with bronchitis, so, of course, they have taken my mind off it all. My son is at present away at school. It is all very mysterious to me. . . . I am thankful in one way that dear Mother has been spared all this worry and trouble. If she had been alive it would have been dreadful for her, and this would have made her very ill I am sure.'

That Sunday, too, there were what next day's *Daily News* described as 'unseemly scenes' at Queen's Road Cemetery, where morbid crowds of sightseers besieged the empty grave —

'The grave was boarded over just as it was left by the police, and even the tin shields which they used to screen the candles and lamps during the exhumation remained by the graveside. The wreaths sent for Mrs Sidney's funeral were removed some feet away. Two young women waited before the cemetery gates were opened in the morning and, as the day progressed, the number of visitors increased until there were more than a hundred people around the grave. Members of the cemetery staff tried to control the crowd, who were walking over neighbouring graves. Some people were even kneeling down to peer into the depths of Mrs Sidney's grave.'

At 4.45 on the afternoon of Monday, March 25th, in a mournful drizzle of rain, Violet and Vera were reburied, and a tantalising paragraph in Tuesday's *Daily Express* volunteered the information that, 'The pathological examination has yielded certain definite results.'

Impatiently, Croydon sat back to await the revelations of the second sitting of the coroner and his jury.

II

The inquest on Violet Emilia Sidney, which had been adjourned on March 8th, was resumed at 10.30 a.m. on Thursday, April 4th, 1929, at the old Croydon Workhouse. A gauntly institutional building of dark brick, whose great, square clock-tower bore the date 1865, the place loomed like a sepia blot on a green landscape. It had been optimistically redesignated the Queen's Road Homes, but this euphemism did little to propitiate the aura of Dickensian despair that seemed, in the course of sixty years, to have soaked into its very bricks.

The coroner's court was convened in the dreary, ground-floor boardroom, which ran the length of the left wing of the building, and not even the view from its windows of a lovely green lawn, with coolly plashing fountain and spring-decked trees, could disperse the heavy legacy of melancholy which weighted the air.

The coroner, Dr Henry Beecher Jackson, a short, clean-shaven man in early middle age, took his seat at the head of a green-baize-covered horseshoe table. The witnesses sat opposite, half-a-dozen yards away, with the light from the four windows full on their faces. On the coroner's right were the jury, and on his left, placed in rows against the green-painted walls, were chairs for fifty or sixty spectators. Near Dr Jackson sat Mr William Arthur Fearnley-Whittingstall, the barrister representing Grace Duff, Thomas Sidney, and William Stafford Sidney — Violet Emilia Sidney's brother-in-law and executor. Fearnley-Whittingstall was at that time only twenty-six, tall, thin, pallid and deceptively boyish-looking. He had been practising at the Bar just four years, but, as events were to prove, he was an advocate of rare brilliance, who, but for his early death, would undoubtedly have graced the bench of the High Court.

Dr Jackson cleared his throat.

The murmur of excited chatter died away.

Silence.

The boardroom clock ticked evenly. Outside the window, branches swayed and a bird was singing. There was the distant droning of an aeroplane.

In a quiet, clear voice, the coroner began his address to the jury, outlining the history of Mrs Sidney's sudden illness and death.

The first witness to be called was Mr Thomas Sidney. A tall, good-looking man of thirty-nine, carefully dressed, clean-shaven, his hair just turning grey, Tom Sidney moved across the court and, at 10.45 a.m., sat down in the witness-chair.

He had, he said, lived with his mother prior to his marriage in 1922. His present house was near hers, and he had seen her at least every day, and sometimes twice a day, since his sister, Vera's, death. Mrs Sidney had been grieving very deeply for her daughter, but he did not observe any signs indicating that her mental condition was not normal. She had complained of giddiness and that she did not seem able to concentrate her thoughts, but she had never suffered from delusions, or had any treatment for mental illness. He did not know of any insanity among her near relatives. He had never heard her threaten to take her own life, nor had she ever attempted to do so.

Shortly before Vera's death, the last of Mrs Sidney's best friends died, and at Christmas 1928 she told him that she was now alone in the world except for her immediate family. But, these sad losses aside, she had no cause for worry, and was in comfortable financial circumstances. She was a member of the Church of England and was very much against suicide, which she considered to be morally wrong. He thought, in fact, that she was most unlikely to commit suicide.

Although he knew that his mother had tried two or three medicines for constipation, he did not know that Dr Elwell was attending her officially, or that he had prescribed a tonic for her. Nor did he know that his mother was taking medicine until she told him so on the second day before her death. He thought that the day of her death was the first morning he had failed to visit her since Vera's funeral.

He went to tea with her on March 4th, the day before she died. That afternoon they had a visitor from the local church, St Peter's.[1] This rather upset his mother, as they were in the

---

[1] Mrs Elsie Adelaide Anderson, wife of the Reverend Richard William Eric Anderson of 18b Selsdon Road, South Croydon.

midst of a business discussion concerning Vera's will, of which he was co-trustee and executor with his sister, Mrs Grace Duff. He had tried to make hints for the visitor to go, but she was one of those who would not take a hint. Under Vera's will his mother had a life interest on £2,000, which, in the event of her death, was to be equally divided between Mrs Duff and himself.

Since he had ceased to live with his mother, he had had no key to her house. Neither, to his knowledge, had Mrs Duff.

Mrs Noakes and Mrs Sidney were, to the best of his belief, on good terms.

After the lunch adjournment, the coroner questioned Tom Sidney closely on the subject of the medicine-bottle.

He replied that Dr Elwell had told him that there was nothing injurious in it, and after that he had thought that his mother must have been accidentally poisoned because of a dirty medicine-bottle.

When he had been under examination for four hours, Sidney, who was obviously growing tired and irritable, told the coroner: 'After an examination like this it is remarkable if you don't get fed up and tie yourself up. It is a fearful strain on the memory.'

'I don't expect you to remember all the points,' responded Dr Jackson, 'but the whole object of this inquiry is to find the cause of death, and it can only be found on evidence given in accordance with recollection of witnesses. Lots of these points have to be put in detail, and I quite understand if you are unable to recollect all the details.'

This closed the examination of Thomas Sidney. It was then 4 p.m.

Time for only one more witness to be heard that day — Dr John Archibald Binning.

The coroner asked him if he had thought that Mrs Sidney might have been suffering from ptomaine poisoning from the food that she had had at lunch.

Binning said that he had, and that he collected samples of the remaining portions. He had also taken the medicine-bottle and locked it in his consulting room. He later handed it to the coroner's officer.

The inquest was then adjourned for eight days.

III

When the third sitting of the inquest on Violet Emilia Sidney opened on Friday, April 12th, Thomas Sidney was recalled. He deposed that he was present at Queen's Road Cemetery at 2.45 a.m. on Friday, March 22nd, when a coffin which he had identified as that of his mother was exhumed. He followed the coffin to Mayday Road Mortuary, where it was opened in his presence, and identified the body which it contained as that of Violet Emilia Sidney.

While Mr Sydney Gardiner, of 59 Selshurst New Road, South Norwood, undertaker's assistant in the employ of Messrs J.B. Shakespeare, funeral directors, of 67 George Street, Croydon, gave details concerning the funeral and exhumation, Mrs Duff, who was sitting in the seats reserved for witnesses, left the court and remained in the corridor until Divisional Detective-Inspector Frederick Hedges began his evidence.

Inspector Hedges told of the various bottles, tins and other articles which the police had collected from Mrs Sidney's home, Dr Binning's surgery, the gardener, Arthur Henry Lane's, house, Mr F. S. Rose's George Street pharmacy, and Grace Duff's and Tom Sidney's houses in March. Referring to the tin of Eureka weed-killer removed from Tom Sidney's tool-shed, Hedges admitted that it was Mr Sidney himself who first drew his attention to the fact that the weed-killer was in his possession.

Next came John Henry Baker, of 4 Farnley Road, South Norwood, mortuary attendant at the Mayday Road Hospital. While Baker was giving his formal evidence, Grace Duff, who had been sobbing for some minutes, suddenly rose, half-crossed the court, and asked, 'May I go out for one minute? It is too awful.'

'Yes, certainly,' nodded Dr Jackson.

After lunch, Thomas Sidney was brought back at the request of his counsel, Mr Fearnley-Whittingstall, who proceeded to question him with regard to the tin of Eureka weed-killer which Inspector Hedges had removed from his home on March 20th.

He stated that one evening when he returned home his wife had told him that the police had been round wanting to know whether poison of any kind was kept on the premises, and that she had forgotten to mention they had some weed-killer.

In fact, he had been using weed-killer for about fifteen years, and the last occasion on which he bought a tin was some eighteen or nineteen months ago.

'I have bought a tin every other year,' he said. 'In my mother's house you will see one or two empty tins which were used when I was living with her.'

The coroner interrupted to ask Inspector Hedges: 'Did you see one or two empty tins at 29 Birdhurst Rise?'

'Yes, there is an old rusty tin there.'

Tom Sidney interposed that the tin in question was a very old one. 'It might be possible to extract some poison from it, but I don't want to complicate the case,' he added.

'We don't want to complicate the case,' agreed the coroner, 'but if the tin is there we want to know, because that is the house where the death took place. Suppose the tin is empty now, it doesn't follow that the tin was empty before Mrs Sidney's death.'

Hedges broke in with, 'I should say that it has been empty for years. It was all rusty inside.'

But the coroner was not satisfied. 'It may be, but there might be poison in the rust.'

'It had not been disturbed.'

'It is difficult to say whether it had not been disturbed,' insisted the coroner. Then, turning to Sidney, 'When did you last see the empty tin?'

'Last Wednesday [April 10th] in the tool-shed at 29 Birdhurst Rise.' He did not remember seeing it before, but felt sure that it was one which he had bought when he lived with his mother, and which he had used for her garden.

In answer to Mr Fearnley-Whittingstall, Sidney confirmed that immediately his wife told him of the police inquiries, he got in touch with them and informed them of the Eureka weed-killer and the rat-poison which he had in his possession.

Fearnley-Whittingstall moved on to the subject of Vera Sidney's will. Sidney told the court that his sister, Mrs Duff, received £2,000 on Vera's death and that he received £1,000. 'I made a mistake last week when I said Vera left £2,000 to Mother for life. That was optional. It was an absolute gift, but Vera expressed a wish that the money should be divided at her death between Mrs Duff and myself. That was how the error arose.'

Vera left her residuary estate to be divided between Thomas Sidney's children and the children of Grace Duff. The total value of that estate was a little more than £7,000, and there were some other small legacies.

Dr Robert Matthew Brontë, the pathologist, then came into court.

On March 6th, he had made a post-mortem examination of Mrs Sidney at the Mayday Hospital Mortuary. The deceased was a medium-nourished female, and there were no marks of violence. The heart muscle was in a condition known as brown atrophy, and there was marked atheroma of the arteries. The lungs were ballooned at the margins, but there were no haemorrhages. The stomach was empty and showed a slight reddening. The small intestine exhibited similar reddening. The large intestine contained liquid, and presented signs of irritation. The spleen displayed evidence of chronic inflammation.

When Brontë had completed this brief résumé of his findings, the coroner told him, 'I do not propose to ask you any more today. You will, of course, have to be recalled as to the cause of death.'

Last witness of the day was Dr John Henry Ryffel.

He reported the results of his analysis of the various organs from Mrs Sidney's body, and the contents of the bottles and tins handed to him by the police and the coroner's officer.

In the skin, hair, viscera and othe rparts he had found a total of 3·48 grains of arsenic. He thought that the deceased must have had the fatal dose not more than twelve hours before her death because, although arsenic was a rapidly eliminated poison, there was a relatively large amount still remaining in the intestine and its contents. He did not think that she had had any doses prior to the fatal one, because if small doses of arsenic were introduced over a period of time it was eliminated by way of the hair and finger-nails. He had analysed Mrs Sidney's hair and nails, and found no evidence of such a process having taken place. The liver was richest in arsenic. Next came the small intestine and its contents, and then the heart. The finger and toe nails contained more arsenic than the hair.

The Eureka weed-killer contained 291 grains of arsenic per solid ounce. The Noble's liquid weed-killer contained 140 grains of arsenic per fluid ounce.

The only articles, other than the samples of the weed-killers , in which he had found arsenic were Mrs Sidney's medicine-bottle, and the wine glass in which she had taken her Metatone.

In the medicine-bottle was a deep-red fluid containing one grain of arsenious oxide. There was only a quarter of a teaspoonful of liquid remaining in the bottle. That meant that there would have been 8 grains of arsenic in two teaspoonfuls — the prescribed dose of Metatone.

He had observed a white-coloured sediment round the sides of the interior of the bottle. It was, however, only slight, and he did not agree that it was like sago grains.

He had made certain experiments with a view to finding out whether such a sediment could be produced by mixing weed-killer with Metatone. First, he mixed approximately equal volumes of Noble's liquid weed-killer and Metatone. The only changes that he noticed in the Metatone were a slight change in colour and a certain cloudiness. There was no sediment formation. He then mixed some Eureka weed-killer with Metatone, using a small quantity of Metatone and about one quarter of the same volume of weed-killer. He mixed them in a beaker, corked the mixture and allowed it to stand. The powder dissolved slowly, and there was a distinct cloudiness about the liquid. The resultant mixture roughly corresponded in appearance with the liquid in Mrs Sidney's medicine-bottle.

After stating his opinion that the cause of Mrs Sidney's death was acute arsenical poisoning, Dr Ryffel, replying to Mr Fearnley-Whittingstall, explained that the form of arsenic used

in medicines was sodium arsenite, whereas the form found
in this case was arsenious oxide. The ordinarily fatal dose of
arsenious oxide is 3 grains. In this case, he was sure that at least
5 grains must have been taken.

IV

Sitting Four. Wednesday, April 17th, 1929.

Before the start of the proceedings, a tin drum of Noble's
liquid weed-killer, a tin funnel, and a basket containing several
bottles were carried into the court.

Arthur Henry Lane, old, deaf and almost blind, described as
a jobbing gardener, living with his wife at 17 Mansfield Road,
South Croydon, shuffled uncertainly to the witness-chair.

He had worked for Mrs Sidney at 29 Birdhurst Rise for ten
years. Throughout the last winter he had been going there for
half a day each Saturday morning. He also did jobbing gardening for Mrs Duff from time to time, the last occasion being
about October 1928. He was absolutely certain that he had never
used any weed-killer at Mrs Sidney's, and that Mrs Sidney never
kept any on the premises.

The coroner was handed a small tin by Inspector Hedges. This
was the tin to which he had referred at the previous sitting, and
which Hedges had collected from the garden shed, by the side
of Mrs Sidney's house, on the evening of April 12th.

Dr Jackson poured some carrot seeds out of it into his hand,
examined them, then passed the tin across to Lane.

'Do you remember seeing that tin before?'

Lane, who was actually extremely deaf, was some time in
answering, and, very unpleasantly, Dr Jackson remarked, 'You
have got deafer this last two minutes. Do you swear you have
never seen that tin at Birdhurst Rise?'

'Yes, sir,' mumbled poor Lane.

Asked what he had used to kill the weeds at Birdhurst Rise,
Lane said that Mrs Sidney had used salt.

The coroner spent some minutes trying to learn from him
when he was last inside Number 29. The old gardener was sure
that he had not been in the house since Vera Sidney died. For
about two months before Mrs Sidney died he had been having
his lunch at Birdhurst Rise, but he used to eat it in the garden.
If it were raining he had it in the shed.

The drum of Noble's liquid weed-killer, with the funnel on
top, was then produced, and Lane stated that he had had that
in his possession for about six months. Mrs Duff had had the
drum in her garden, and told him to take it away as it was
dangerous stuff with children about. He took it straight to his

house that day and kept it in a shed at the bottom of his garden until he handed it over to the police on March 10th last.

The coroner looked at Lane severely.

'Was the tin corked when Mrs Duff gave it to you?'

'No,' said Lane promptly.

The reply seemed to annoy Dr Jackson.

'You are answering your questions much too casually,' he reproved sternly. Then, in an even voice and with a carefully assumed air of patience, repeated, 'Can you remember if there was a cork in that tin when you received it from Mrs Duff?'

And in his turn, Lane repeated that there was not. As an afterthought, almost as if he were consciously trying to please the coroner, he added, 'There was a funnel in it, though, and I managed to carry it home without spilling a drop on the way.'

But the coroner was not to be appeased. He seems to have taken a dislike to Lane. 'Was that not a rather silly thing to do?' he observed acidly. 'You knew it was dangerous stuff.'

Pretending that he had not heard — and perhaps he hadn't — Lane went on to tell how, subsequently, he had used a little of the weed-killer to poison meat for rat-traps which he used in the shed at his own house. He had never known Mrs Sidney to do any gardening, other than a little weeding. All sorts of vegetables, including carrots, were grown in her garden. She bought the seeds, but he dug the ground and sowed them.

The coroner pointed out that there was a packet of carrot seeds in the weed-killer tin and wanted to know if Lane could explain how it had got there.

Lane could not.

Mrs Kathleen Noakes, cook-general to Mrs Sidney, was the next to be questioned. She was a married woman, but her husband, Robert Henry Noakes, of Portsmouth, who was an A.B. seaman in the Royal Navy, had taken divorce proceedings against her. She had been employed by Mrs Sidney from August 31st, 1928, until the time of her death. In October 1928, she gave notice of leaving Mrs Sidney's service on the following November 29th, but stayed on to give her an opportunity to find a replacement. She was, at present, living at 44 Scarbrook Road, Croydon, the home of Mr Ernest Albert Carey.

After Miss Vera's death, she and Mrs Sidney were the only persons living in the house. She liked her mistress very much and was quite happy in her place. Mrs Sidney grieved very deeply for Miss Vera, but had become reconciled to her loss. She did not think that her mistress had any worries. Her mental faculties were quite keen right up to the end, and she was perfectly sane.

Then, with great emphasis: 'I shall never think that she took her own life.'

Mrs Noakes described how she had turned out the dining-room on February 27th. Her mistress removed the things from the sideboard, and put them on the table before she started to sweep. Mrs Noakes had put them back after she had finished sweeping, but did not at that time see a medicine-bottle, wine glass, or any tumbler or drinking-glass. She remembered Dr Elwell's calling on Mrs Sidney about a week before she died. After he had gone, her mistress told her that he had suggested a tonic for her. She had then said, 'I don't think medicine is much use to me.' Mrs Noakes asked her why, and she replied, 'When one's inside is upset,' and explained that she was constipated. Mrs Noakes added that Mrs Sidney told her that she had asked Mrs Duff to bring her in some senna pods, and that she had seen her mistress making the senna herself in the dining-room. Shortly after this conversation a message-boy came to the door with two small packets, one of which looked like a medicine-bottle. Mrs Noakes put the packages on a tray and took them straight to her mistress in the drawing-room. 'That's my medicine,' she said. Mrs Noakes had never actually seen Mrs Sidney take any medicine. The first time that she saw the medicine-bottle held up by the coroner was after Mrs Sidney had taken the last dose on March 5th. It was then standing on the silver-crowded sideboard, near where Mrs Sidney had placed the wine glass. She did not then notice how much medicine was in it.

Questioned about the visitors to Mrs Sidney's house, Mrs Noakes listed them carefully. Mr Thomas Sidney came there a lot. Also Mrs Duff. They appeared to be very attached to their mother. Mrs Margaret Sidney and Mrs Duff's children used to come, too. Apart from the wife of the new curate of St Peter's, who stayed to tea on March 4th, Mrs Sidney had not had any visitors who had had a meal, of any kind, with her for some weeks before her death.

On March 4th Mrs Sidney retired to bed as usual at 10 p.m. When she said goodnight to Mrs Noakes she seemed to be fairly well, though still upset over the death of Vera. Mrs Sidney had not been eating much, and Mrs Noakes tried to persuade her to have her breakfast in bed next morning. But she refused, saying that she was afraid that if she stayed in bed she would become weak and not be able to get up again.

Mrs Noakes heard nothing of her mistress during the night. She got up at 7.15 a.m. on March 5th, and at 8.15 a.m. heard Mrs Sidney leave her bedroom to go to the bathroom. She came downstairs at about nine o'clock.

Mrs Noakes then went on to describe the events of March 5th.

When she had finished the coroner asked, 'So far as you know, was there any poison in the house while you were there?'

'No, sir, not so far as I know.'

And that was that, until 10.30 a.m. on Monday, April 22nd.

V

According to the coroner's schedule, the first witness on the morning of the fifth sitting of the inquest on Violet Emilia Sidney should have been her brother-in-law, Mr William Stafford Sidney, but it was explained that he was unable to be present until later in the day. Instead, amidst a rustle of excitement, Mrs Grace Duff, clad in deep mourning, took his place.

She began her evidence by telling Dr Jackson that she used to visit her mother practically every day. In the morning she would call in to see if there was any shopping she could do for her, and very often she would look in during the afternoon, or later in the day, as well. On her morning visits she usually saw her mother in the dining-room and in the afternoon in the drawing-room. The visits were not generally lengthy ones, as she had her own family to look after. Her mother never suffered from any mental illness or delusions. She was a healthy woman of late years, though about twelve months ago she had suffered with high blood pressure.

As she gave this evidence Mrs Duff displayed great emotion. There were tears in her eyes and she spoke in a low voice.

The coroner wanted to know if she had ever heard her mother threaten to take her own life.

'Never.'

'Did it ever occur to you she might do so?'

'No. Just the night Vera died. She was beside herself; but never since. I am perfectly sure Mother was much too good and religious to do such a thing.'

'Did you think that your mother might have contemplated suicide on that night?'

'On the night Vera died she locked her door. The nurse and I were terrified outside, but it was all right.'

At this juncture Mr Alan Glyn Jones rose, saying that he appeared for Mr F.S. Rose, the Croydon chemist, whose evidence, if possible, he would like to interpose, as he was a very busy man.

The coroner agreed, and Mrs Duff stood down.

Frederick Sandford Rose was a pharmacist, carrying on business at 110 George Street, and residing at 88 Addiscombe Road, Croydon.

From time to time he made up prescriptions for Dr Elwell. He saw one for Mrs Violet Sidney on February 25th. The prescription was for Metatone, a patent medicine manufactured by

Parke Davis & Co.[1]

He dispensed this prescription of Dr Elwell's himself from a
large, brown, 80-ounce stock bottle. All he did, was to pour
four ounces from the big bottle into a 4-ounce medicine-bottle.
It would have been practically impossible for there to have
been any sediment or precipitate in the Metatone when it was
in the big bottle, and he could swear to the fact that the Metatone was perfectly clear after he had dispensed it into the
smaller bottle, because he had held the bottle up to the light
in the dispensary.

The bottle was sent to Mrs Sidney that same day. The
stock-bottle from which he had dispensed the Metatone was at
that time nearly full. He subsequently dispensed practically all
of it, and had not had any complaints from any other customers.
Dr Elwell had also prescribed some tablets for Mrs Sidney,
which were sent out at the same time as the Metatone.

'Would it,' the coroner inquired, 'be possible for any arsenic
to get into Mrs Sidney's medicine-bottle by mistake'

'It would be impossible — absolutely impossible.'

What other reply would Mr Rose be likely to have vouch-
safed to a question like that?

By now Mr William Stafford Sidney had arrived.

'I live at 19 Royal Avenue, Chelsea. I am a member of the
London Stock Exchange. Mrs Sidney was my brother's widow.
She had made her last will on June 13th,1927, appointing her
daughter, Vera, and myself as executors.'

What he had to say made dull, legalistic hearing.

By that will she gave him £100 free of legacy duty, and to
Vera Sidney such furniture, plate and articles of domestic use
as she might select. The remainder of her furniture, plate and
other articles, she bequeathed to her daughter, Mrs Grace Duff,
and her son, Thomas Sidney, in equal shares. Her jewellery, and
various other articles of personal use, she gave to Mrs Duff and
Vera Sidney in equal shares. Her residuary estate she gave to
trustees, to be divided equally between Mrs Duff, Vera Sidney
and Thomas Sidney. That residuary estate amounted to something between £9,000 and £9,500, including the sum of £2,000,
which she would receive on the death of her daughter, Vera.

Grace Duff then resumed her evidence.

Yes, she was co-trustee and executor, with her brother, of
Vera's will. In connection with the investment of Vera's estate,
Tom Sidney had said, 'I am going to sell so-and-so'. He had

---

[1] Metatone contains various glycerophosphates, calcium, man-
ganese, potassium, sodium, strychnine, nucleinic acid and vitamin B.
It does not contain any arsenic, and the proportion of strychnine is eight
two-hundredths of a grain to every fluid ounce.

said that his mother wanted him to sell something. Mrs Sidney was apparently keen to keep some things and sell others, but there had been no disagreement of any kind between Tom and his mother.

Witness knew that after her sister's death Dr Elwell visited her mother and prescribed medicine for her, and Mrs Sidney had told her that she was taking a tonic. When she called at her mother's on the morning of March 5th, she mentioned to Grace that she had not taken a dose that morning.

Coroner: 'Did your mother go upstairs?'

Mrs Duff: 'She may have, I can't take an oath on it. It could only have been for a little time, because I wasn't long in the house.'

Coroner: 'Where did you leave your mother?'

Mrs Duff: 'I thought I left her in the hall, but I won't be sure. She was talking about some black patterns.'

Asked where her mother would be likely to keep the medicine-bottle, Mrs Duff was equally vague.

'I don't know, I'm sure. I somehow feel that if it had been standing on the sideboard I should have seen it, but I didn't see it there. There was a little cruet cupboard in the sideboard that she could have kept it in.'

The first time she remembered seeing the medicine-bottle was just after 1 p.m. on March 5th, when she saw it on the sideboard. Once before she had seen a medicine-bottle on a chest of drawers upstairs, but she thought that it was a bigger one than that containing the Metatone. After Mrs Sidney's death, Mrs Duff's son, John, told her that one day when he had run upstairs to get something for his grandmother he had seen a bottle with some dark-red fluid in it standing on the chest of drawers in her bedroom. He could not remember the day.

When her mother died, there was no thought of criminal poisoning in Mrs Duff's mind. Mrs Sidney had left no letter or note to throw any light on the cause of her death.

She did not know whether or not her mother's life was insured. She knew that she had made a will, but had no definite knowledge of its provisions, though her mother had once said that she did not think it fair to make differences between children. She thought that Mrs Sidney's estate would amount to about £4,000 or £5,000. Before she died, her mother was helping her financially — 'She was giving me £50 a year, and making me odd presents of money as well. If I had any pressing bill she would settle it for me. She preferred it that way because she thought I was rather extravagant.'

The drum of Noble's liquid weed-killer was then placed on the table. 'Do you recognize that tin?'

Mrs Duff told the coroner that she did. It had been bought

by her husband and was kept in the cellar at Hurst View. It was
left there after her husband's death and she never gave it another
thought until August 1928, when she moved to 59 Birdhurst
Rise. She then gave it to Mr Lane, who had taken it away six
months ago. After that, she had no form of arsenic in her
possession.

Coroner: 'Did you know that your brother, Mr Thomas
Sidney, had a tin of weed-killer in his possession?'

Mrs Duff: 'No.'

The foreman of the jury, Mr McConnell, passed a written
note to the coroner. He read it. 'The jury want to know if on
March 5th, the day of her death, your mother gave you any
money to make the purchases for her?'

'No, she settled up when I came back.'

The jury also asked: 'Was medicine of any sort ever given
to, or prepared for, Mrs Sidney by Mrs Duff, or any other
member of her family?'

'No. I have never given her any, or prepared her any, and so
far as I know no member of the family has done so,' was the
answer.

The foreman of the jury stood up.

'Was the deceased of a secretive nature?'

Mrs Duff seemed to be weighing the question and its implica-
tions.

'She was reserved and old-fashioned, and I should think she
would have preferred to have taken her medicine alone. I
shouldn't call her 'secretive' exactly, but she would be more
inclined to be reserved about taking medicine than most
people.'

One of the jurymen: 'What I want to know is, would Mrs
Sidney take medicine four times a day without telling anyone?'

Grace Duff turned her head so that she was looking him
straight in the face. 'I don't think she took it four times a day.
The last day of her life I said to her, "Did your first dose taste
nasty?" She said, "I have never taken it before today."'

When Mrs Duff finished her evidence she had been in the
witness-chair for the best part of four hours.

She was tired. The coroner was tired. The jury were tired.

Dr Jackson announced that there would be a ten-minute
break. Just long enough for a smoke and to stretch one's legs.

Then it was time for the next witness — Dr Robert Graham
Elwell, of 14 Addiscombe Road, East Croydon.

When he saw Mrs Sidney on February 27th, she told him
that she had taken the medicine which he had prescribed.

On March 5th, he examined her heart and tested her blood
pressure. It was 150, which was quite good. Previously it had

been as high as 170. Her pulse, too, was quite good. She said she was feeling pretty well, but had had a cold. He asked her about the Metatone, and she confessed that she had not been taking it regularly — 'I smiled and said, "It won't do you much good if you don't take it." Prior to March 5th, she had never complained to him of vomiting or diarrhoea.

The next that Dr Elwell heard of Mrs Sidney was when he got back to his house just after 3 p.m. that day. There was a telephone message for him to ring up Dr Binning at Mrs Sidney's house. He did so, and Binning told him that Mrs Sidney was very ill and asked him to come around as soon as possible.

Elwell arrived at Number 29 at about 3.20 p.m. Binning told him that he had given the patient sodium bicarbonate. She had a pulse, but her temperature was below 96 degrees, indicating great collapse.

Elwell asked her if she had any pain.

'No pain,' she replied, 'but if I could get something away from here' [indicating the right side of the stomach just below the ribs] 'I should feel better.'

She got a little better at first, and then became worse.

Between 4 and 5 p.m. Mrs Sidney was given an injection of pituitrin, which brought her round for a time.

She did not complain of any pains throughout. She had some tea when she felt better, but about ten minutes after drinking it brought it all up again. It was after that that she collapsed. She passed a very small rice-water motion about the same time that she vomited. That was the only time that Elwell saw her use the bedpan while he was there.

Dr Poynton suggested that the illness might possibly be due to *Bacillus aertrycke* — a common cause of food poisoning — but was unable to make any firm diagnosis.

After her death there was no suggestion that she had had arsenic.

He had never thought that Mrs Sidney was likely to commit suicide.

He concluded his evidence with the admission that acute arsenical poisoning now seemed to him the most probable cause of death.

The sitting had lasted the whole day.

VI

At the sixth sitting of the inquest, on Monday, May 6th, 1929, Thomas Sidney, Mrs Noakes, Inspector Hedges, Samuel John Clarke, Dr Ryffel, Dr Brontë, Dr Binning and Dr Elwell were all recalled for further examination.

Back into the witness-chair went Tom Sidney. He was closely examined by the coroner as to his financial position before his mother's death. He was adamant that he had been in no money difficulties; his business had, in fact, rather improved.

On the morning of March 5th he took his little daughter, Virginia, out for a walk. They went along Birdhurst Rise and passed Number 29 at about five minutes to one, but did not go in, not even into the front-garden. — 'She is a very noisy little girl, and she got on my mother's nerves very much indeed, and that was sufficient reason for not going in.'

He then referred to his visit of the previous day, March 4th, when Mrs Anderson, the curate's wife, was with his mother for an hour, and said that he was with them in the drawing-room the whole time. His mother's house was a very dark one, and a stranger would have difficulty in finding his or her way about inside it if the doors were shut. It was quite impossible for the curate's wife to have touched the medicine-bottle. He took her to the door, and saw her leave.

He told Dr Jackson that he had known for a year or eighteen months before her death that his mother had made a will under which he and his sisters would benefit in equal divisions. He thought that she was worth between £8,000 and £9,000. He did not know of any insurance on his mother's life. Besides his professional earnings, he had about £4,500 capital at the time of his mother's death.

Mrs Noakes, called back to the witness-chair, then made a very odd allegation. On the day of Mrs Sidney's death she saw Tom Sidney in the hall of Number 29. He had one of his children with him.

'This is a very serious matter, you know,' warned the coroner. 'If you have any doubt you must not swear to it.'

Mrs Noakes flushed red. 'I have not sworn to it,' she protested. 'I have said to the best of my recollection.'

'You have heard Mr Sidney say he was not inside the house at all until after lunch that day?'

'Yes . . . He was standing at the hall-stand looking in the glass when I came downstairs. He spoke to me and said, "I won't go in to see Mother because it's nearly one o'clock." '

'Can you be quite sure that it was on the day Mrs Sidney died that this happened?'

A pause.

Mrs Noakes, obviously overwhelmed, capitulated. 'No, I can't be sure.'

The coroner produced a statement which Mrs Noakes was alleged to have made to Inspector Hedges on April 27th. It referred to March 5th and read:

'After Dr Elwell had been, and just before Mrs Sidney took her medicine. I was taking in the things to get ready for Mrs Sidney's lunch, when, to my surprise, I saw Mr Thomas Sidney standing in the hall with one of his children. The front-door was closed, and as I had not admitted him, I wondered how he got into the house.'

Mrs Noakes agreed that she could have made a mistake when she said that it was on the day of the death.

But the coroner had not finished with her yet.

'When you saw him in the hall did you think he had come in by the back-door?'

'Yes. The back-door was ajar for the greater part of the day.'

'Anyone could have got in through the back-door, then, without your knowing it if you were not in the kitchen?'

Mrs Noakes nodded. 'Yes.'

Mr Fearnley-Whittingstall rose to cross-examine.

She was, potentially anyway, a hostile witness.

'Did Inspector Hedges ask you any questions when you made this statement?'

'No, sir.'

'Do you mean that you got up and recited this from beginning to end without a break, and he did not ask you any questions?'

'Yes.'

Counsel lifted a quizzical eyebrow. He then picked up a sheaf of papers and read out an extract from one of the pages of Mrs Noakes' statement to the effect that Mr Sidney was given a key after Vera died.

'Did Inspector Hedges not say to you, "Do you know if Mr Sidney was given a key after Miss Sidney died?"'

'I expect he did.'

Not good enough, that grudging affirmative.

'It is such an important point I am going right into it. You first said you were not pumped. You have just told me he did not ask a question from beginning to end. You said you stood up and recited the statement right off. Has Inspector Hedges ever asked you before April 27th whether or not Mr Sidney had been to the house on the morning of Mrs Sidney's death?'

'Of course he asked me.'

That was better.

'How many times?'

'Once, when he took the statement.'

Not good enough, again. In a stern voice Fearnley-Whittingstall repeated the question.

'*How many times has he asked you?*'

'Each time he took a statement.'

Now he was getting somewhere.

'How many conversations has Inspector Hedges had with you since this inquest began?'

'Nothing at all.'

'Oh, no, Mrs Noakes! *How many conversations has Inspector Hedges had with you since this inquest began?*'

Poor Mrs Noakes tried a little bit of evasion.

'They were nothing to do with the inquest, but only a little private matter.'

Up against the force of Fearnley-Whittingstall's powerful personality she had in the end to admit that each day since the inquest opened she had had conversations with Inspector Hedges.

'But not always about the case,' she put in pathetically, trying to salvage something from the wreckage of her denials.

In further cross-examination it was brought out that after seeing Mr Thomas Sidney it was only a matter of seconds before witness went in to lay the lunch; that she could swear that Mrs Sidney did not go upstairs between 12.30 and 1 p.m. on the day of her death; that Mr Sidney could not have gone into the dining-room without seeing his mother, and that she was sure that he did not in fact see her, or Mrs Sidney would have mentioned it.

Fearnley-Whittingstall had thus brilliantly established the impossibility of his client's having had access to Mrs Sidney's medicine that morning, even if he *had* been in the hall of the house.

He now proceeded to demolish the validity of Mrs Noakes' stated recollection of having seen Tom Sidney in the hall at all.

He returned to the vexed, and vexing, question of the statements which she had made to the police.

'How many times has Inspector Hedges asked if Tom Sidney called?'

'Each time he has taken a statement.'

Fearnley-Whittingstall spared her a compassionate, encouraging smile.

'Please answer this question quite candidly. He must have asked you nearly dozens of times whether Tom Sidney had been to that house on March 5th?'

There was no fight left in her.

'Yes.'

'Having asked you dozens of times ever since this inquest opened, all he can get you to say on oath after six weeks is, "I fancy I saw him"?'

'I told them I wasn't sure.'

There were no smiles, encouraging or otherwise, now.

'Having asked you dozens of times ever since the inquest

Number 29 Birdhurst Rise. 'Tall, gabled, and of naked, liver-coloured brick.' Vera and Violet Emilia Sidney died here.

Photo: Tim Petersen

Edmund Creighton Duff. Victim Number One.

Violet Emilia Sidney. Victim Number Three.

Vera Sidney. Victim Number Two.

opened, the best he can get you to say after all this badgering is that you fancy you saw him?'

Before Mrs Noakes could reply, Inspector Hedges, who was sitting near the coroner, jumped to his feet. 'I strongly object to the use of the word "badgering",' he spluttered angrily.

The coroner took his part. 'I do not think the use of the word "badgering" is necessary.'

Fearnley-Whittingstall spun furiously round. 'Mrs Noakes is a witness and I am counsel, and I can use what words I like. I think I am entitled to interpret almost dozens of times asking this question as badgering.'

'Badgering is grossly unfair.'

The words burst from Hedges' lips almost, it seemed, independent of his volition.

The coroner intervened again, asking Mrs Noakes if she had been badgered into making the statement of April 27th.

No. It had been made of her own free will.

'I used the word badger in relation to one particular question,' put in Fearnley-Whittingstall.

'That,' Hedges, his face scarlet with anger, practically shouted, 'is the point I wish to object to, because I have not singled one man out.'

Fearnley-Whittingstall ignored the outburst.

Dr Jackson did his best to pour oil on the troubled waters. 'Mrs Noakes has, I think, made it clear, Inspector Hedges, that you did not question her more about Mr Sidney than anybody else.'

Hedges relapsed into his seat with an eloquent grunt, his ruffled feathers slowly subsiding.

Time for the toxicologist to put in another appearance.

Dr Ryffel produced a medicine-bottle, and held it up for everyone to see.

'This bottle of Metatone and solid weed-killer was mixed on Saturday, May 4th — about forty-eight hours ago. The proportion of solid weed-killer was very high. The appearance is not as when it was mixed — notably the colour of the Metatone, which is somewhat red, has changed to brown. It always does.'

His voice droned on, for all the world like a lecturer addressing a class of soporose medical students.

The contents of the bottle would, he continued, alter entirely in a few days. The sediment in the experimental bottle, although roughly similar to the sediment in the original medicine bottle, was indisputably coarser.

Forty-eight hours previously, he had also mixed Metatone with a slightly more than equal volume of liquid weed-killer. That mixture was nearly clear.

He handed it to the coroner.

'Does that correspond in appearance with the liquid contained in the original bottle?' inquired Dr Jackson.

The colour, he was told, was about right, but the mixture was more fluid, because there was no deposit. That led Dr Ryffel to the conclusion that the mixture found in the original bottle must have been formed by adding some form of solid to Metatone, or, possibly, a solid in a very small quantity of water.

When Ryffel had completed his precise, technical exposition, Fearnley-Whittingstall cross-examined him with regard to his previous evidence of April 12th. The doctor agreed that if Mrs Sidney had taken the exact dose from her medicine-bottle there must have been $2\frac{1}{4}$ teaspoonfuls, containing 9 grains of arsenic, before she took the dose. To get 9 grains of arsenic, 14 grains of Eureka weed-killer would be required.

At this point Fearnley-Whittingstall produced from an attaché-case a pair of scales, Metatone, Eureka weed-killer, and various bottles. These he handed to Dr Ryffel, asking him to measure $2\frac{1}{4}$ teaspoonfuls of Metatone and 14 grains of weed-killer.

The coroner, jury, and Dr Brontë crowded round the Home Office expert as he manipulated the scales.

Presently a small bottle of brownish-coloured liquid was exhibited. It was shaken and corked and Dr Ryffel gracefully retired.

Dr Brontë, briefly recalled, regretted that he did not know the cause of the brown atrophy which he had found in the muscle of the deceased's heart. Some disease in the kidneys either could or could not have been due to a natural cause. But either way it could only have been the result of a chronic action. Acute poisoning by arsenic would not produce brown atrophy of the heart muscle, but chronic arsenical poisoning might. He thought that the changes found in the kidneys and liver could be due to chronic arsenical poisoning. In his opinion, the cause of death was acute arsenical poisoning. He based that opinion on the analyst's report, and on his own microscopic examination of the organs.

Dr Binning was requested to examine the three experimental bottles of Metatone-plus-weed-killer prepared by Dr Ryffel.

The coroner held up the one containing the mixture of Eureka weed-killer and Metatone and asked, 'Do the contents of this bottle resemble the contents of the medicine-bottle which you found at Mrs Sidney's house?' Binning replied that they were similar, but did not entirely correspond. It was primarily a colour difference. Although they closely resembled each other in viscosity, the contents of the bottle produced were browner. Also, the sediment in the original bottle was finer. As to the mixture of liquid weed-killer and Metatone, he did not think that this corresponded with the appearance of the contents of the original bottle.

When the foreman of the jury asked whether the mixture made in court by Dr Ryffel resembled the contents of the original bottle, Dr Binning shook his head. 'No, not at all.'

Finally, Dr Elwell gave it as his view that, of the three experimental mixtures, the first mixture of Eureka weed-killer and Metatone most closely resembled the contents of Mrs Sidney's bottle of tonic.

VII

A week later, on Monday, May 13th, the inquest court met for the seventh time. The sitting was mainly concerned with the taking of medical evidence.

Dr Herbert William Southgate, the Croydon Borough Pathologist, testified that in the course of a bacteriological examination of certain organs from Mrs Sidney's body he had searched for signs of food poisoning, but had found no abnormal organisms present. He made microscopical sections of the organs, and gave them to Dr Brontë.

Dr Brontë confirmed that he had received the sections from Dr Southgate towards the end of March, and had examined them under the microscope. The sections were of heart muscle, kidneys, spleen, liver and intestines. Brontë thought that Mrs Sidney must have had a dose of arsenic prior to the one which caused her death. He based this on Dr Ryffel's finding of arsenic in the nails and hair.

The coroner pointed out that Ryffel's report had specifically stated that the arsenic found in the deceased's hair was negligible.

Brontë countered that only a very small quantity of hair was tested, and that if a greater quantity had been examined a larger proportion of arsenic might have been found.

'How long would you say, Dr Brontë, that she must have had arsenic prior to March 5th?'

'Five to seven days,' was the answer.

Brontë was persuaded to amplify. The average growth of the finger-nail in the case of a healthy person is an eighth of an inch per week. In an old person or sick person, growth is not so rapid. In Mrs Sidney's case, arsenic had been discovered at the top of the finger-nails. It had had to be brought from the blood into the skin, and from there into the base of the nail. He calculated that in order to reach the part of the nail examined, the arsenic would have required a period of between five and

seven days. He was satisfied that a single fatal dose of arsenic
could not account for the presence of the poison in the hair
and nails. Mrs Sidney must, therefore, have had previous non-
toxic doses. But the mere fact that anyone showed arsenic in
the hair or nails did not necessarily mean that there was any
arsenical poisoning. It might have been taken medicinally.

Not really very illuminating.

The coroner produced the bottle which had contained the
Metatone which Mrs Sidney had been taking, and asked Dr
Brontë if he thought that it would have been possible for the
poison to have remained at the bottom of the bottle, so that it
was toxically concentrated in the last dregs of the medicine
only. In which case, the last dose but one of the medicine would
produce no vomiting.

Brontë considered that to be perfectly possible, and that the
finding of the arsenic in the nails and hair would imply that some
of the arsenic was in solution in that bottle.

'I think,' commented Dr Jackson, 'that is going rather far.
It would only prove that she had had arsenic before.'

'I did not say *prove*, sir.' The coroner had trodden on the
pathologist's professional toes. 'The last dose but one might not
contain sufficient arsenic to cause any symptoms.'

Then, slowly, articulating carefully as though explaining to a
slightly backward child, Brontë pointed out that the last dose
might be fatal because of its insolubility. If there were arsenic
in the last two doses and it was insoluble, the last dose but one
would produce no symptoms. But if the arsenic *were* soluble, it
would produce symptoms.

'I say that with the greatest confidence in the accuracy of the
statement,' he added with heavy dignity.

Tempers were now becoming a little frayed on both sides.

'I don't see how you can do so with confidence,' objected
the coroner. 'It is a matter of opinion.'

'It is not a question of opinion, but of proven fact,' thun-
dered Brontë.

'Would it be at all likely to happen if the dose was poured
from the bottle into a glass in the ordinary way?'

'It would not be at all likely unless the arsenic was insoluble.'

Dr Jackson remained unconvinced. 'It all depends upon the
quantities. You may have a fairly sharp line where the sediment ends.'

But Brontë was not going to budge an inch. 'It all depends on
the substance which is sedimental,' he retorted irritably.

Then, with the air of a man issuing a challenge: 'I have no
doubt that I could pour out the top two teaspoonfuls of a bottle
containing four teaspoonfuls without disturbing the sediment
in the bottom two teaspoonfuls.'

Fearnley-Whittingstall was up in an instant, quick to press a possible advantage.

'In your opinion was the arsenic in the bottle of a soluble or insoluble form, Dr Brontë?'

'I cannot express any opinion on that. I refuse to express an opinion simply because I cannot. If the bottle had never been shaken and insoluble arsenic had been used, it would sink to the bottom. If it were soluble, it must be evenly distributed. We are dealing with the lower physics which will not allow contradiction.'

Brontë agreed with Fearnley-Whittingstall that arsenic in medicinal doses did improve the health.

Dr Jackson looked up from his papers. 'Do you suggest it was arsenic which caused her to get a little better and to become more cheerful during the last fortnight?'

If it was sarcasm Dr Brontë refused to see it as such.

His poker-faced reply: 'Arsenic could have that effect, together with other factors.'

Answering a juror, Brontë suggested that Mrs Sidney might not have used a spoon to take her medicine, but might have poured it straight into a glass. In that case, if the arsenic were in an insoluble form, it would be a heavy matter and would settle at the bottom. If, on the other hand, a spoon had been used, the medicine would have been more shaken up.

Tom Sidney interposed that he had in fact found a teaspoon beside the medicine glass after his mother's death. 'Unfortunately, I washed it only a few days ago.'

Fearnley-Whittingstall informed the coroner that Mr Sidney and Mrs Duff had acquiesced to evidence being given as to the state of their respective bank accounts, and Rupert Harry Fortnum, manager of the Brighton Road branch of Barclays Bank, South Croydon, came forward to say that Mr Thomas Sidney had had an account there since 1918, and Mrs Duff since 1926. Both accounts had always been quite satisfactory.

At the conclusion of Mr Fortnum's evidence, the coroner adjourned until the morning of Wednesday, June 12th. 'There will not be much more evidence to take, as far as I know at present,' he added.

VIII

For reasons which we shall see later, the adjournment was even longer than the proposed month, and it was not until Thursday, June 27th, that the court assembled for its eighth sitting.

It opened with Dr Ryffel in the witness-chair again. The

coroner was anxious to make it clear to the jury, if possible, whether the arsenic which was found in the bottle of Metatone could have been there when the last dose but one was taken by Mrs Sidney. 'When you received the bottle its contents consisted of some deep red fluid and whitish sediment?'

That was so, but Ryffel could not be definite as to whether or not the sediment contained arsenic, because he did not separate it from the liquid. On receiving the bottle he first added water to it and shook the mixture. The sediment, readily soluble in water, then dissolved. The sediment, whether it contained arsenic or not, was, therefore, soluble in a diluted solution of the medicine in the bottle. The fluid thus obtained contained arsenic in strong solution.

The coroner placed a wine glass before him. When Ryffel first received it, it had had some sticky liquid adhering to it. The material had dried somewhat, but there was practically no deposit. It appeared to be the same as the liquid in the bottle, except that it was more brownish in colour. He accounted for this difference in colour by the fact that it had been exposed to the air, and that he had received it four days after the bottle of medicine. There were also a few specks of sediment on the glass. He tested the liquid in the glass, and it was rich in arsenic. There was so little sediment on the glass that it could not possibly have accounted for the total strength of arsenic found. The strength of the solution in the liquid was such that if Mrs Sidney was taking doses of two teaspoonfuls at a time, the dose before the last *must* have produced obvious symptoms of poisoning, unless some of the arsenic was put into the bottle after that dose was taken.

In his view, the arsenic found in Mrs Sidney's nails might have been taken in the last dose of medicine, about six hours before death. It did not to his mind prove that she had taken any previous doses of arsenic. In this Dr Ryffel was completely at odds with the opinion expressed by Dr Brontë.

In his experiments, Ryffel had obtained a slight sediment by allowing a mixture of Metatone and liquid weed-killer to stand for some time. He had not found any sediment forming in as short a time as four days. He did not think that he had found any in less than a week — and that despite the fact that there was more liquid weed-killer than Metatone in the mixture.

The coroner wondered if a person taking a mixture of Metatone and weed-killer would be likely to comment on the grittiness of the mixture.

Ryffel thought that a mixture of Metatone and liquid weed-killer would not feel gritty. Arsenic in an extremely fine powder would not make it feel gritty, but a coarser powder would.

A large, green-striped tin of Eureka weed-killer was produced.

Ryffel peered at the white powder inside it. He noted that some was very fine, and some coarse and caked in the tin. The tin was handed round among the jury, several of whom tested the texture of the powder with their fingers. Dr Ryffel took some of the powder from the tin. 'The contents of this tin certainly feel gritty,' he commented.

Now came the cross-examination of Dr Ryffel by Mr Fearnley-Whittingstall. It began gently enough, but ended on a note of devastating crescendo.

'Can you tell the jury how much arsenic you found in the wine glass?'

'I cannot exactly.'

'Did you measure it or weigh it?'

'I did not weigh it.'

'Did you make any calculation to discover the quantity?'

'No.'

'Or the quantity of undissolved sediment?'

'That would be quite impossible. There was practically no sediment in the glass.'

'It would be equally impossible to say how much arsenic was sediment, and how much dissolved?'

'I am speaking by impression and not by weighing. I can't give figures.'

'How did you tell there was much more dissolved than there was sediment?'

'Because there was little sediment. I have no figures. I am simply saying the impression I got was that the fluid in the glass was rich in arsenic.'

Then, suddenly, Fearnley-Whittingstall let fly: 'Is this a fair epitome of your cross-examination: that you do not know how much arsenic there was: you do not know the proportion between the arsenic and the liquid: and yet you say, "From the strength of the solution, I say that the last dose but one must have produced symptoms of poisoning, unless some arsenic was put in after the dose was taken"?'

Slightly stunned, all that Ryffel could reply was, 'I do not know exactly.'

'You were speaking from a rough impression?'

'I have a mental picture.'

Dr Ryffel elaborated. Very roughly, it was his impression that there might have been a quarter of a grain of arsenic in the wine glass.

Counsel asked: 'Will you agree that arsenic is one of the most widely distributed elements?'

'No.'

Fearnley-Whittingstall held up a red-covered book which, according to him, was 'the standard work, which is to the chem-

ist what the Bible is to the parson.' He then quoted from it:
'Arsenic in small quantities is one of the most widely distributed
elements.'

Ryffel: 'I venture to say that the author has not quite said
what he meant.'

Fearnley-Whittingstall: 'You mean that he has not said what
you meant.' (laughter)

Dr Ryffel agreed that it was difficult to find a mineral substance entirely free from arsenic, and that all the facts about
arsenic were not yet known to science.

The coroner broke in with: 'In spite of all that has been said,
you still adhere to your opinion that arsenic in the liquid in the
wine glass was in quite strong solution?'

'Yes. I have no doubt about it.'

Dr Ryffel retired.

Inspector Hedges then intimated that he had received information as to the purchase of a tin of Eureka weed-killer by Mr
Thomas Sidney. The tin, which cost three shillings, was bought
on September 26th, 1927, at Boots the chemist's in Croydon.
Mr Sidney was known at the shop and had given his correct
name and address and signed the register.

The coroner made a great show of his desire to be fair. 'I
only bring this out because Mr Thomas Sidney could not
remember where he bought the tin, or when. I think it is only
right that you should know there has been no secret purchase
of anything, but that it was bought in the ordinary manner
from a chemist in Croydon.'

Miss Clara Caroline Collett, of 31 Lebanon Road, Croydon,
then came forward.

She had been employed by Mrs Sidney as a domestic servant
from May 1927 until August 1928, and was the first of a posse
of servants, past and present, in the Sidney and Duff households
who found themselves all-unexpectedly called upon to pass
judgment on their master and mistress and the manner in
which they privately comported themselves.

Miss Collett was the predecessor of Mrs Noakes, and had
secured her place through Dale's Registry Office. She described
the relationship which existed between Mr Thomas Sidney and
his mother as rather more affectionate than that which existed
between the average mother and son, and the relationship between Mrs Duff and Mrs Sidney as affectionate also. There was
never any quarrelling, and they were a happy and united family.

Mrs Sidney did not seem at all eccentric in any way. On the
contrary, her brain was very keen. She was not the sort of
woman likely to take her own life.

Miss Vera Sidney was also a woman of strong character.

Mrs Duff entered Mrs Sidney's kitchen only once in the

fifteen months that Miss Collett was employed at Birdhurst Rise. That was when she came to the house after Major Duff died and went into the kitchen to tell Miss Collett of her husband's death, knowing that she would sympathize.

Miss Collett had never seen Mr Thomas Sidney in the kitchen.

During the afternoon, the coroner summoned Dr Brontë back to ask: 'Can you say with certainty, on the evidence you have read, that arsenic must have been added to the contents of this bottle after the initial dose of Metatone had been taken?'

Dr Brontë was satisfied that he could. If the whole of the arsenic was in the bottle from the beginning, then the first few doses must have caused obvious symptoms of arsenical poisoning. If the whole of the arsenic had been in soluble form when the bottle was delivered to Mrs Sidney, and she had taken her medicine as instructed, there would have been an almost-saturated solution of arsenic in the bottle in less than three days.

There was prolonged laughter when Mr Fearnley-Whittingstall, cross-examining Dr Brontë, delivered himself of the following: 'You have read Dr Ryffel's evidence this morning. If an unknown amount of water was added to an unknown amount of medicine, containing an unknown amount of sediment, which contains an unknown amount of arsenic, of which mixture an unknown amount was drunk, an unknown amount dissolved, and an unknown amount left, with an unknown amount of arsenic and an unknown amount of sediment, would you consider that sufficient data on which to form a theory to put before a jury such as Dr Ryffel formed?'

Brontë blinked, seemed to be staggering a little mentally, and admitted, 'I am afraid I cannot follow the question. There are so many "unknowns" about it that my answer will remain unknown.'

Fearnley-Whittingstall said that he would like the question and answer to be recorded on the depositions. 'I am rather proud of it,' he added with a laugh.

The coroner confessed that he had been unable to take the question down, and suggested to Dr Brontë that his answer was, 'I cannot answer the question.' Brontë agreed, and then he, the coroner and Fearnley-Whittingstall joined together in an endeavour to reconstruct the question to which it was the answer.

The Croydon chemist, Mr Frederick Sandford Rose, made a brief re-appearance to describe some experiments which he had made to test the comparative solubility of various arsenical compounds in water and in Metatone. He had found arsenious oxide to be less soluble in Metatone than in water, and that Eureka weed-killer was also more soluble in water than in Metatone.

Tom Sidney was brought again to the witness-chair, but had

no sooner sat down than the coroner decided to recall Grace
Duff instead.

The questions put, and the answers supplied, were run of the
mill.

No, she had never had any arsenic in her possession in any
other form than liquid weed-killer.

'Yes, she had bought her house at 59 Birdhurst Rise and had
given, she thought, £650, leasehold, for it. She had spent over
£200 on doing it up. The lease had an unexpired term of fifty-
five years to run, at a ground-rent of £10 a year.

She was not in debt at the time of her mother's death, nor
was she being pressed by creditors.

The coroner asked: 'Do you know what happened to your
mother's cat after her death?'

'My brother had it destroyed,' said Grace.

'Destroyed?'

'Yes, sir. I was going to have it, but my brother thought it was
not healthy with the children and the other animals.'

And with the speaking of poor Bingo's epicedium that day's
proceedings reached their solemn close.

IX

The ninth and last sitting of the inquest on Violet Emilia
Sidney was held on Wednesday, July 31st, 1929.

Turning to the jury Dr Jackson began his summing-up.

'You must,' he told them, 'find your verdict entirely on the
evidence you have heard, and you must disregard any rumours
you may have heard.'

After a brief recapitulation of the evidence, the coroner
offered four alternatives for their consideration.

1. That Mrs Sidney added the arsenic to the medicine
   herself, and took it to kill herself. That is, either that she
   committed suicide, or, not being of sound mind, she killed
   herself.

2. That the arsenic got into the medicine in some way of
   which there was no evidence, accidentally.

3. That the arsenic got into the medicine through the criminal carelessness of somebody else. That would be man-
   slaughter.

4. That Mrs Sidney was poisoned by somebody else, who put
   the arsenic into the medicine with intent to kill or cause
   grievous bodily harm. That would be murder.

Considering the first, he pointed out that Mrs Sidney had no one living in the house with her at the time of her death except her servant. Her daughter, Vera, to whom she was devotedly attached, had died on February 15th, and she had been grieving deeply and had often been heard to say, 'I don't know how I can go on living without her.' According to her surviving children, however, Mrs Sidney was beginning to appear more reconciled to Vera's loss, and was starting to look towards the future.

Her children said that she had no other cause for worry, had never suffered from delusions, had never been under treatment for mental illness and had never threatened to take her life. She had, in fact, specifically stated that she regarded suicide as morally wrong.

You could hardly say that these facts pointed strongly to suicide. It seemed very unlikely that she would have put poison in the medicine-bottle. There was nothing to support the suicide theory in conversations that she had after she had taken the fatal dose. She complained of the taste of the medicine and said it had been poisoned. If it was suicide one would suspect that she would either have confessed her action, or else tried to conceal that she had taken poison.

'It is a question for you to decide, and in balancing the facts, you should bear in mind that in many cases the mind of the suicide is abnormal and that not infrequently the nearest relatives have never realised it. In many cases such a person is capable of extraordinary conduct, inexplicable to the ordinary mind.'

As to the second alternative, there was no evidence of arsenic's having got into the medicine accidentally, or of any arsenic on the premises at 29 Birdhurst Rise, apart from the few specks in a small quantity of powdered rust found in an old tin in the garden shed. How could arsenic get into the medicine-bottle accidentally after the previous doses had been taken — and yet before the last dose? The only way that suggested itself was if, perhaps, there was arsenic by accident in some liquid which Mrs Sidney thought was water, and which she used to dilute the last dose of medicine. But there was no evidence that this was what happened.

Neither was there any evidence to suggest that the arsenic got into the medicine as a result of the criminal carelessness of somebody else. The coroner thought that the jury must be quite satisfied that the arsenic was not in the bottle when it was delivered to Mrs Sidney's house.

The great question was the fourth: that Mrs Sidney was feloniously poisoned by somebody else.

'This involves inquiry into the members of the family and visitors to the house, and also the possibility of some person outside the family getting access to the bottle of medicine. One of the strange features of this case is that there is no one who admits to having seen the medicine-bottle from the time it was delivered to Mrs Noakes and handed by her to Mrs Sidney, till the time when the last dose was taken. This fact appears less strange when it is remembered that Mrs Sidney was a methodical woman, and might have always put the bottle back in the side-board after taking her medicine.

'Who could have had access to that bottle? It would have to be someone who knew where Mrs Sidney kept it, and none of the witnesses at this inquest admits having known where it was kept. If the deceased was poisoned by somebody else, that somebody is very likely to deny knowledge of where it was kept.'

The jury would need to consider the servant living in the house, relatives frequently visiting it, and, conceivably, other visitors.

Mrs Noakes seemed to have been fond of Mrs Sidney and was about to leave her service to live with a friend. Why should she poison the medicine? There was no evidence that she did. There was no evidence of any motive, either of ill-will or expected benefit.

Mr Thomas Sidney's children were so young that the jury would no doubt rule them out.

Of Mrs Duff's children, the jury would have to ask themselves why on earth should they poison their grandmother's medicine? There was not a scrap of evidence that they did, nor any motive for their doing so.

There was also a daughter-in-law, Mrs Margaret Sidney. She might have benefited indirectly under Mrs Sidney's will, but was that an adequate reason why she should do this? Further, there was no evidence at all, to implicate her.

'We may turn to the daughter, Mrs Duff.

'There is nothing to show that Mrs Duff had any ill-feeling, or reason for ill-feeling, against her mother. All the evidence points the other way. She knew her mother had made a will, but she says that she had not seen it, and her mother did not tell her of its provisions. It was only natural that as a daughter she should benefit under that will. But do you consider that an adequate motive for poisoning her mother's medicine? She was far from being in want. She was in no financial difficulties.

'The absence of adequate motive is not conclusive that a person did not commit the crime. You cannot look into the minds of human beings. There are people, apparently sane, who have been known to have a devilish delight in killing others without any motive capable of proof.

'You have seen this woman, heard her, and heard of her from those best qualified to judge. She had, in a sense, the opportunity to poison, but have you heard any evidence which would explain any motive? She appears to be, although perhaps emotional, a truthful witness, and you must remember the conditions under which she appeared before you. It is also for me to tell you that there is not a tittle of evidence of administration. The most that the evidence comes to is opportunity of doctoring the medicine, and access several months ago to a form of arsenic in solution which, according to the evidence before you, was too weak a solution to produce the observed strength.'

Finally, there was Mr Thomas Sidney.

At times he had not seemed to appreciate the gravity of the inquiries. The jury had seen and heard him, and perhaps had formed a judgment as to his veracity. In case they should think that he was not the most truthful of the witnesses before them, he would impress upon them that they could not draw any inference of murder from that.

At this Tom Sidney interposed angrily, 'Is there any evidence, Dr Jackson, that I have not told you the truth in these inquiries?'

'I must ask you not to interrupt,' snapped the coroner.

Continuing, Dr Jackson said that what he had stated regarding the mutual affection of the members of this family applied to Mr Sidney. He appeared to have been devoted to his mother, and there was apparently no evidence of ill-feeling. He thought she was worth between £8,000 and £9,000, and it was only natural that he, too, should benefit upon his mother's death. Was that an adequate motive for the crime of matricide for one in no financial difficulties? Both he and Mrs Duff would shortly have something coming to them under Vera's will. He, too, had, in a sense, opportunity to poison, and he had in his possession weed-killer. In his case also, however, there was no tittle of evidence of administration.

'I think there is no one else. You must bear in mind that impossibility of doctoring medicine or administering poison is quite conclusive. Possibility of administering poison or doctoring medicine is not evidence that it *was* administered or poison. I think it right to tell you that there is no evidence, in my judgment, which singles out one member of the family as poisoner. Unless you are certain in your own mind that a particular individual is responsible, and that certainty rests on the sworn testimony, you ought not to name any person in the verdict.'

Dr Jackson's summing-up had lasted for fifty minutes, and, after he had explained to them that they were perfectly entitled to reject any of the views that he had expressed if they thought that he was not right, he told the jury to retire to consider their verdict.

They returned after an absence of thirty minutes, and the

foreman announced their finding as follows:

'Mrs Sidney died from acute poisoning by arsenic.'

Coroner: 'You should put a second paragraph to your verdict that she was murdered by some person or persons unknown, if that is what you mean. You are supposed to add a second paragraph classifying your verdict, if you can.'

Foreman: 'The question is: Does a verdict of murder exclude the possibility of suicide?'

Coroner: 'Suicide is self-murder, and it is rather a difficult question to answer. I think murder, as commonly accepted, is murder by some person other than the deceased. I think you should show you had the possibility in mind. You can say the cause of death was acute arsenical poisoning, and that there is not sufficient evidence to show whether she killed herself or was murdered by some other person or persons unknown. It is a question for you whether you mean to leave the question of suicide open. If you do, I think you should say so.'

And that was what the jury said.

Mrs Grace Duff broke down and wept.

The inquisition was closed.

The riddle remained a riddle.

5

INQUEST ON VERA

I

Throughout the four months that he had been holding the inquisition into the sudden death of Violet Emilia Sidney, Dr Jackson had also been conducting an inquest on her daughter, Vera Sidney.

This, too, had been held at the Queen's Road Homes, though with a different jury. Otherwise, the legal personnel and many of the witnesses were the same, and Mr Fearnley-Whittingstall again represented the interests of Thomas Sidney and Grace Duff.

The inquest on Vera had been opened at six o'clock on the evening of the day on which her body had been exhumed — March 22nd, 1929, but at that first sitting only evidence of identification was taken. What may be termed the inquest proper, began at 10.30 a.m. on Thursday, April 18th, 1929.

Pale-faced and appropriately dressed in deepest mourning, Vera's sister, Mrs Grace Duff, took her place as the first witness.

She described Vera as a healthy woman, fond of sport, particularly golf, who drove her own car. She was of a cheerful temperament on the whole, and Mrs Duff had not noticed any change in her in that respect prior to her last illness. She had never had any mental trouble, and had, so far as witness knew, nothing to worry her, except perhaps her health. She had, admittedly, been a little concerned about that in recent months, because she felt that she could not do quite so much as she used to. She had been very anaemic latterly, and her heart had received a strain during the war, so that she was really more delicate than most people knew. She had never threatened to take her own life, and Mrs Duff was utterly convinced that she would never do so.

There were tears in Grace Duff's eyes as she recalled how, on the evening of the Sunday before Vera died — February 10th — she saw her at 29 Birdhurst Rise. She was then 'fairly all right', although she had not been feeling well for some days and had a heavy cold. She said that her bones were aching and she thought she had a touch of rheumatism.

Mrs Duff did not think that she saw Vera on the Monday, February 11th, although it was just possible that she saw her in the morning. She certainly did see her — twice — on the Tuesday, when Vera was in bed, having been sick all night. She stayed with her for a quarter of an hour or so in the early afternoon. Vera then told her that Mrs Noakes and Bingo, the cat, had also been sick.

Dr Jackson's manner was gentle and sympathetic. 'When she told you that she had been sick all night, the cook had been sick, and the cat had been sick, did you make any inquiries as to what your sister and the others had been eating?'

'I thought it was a sort of general 'flu going through the house, but I did ask what they'd been eating.'

Mrs Duff added that her sister had had soup, but that Mrs Noakes had been sick *before* she had any soup. Whether Bingo had had any soup she could not say, but it would be a funny thing to give a cat. When she asked Vera what she had been eating Mrs Sidney was there, and Grace had caused a laugh by saying to her mother that it must be the 'flu, because the cat had the 'flu, and she thought they all had it.

On the Tuesday evening — February 12th — Vera told Grace that she had got up, but that she had had to return to bed. On that occasion Mrs Duff stayed with her only a few minutes.

'It was very, very cold. I knew that Vera worried about her car, and I really popped in to see if I could empty the radiator for her, but she said I didn't know enough about cars.'

Vera had said that she had taken the soup, after which she was sick, at supper-time on the Monday.

On the Wednesday morning — February 13th — Mrs Sidney visited her daughter, Grace, at 59 Birdhurst Rise, and said that she was very worried about Vera, who had gone out to attend to her car, and was still out. She also asked Grace if she would meet Auntie Gwen at the station, as she did not think that Vera was well enough to go. When, later, Grace saw Vera at her mother's home with Auntie Gwen, she was looking very ill. She said she felt rotten because she had been turning the starting handle of the car. In the end she had felt so bad that she could not go on with it any longer. 'I'm not going out of this house again today for anyone,' she had said.

Mrs Duff next saw Vera on the morning of Thursday, February 14th. She was then in bed and 'looked awful.'

Answering the coroner, Mrs Duff said that she did not think her sister's life was insured. She knew that she had made a will and thought that she was very likely to benefit under it. She had never actually seen the will, but had heard Vera say that she was going to leave her mother enough money to keep on the house. She thought that Vera was worth about four or five thousand pounds.

'Had you any suspicions at the time that your sister's illness was due to any other cause than natural disease?'

'Well, you see, I was just a little bit suspicious about the soup and the veal. I wasn't sure that she hadn't had something that disagreed with her — just a little bit dubious.'

'Had you heard about that time that there was a good deal of gastric influenza about?'

'Yes.'

The second witness was Dr Elwell.

He had attended Miss Sidney for an influenzal chill in February 1928, and did not see her again professionally until the evening of February 13th, 1929, when he received a message requesting a domiciliary visit.

He arrived at the house that Wednesday at 9.05 p.m., and found the deceased in bed, sitting on a bedpan, with a basin beside her, containing frothy, mucous vomit. She appeared as if she could vomit again on the slightest provocation. She was suffering very markedly from collapse, and no pulse could be felt in either wrist. Her temperature was 102°F. He gave her some bicarbonate of soda which, together with some champagne that her mother gave her, she promptly brought up. She was continually straining, and passed two small, watery motions. He did not leave the house until midnight, when the diarrhoea and vomiting appeared to have subsided. He returned just over an hour later and, as Vera was in severe pain, gave her an injection of one-eighth grain of morphine hydrochloride, hypodermically.

Dr Elwell next saw Vera at about 9 a.m. on Thursday, February 14th. She was still very collapsed, her temperature 100°F., and she complained of pain in her legs. She had a recurrent catching of the throat. Her pulse had not come back. Elwell consulted with Dr Binning, and they decided to call in a specialist, Dr Charles Bolton, an authority on gastro-intestinal disease.

Elwell remained with Vera nearly all that day. She told him that she thought she had a chill. Nothing was said about anything that she had eaten having upset her.

So far as he could judge, Vera and her sister, Mrs Duff, were on excellent terms, and very much attached to each other. He knew Vera fairly well and she used sometimes to do massage cases for him. The question of food poisoning or other poisoning had not entered his mind, and he did not notice any signs suggesting chronic arsenical poisoning. He did not take any sample of vomit or stool. She was passing what looked like rice-water vomit and stools, but there was no haemorrhage.

Miss Sidney was not at all the sort of person likely to take her own life.

Replying to Mr Fearnley-Whittingstall, he said that he had not noticed any eruption or irritation of the skin. The patient had not complained of thirst. Her heart was very badly dilated. She had no pulse, and he could just count the heart sounds with a stethoscope. It was such an acute dilation that it probably would not occur in a heart which was very strong to begin with. Deceased's eyes were not watery, so far as he observed.

After a brief consultation in the corner of the court with Inspector Hedges, the coroner asked: 'Would you say that all the symptoms that you observed in Miss Sidney's illness were consistent with acute arsenical poisoning?'

'In my opinion they were not. The temperature was a most puzzling point about her.' It was enormous for a poisoning case.

He was not sure that he had ever seen a case of acute arsenical poisoning before.

II

The third sitting, on Saturday, April 27th, opened at 10.30 a.m. with the taking of formal evidence of the exhumation from Mr Sydney Gardiner, undertaker's assistant, and Tom Sidney.

That disposed of, accompanied by a buzz of interest, the celebrated pathologist, Sir Bernard Spilsbury, walked with brisk, businesslike steps to the witness-chair.

He had attended the exhumation on March 22nd, and afterwards conducted a post-mortem examination of Miss Vera Sidney. The clothing in which the deceased was buried was clean and dry. Portions were removed and kept for examination.

Deceased was a well-nourished and well-developed woman, about 5 feet 5 inches in height. The surface of the body was dry. The brain was of a normal colour and contained clotted blood. The heart weighed 11 ounces, was enlarged and well covered in fat. There was some congestion at the rear of the lungs. There was a little clear fluid in the peritoneum. The liver weighed 46 ounces, and was soft and pale. The kidneys were small, weighing 8 ounces together, and were pale. There was a small amount of thick, dark-brown fluid in the stomach. The lower part of the small intestine showed areas of congestion. The large intestine showed areas of congestion and was a bright red. A microscopic examination showed advanced fatty degeneration of the heart, liver and kidneys.

'The cause of death, in my opinion, was syncope, due to fatty degeneration of the heart, liver and kidneys. I found no disease which would account for these facts. There was a condition which suggested the action of some gastro-intestinal irritant. A feature of the post-mortem examination, confirmed by microscopical examination, was the comparative absence of post-mortem degeneration, which was remarkable in a body exhumed five weeks after burial.'

At that, Fearnley-Whittingstall was on his feet.

'Sir Bernard, the state of the body, you say, was remarkable for five weeks after death?'

'Yes.'

'Could that be accounted for by the airtightness of the coffin?'

'No, sir, no.'

'You noticed there were some hyacinths in the coffin, held by the hand?'

'I noticed some flowers.'

'Did you notice that the hyacinths showed almost no sign of having withered?'

Sir Bernard, cautiously: 'They were withered to a certain extent.'

'I am suggesting that the airtightness of the coffin kept the flowers fresh.'

'Yes, I think that is so. It would keep them from drying.'

Now, gently, the question up to which all the others had been leading . . .

'The airtightness would in some way affect the preservation of the body?'

'Oh, yes.'

That was it. Point made.

Fearnley-Whittingstall sat down.

At the afternoon session, Dr Ryffel presented his report of the analysis which he had made of the organs from Vera Sidney's body.

He found in the liver ·255 grain, or a quarter of a grain, of arsenic in the form of arsenious oxide. In the kidneys ·012 grain. In the heart ·019 grain. In the spleen ·0014 grain. In the stomach ·012 grain. The contents of the stomach were sparse, and contained only a small proportion of arsenic, which amounted to ·0005 grain. In the small intestine ·019 grain. In the large intestine ·025 grain. In the rectum ·0094 grain. In the brain ·009 grain. In the bones ·019 grain. In the muscles ·93 grain. In the pleural and peritoneal fluid ·003 grain. The total amount of arsenic found was 1·48 grains of arsenious oxide. The skin and lungs were not supplied, but might be assumed to contain ·05 grain. The hair of the head contained only the slightest trace of arsenic, but the toe and finger nails contained 2 parts of arsenious oxide per 100,000.

The amount of arsenic accounted for was not a poisonous dose. But, allowing for the fact that the deceased lived for thirty-six hours after her attack of sickness, and the quantity of arsenic that must have been eliminated from the body during that time, if that sickness was the result of arsenic, the original dose must have been over 5 grains, which was a fully poisonous dose.

If the whole of her illness, which started three days before her death, was consequent upon the taking of arsenic, then the total must have been still larger.

Dr Ryffel could not specify in what form the arsenic was taken, except that it was some form that was absorbable. Some compounds of arsenic were not. He was unable to say whether, in this case, it had been in solid form or in solution.

Fearnley-Whittingstall's turn to question him.

'Can you say whether it was a fatal or non-fatal amount that was absorbed? That is impossible in your calculations?'

'I do not agree. The interval was thirty-six hours. If you find $1\frac{1}{2}$ grains in the body at the end of thirty-six hours, with elimination taking place at that time, I think it is fair to suppose, speaking roughly, that 3 grains were absorbed.'

'What would you regard as the minimum fatal dose of metallic arsenic?'

'A matter of luck.'

'Of white arsenic?'

'Three grains, I believe — that is of arsenious oxide.'

Tom Sidney now stepped up to the witness-chair to tell the court that his sister had lived the whole of her life with their mother, and that the two were on very affectionate terms, always interested in each other's affairs. He and Mrs Duff were also on good terms with Vera, and so, as far as he knew, was Mrs Noakes. No near relative had ever suffered from unsoundness of mind,[1] or taken his or her own life.

III

The examination of Tom Sidney continued on Wednesday, May 1st, when the fourth sitting of the inquest on Vera was convened, and there were several stormy passages between him and the coroner.

Sidney had made certain statements to Inspector Hedges in the presence of Inspector Morrish on March 7th and 9th. What those statements amounted to was that he had been taken ill in Edinburgh on Friday, February 8th, 1929. He had arrived back in Croydon very late on the Saturday night, and was examined by Dr Binning. The next day, Sunday, February 10th, he stayed in bed all day. Then, on the morning of Monday, February 11th, he went for a long walk by himself; returning from which, he went to bed. That Monday evening he gave an entertainment at the Connaught Rooms, Holborn. He was taken ill during the performance: his voice gave out, and he had to go home and retire to bed, where he stayed until midday on

---

[1] This is not in fact strictly true — see page 155.

Wednesday, February 13th. The first occasion upon which he saw his mother after his return from Scotland, was Tuesday, February 19th, the day of Vera's funeral. He had first heard that Vera was ill on Thursday, February 14th, when, at about midday, Mrs Duff called and told him. He last saw Vera on the previous day, Ash Wednesday, when she called at his house at about 12.30 p.m.

The coroner was silently reading one of the long, typewritten statements, when Sidney asked if he could see them.

'Oh, yes,' answered Dr Jackson, 'but I don't propose to ask you anything about them.'

Sidney was reading from a copy of one of the statements, when he pointed out that it might be read in two ways.

'Don't bother about that,' advised the coroner.

A minute or two later, Dr Jackson requested him to read from a particular page of one of the statements.

Sidney looked puzzled. 'Certainly this statement . . . here . . . I don't know whether it was an error on my part, or . . .'

The coroner interrupted him. 'You pick out the very part I was going to question you about.'

'There is one qualification I want to make with regard to this statement of March 7th,' Sidney went on. 'The reference to my sister on February 13th.'

Dr Jackson was watching him closely. 'This is very important to my mind, and I must get it down. You say in your first statement:

"First, I wish to speak of my sister. On February 13th, 1929, she called upon me about 12.30 p.m. At that time I had had a week indoors from influenza. I said to her, 'I am surprised to see you, as I was told you were ill.' She said, 'I am all right now and I am running round to see my car.'"

'Is that what you said?'

'Most likely it is,' replied Sidney.

'This is a very important matter, as a matter of fact.' The coroner did not appreciate his seeming casualness. A few seconds later he read out from the first statement: 'At that time I had had a week indoors from influenza.'

'That statement can be qualified. I had not my diary with me when I made the statement.'

'It is a perfectly plain statement.'

'I made it in a haphazard way. I didn't know that they were going to exhume my sister and find arsenic in her body, and neither did I know that this was going to be brought up.'

'Then what do you say this statement refers to?'

'I say it refers to a period when I was a week indoors with influenza. I do not say that the week started or ended on

February 13th. I hadn't my diary with me.'

'Why did you say that on February 13th you had had a week indoors from influenza, when you had been out for a two hours' walk on February 11th — two days before?'

'Well, I think, honestly, you are straining at the gnat. I was speaking back about a fortnight. I didn't qualify that date. I meant that at that time I had had a week indoors. I still say this statement was correct.'

The coroner was busily writing when Sidney called across, 'I don't want that put down.'

'You have said it. It is your explanation.'

'I think it has been qualified. I must have counsel's advice. It is putting an entirely different interpretation on my statement.'

'Is it correct or incorrect?'

'I think you can qualify it in two different ways.'

Sidney refused to be held down to any particular date as to when his influenza attack had started.

By now the coroner was getting thoroughly ruffled. 'Why did you first speak of your sister in that statement?'

'I didn't know at the time that they were inquiring about Vera's death. Inspector Hedges put those words into my mouth. I didn't wish to speak about Vera. I do think they should be more careful in putting down answers, because I didn't know this matter was going to be brought in front of a jury.'

'Wait a minute. Not so fast. I have to put it down,' said Dr Jackson testily.

'I don't *want* it put down.'

'It doesn't matter what you want put down. It must be put down. You are here to give evidence. Did you know that the police were inquiring concerning Vera's death?'

'No, sir.'

'Only about your mother's death?'

'Yes. We had no idea that anything special was being inquired into. We didn't think of anything but a natural death.'

'That, of course, has an important bearing on the statements. Do you suggest that the inspector put words into your mouth?'

'Oh, no. Just a phrase. He helped me to frame my answers here and there. That's all.'

Mr Fearnley-Whittingstall now entered the fray.

'If a great deal is to turn on this meticulous examination and questioning, I would ask Inspector Hedges to leave the room.' Then, referring to the disputed statement: 'Let us have Inspector Hedges if it turns on this statement, "First, I wish to speak of my sister," which smacks of Scotland Yard.'

By this time in despair, Tom Sidney explained that he did not want an erroneous idea to get into the heads of the jury and stay there. 'It is a month later that I made this statement. I have this terrible tragedy on my mind. My sister and my mother are gone. My whole life is upset.'

But Dr Jackson is like a bulldog. 'If you did not know they were inquiring into Vera's death, you knew they were inquiring into the death of your mother?'

'Yes,' says Sidney desperately.

'Is it not important, then, that your answers should be accurate?' persists the coroner.

'My answers were accurate.'

'Do you not think the statement is very misleading?'

'It was made months ago. It is rather vague.'

'I should think it was very definite. You are trying to make it vague. In plain English it is very definite. With regard to the walk on the morning of February 11th, where did you go?'

Sidney regretted, he was afraid he couldn't remember. Usually he walked seven or eight miles. He was ill at the time, and was taking an extra long walk in order to get himself in as good a condition as possible.

Asked whether he went to his mother's house that day, he regretted again, he was not sure. But of one thing he was certain. He did not go in. 'I'm sure I didn't, because I was supposed to be suffering from illness and I wouldn't like to infect my mother with it.' Then, bitterly: 'I wish I had gone in, because as far as I can see they are trying to prove or disprove that I had anything to do with this poisoning.'

'Unfortunately we have to do so,' commented the coroner.

'My only regret is that it has to be done in public,' was Sidney's tart response.

Then came a sharp exchange between Fearnley-Whittingstall and Inspector Hedges.

Fearnley-Whittingstall was quietly reading a statement made by Mr Sidney, when Hedges loudly objected that he thought that it was not right that he should read the whole thing.

'The coroner is conducting this inquiry,' snapped Fearnley-Whittingstall.

Undaunted, the Inspector was making a further protest when Fearnley-Whittingstall, who was continuing to read the statement, interjected sharply, 'One minute, Mr Hedges. The coroner has to decide this point.'

Dr Jackson and counsel then went to a corner of the room and spoke together, and Fearnley-Whittingstall intimated that he had read the statement and did not want to see any more of it.

Pressed by the coroner, Sidney was positive that he did not leave his house on Wednesday, February 13th. 'I never even dressed that day.'

'Last time you were sure that you did not leave your house

on Tuesday, the 12th. How can you be sure you did not leave the house on Wednesday?'

'Because it was the day I realised I had made myself much worse by going out.'

'You previously stated that you did not go out on Tuesday, and that you were in bed from the time of coming in on Monday night until midday Wednesday.'

'To the best of my belief, I was.'

'But today you admit that you are not sure. How can you be sure about Wednesday when you previously swore that you did not go out on the Tuesday?'

'Did I swear?'

'You did. All your evidence is on oath. I have warned you to be careful. If you are not sure of a point you must say so. We don't want misleading evidence. Why are you more certain of Wednesday than Tuesday?'

'If I was not certain about the Tuesday it was because when I came home I saw against Tuesday a small expenditure in my account book. I could not account for that from memory, and it is just possible that I went out that morning and spent some money.'

'Your evidence previously given was entirely wrong?'

'Not entirely wrong.'

'Well, certainly wrong in connection with Tuesday?'

'Yes.'

'I think I am justified in saying that your evidence is entirely wrong. You said you were in bed.'

'I don't want to tell lies so that it will appear in the papers, and for someone to say they saw me walking down the road.'

'I am not suggesting you want to tell lies. I believe you are as anxious as anyone to help us to get the truth in these matters. I suggest that it was a mistake and that we cannot rely on your evidence as a statement of fact.'

And that brought the day's somewhat fraught hearing to an end.

IV

'I am here because I am subpoenaed, but I don't feel very well this morning. I will answer questions to the best of my ability, but I don't want to be bullied. I can't stand it.'

Thus, Mrs Kathleen Noakes at the commencement of the fifth session of the inquest on Vera Sidney on Thursday, May 9th.

'It is not a question of being bullied.' Dr Jackson's manner was soothing. 'But you may have to be cross-examined. I will probably take your evidence up to twelve o'clock, and then give you a rest, recalling you later if necessary.'

According to Mrs Noakes, on the Sunday before Miss Vera died (February 10th) she had come down to breakfast complaining of a cold in the head and saying that she was going to stay indoors that day. She had her lunch downstairs, but she did not have any soup. In the evening she said that she still felt very seedy.

On the Monday (February 11th), Miss Vera went to Oxted for lunch[1], and returned in time for tea, having it, as usual, in the drawing-room. She did not seem worse or better than she had been in the morning. That night she had supper with her mother in the dining-room.

'Now I want you to be very careful about this,' Dr Jackson warned solemnly. 'If you cannot remember certainly, you will tell us so. If you can, I shall be glad. Who prepared the soup Miss Vera had for supper on February 11th?'

'I did.'

'Was it after supper on Monday night that Miss Vera vomited?'

Mrs Noakes hesitated. Looked troubled. 'I'm not quite sure. To the best of my recollection it was Tuesday.'[2]

At this point the coroner suggested that she should leave the witness-chair and have a rest.

Her place was taken by Dr Binning.

He started off with the admission that he had never previously attended a case of acute arsenical poisoning. The remainder of his evidence was, at this stage of the proceedings, formal.

Mrs Noakes returned to the witness-chair, refreshed after the lunch interval.

She spoke of making soup for Wednesday's lunch on Tuesday (February 12th), the day before. Referring to that Tuesday, she unfortunately could not remember whether Miss Vera had soup for supper or not. Mrs Sidney never took any soup, because she liked it thick, and Miss Vera always had it thin. When witness left the house for her afternoon off at three o'clock on Sundays, she would leave the soup in the saucepan on or near the gas-ring in the scullery. When she made soup for two days, whatever was left over after the first day was kept in the pantry in the cellar. This pantry was one of three cellars. The door leading to the cellar stairs was in the passage leading from the back-door.

[1] Mrs Noakes subsequently amended her statement. She had got mixed up about Miss Vera's movements that Monday, and it must have been on another day that she went to Oxted.

[2] Mrs Noakes later admitted that she had made a mistake and that it was on the Monday night, and not the Tuesday night, that she, Vera, and the cat were all sick.

The back-door was often left ajar, and anybody could get into
the house. If anyone opened the door to the cellar it would
make the kitchen dark.

The coroner: 'Can you be sure that the soup you had on
the night that you and the cat were sick was made on the day
you had it, or was it made the day before? Which portion was
it?'

'It was the second portion.'

'You are quite certain, are you, that what you gave to the cat
was the last drop of that batch of soup?'

Mrs Noakes was emphatic. 'Yes.'

She agreed that if she and the cat were sick on the Monday, it
would be after the soup she had made on the Sunday (February
10th). Into the soup which she made on Tuesday (February
12th), she put carrots, turnips and onions, some soup powder
and the remains of some boiled veal, left over from the previous
Friday or Saturday, which Mrs Sidney told her to put in. Some
of the Symington's soup powder from the same packet was, on
March 9th, handed to the coroner's officer.

Dr Jackson told the jury, 'It has been analysed, and there
is no arsenic in it.'

Mrs Noakes had been in the witness-chair all day except for a
few minutes, and she looked pretty washed out. Her evidence
had not been completed, but the time had come to adjourn.

V

The interval between the adjournment of the fifth sitting
and the resumption of the inquest on Vera Sidney on June 1st,
was a long one, and throughout those three weeks a great many
things were happening.

At about seven o'clock on the morning of May 18th, two
grave-diggers at Queen's Road Cemetery removed the carved-
angel headstone, and set to work to open the grave of Edmund
Creighton Duff. Following police consultations which had gone
on until after midnight on May 17th, the Home Office had
authorised an exhumation.

Presently, two police sergeants arrived to supervise the digging.
Later, they were joined by Mr Douglas James Shakespeare, the
undertaker, Dr Binning, Detective-Superintendent William Frederick Brown of Scotland Yard, Detective-Inspectors Hedges and
Morrish and Detective-Constable Carl Louis William Hagen.

Later still, Tom Sidney arrived. He was met at the cemetery
gates by the three senior police-officers. He seemed tired but
quite cheerful, and remarked, 'Well, I'm glad it's not three
o'clock in the morning this time!' After looking into the opened

grave, he took up a position so close beside it that when one of the grave-diggers threw out a shovelful of soil it fell at his feet, and he sprang back with a sharp exclamation of horror.

When at last the grave-diggers had exposed the coffin, lying in its bed of damp clay, they did not attempt to remove it, but placed boards over the grave to await the arrival of Sir Bernard Spilsbury.

Sir Bernard came hurrying down the path at 10 a.m. He stood by, notebook in hand, and scribbled down observations on the condition of the soil as the grave-diggers resumed the work of exhumation.

Just as the diggers were straining at the straps to raise the coffin, a short, bespectacled man, carrying a small case, arrived at the graveside. He was Dr Gerald Roche Lynch, senior official analyst to the Home Office. After an earnest conversation with Sir Bernard, he pulled a large notebook out of his pocket and settled down to watch the exhumation, making copious notes concerning the smell of the soil and all such other matters as might have a bearing on the question of poison.

Wooden props had been erected round the grave with a view to putting up a screen of tarpaulin sheets, but the screen was not erected. The exhumation was carried out without secrecy, and several people passing through the cemetery stopped to look.

The clay covering the name-plate on the coffin was scraped away and the particulars on it were identified by Tom Sidney.

Sir Bernard took a quantity of earth and clay from the sides of the wood and put it carefully into a glass jar, which he stowed away in his black bag. One of the grave-diggers filled another jar with earth from the bottom of the grave, and handed it to Spilsbury.

The coffin was lifted into Mr Shakespeare's horse-drawn van, and Tom Sidney, accompanied by Brown, Hedges and Morrish, walked slowly in the roadway behind it as it moved at a funeral pace through half a mile of back-streets to Mayday Road Mortuary.

There the post-mortem examination was made by Sir Bernard, with Dr Brontë, Dr Roche Lynch and Dr Binning looking on. Various organs were removed and sealed in glass jars for further examination by Dr Roche Lynch. The body was put back in the coffin and reburied at 2 p.m. that same afternoon.

Tom Sidney admitted to a *Star* reporter.

'Both Mrs Duff and myself are very pained at this development. Mrs Duff is very upset, and it was quite impossible for her to witness the exhumation today. It would have been too great a strain on her after what she has already endured at the inquests.'

Grace Duff herself was interviewed the following morning by a *Daily Express* reporter who called at her home.

'It is my dearest wish that this dreadful mystery should be cleared up as soon as possible. I want everything to be done that can throw daylight on the horrible things which have happened to us. It was dreadful for me to have the body of my husband exhumed. It seemed such desecration; worse than the first burial. But I am glad they did it if it will help them to discover the truth. We were such a united family — splendid friends. My sister was the kind of woman to whom all went with their troubles — and her life was not half over when she died. This house was bought so that I could be near my mother and sister. My mother simply adored my eldest daughter. We were always running into their house. They were always calling on me. Can you imagine how I miss them now, or how sad I feel when I have to pass their house? They told me they were going to exhume the body of my husband at night, otherwise I would have been there to see it done. How strange are the coincidences which have harmed my family. It has been said that we must have an enemy who has done all this.'

Following the exhumation of Edmund Duff and the medical examination of his remains, a series of consultations were held between the police and the Home Office scientific and legal experts.

These consultations were conducted with the greatest secrecy, but that did not prevent the press from hazarding suggestions as to what matters were being considered at those closely-guarded conferences.

The *Daily Express* of May 23rd understood that:

'a special application will be made to the High Court for an order to hold a second inquest on Mr Edmund Creighton Duff. Action in regard to a second inquest is dependent on the final report of Dr Roche Lynch, the Home Office expert who is carrying out an analysis of certain parts of the body.'

Throughout the following week, the newspapers, starved of factual information, could do little more than speculate.
Said the *Daily News* of May 24th:

'If the evidence is sufficient to raise doubts as to the previous finding of "Natural causes", the Croydon coroner can take action under the Coroners (Amendment) Act of 1926, which provides "Where the Court is satisfied that by reason of the discovery of new facts or evidence it is necessary or desirable in the interests of justice that an inquisition on an inquest previously held concerning a death should be quashed and that another inquest should be held the High Court can exercise its powers.'''

The *Evening News* of May 27th announced authoritatively:

'The reports of Dr Roche Lynch and Sir Bernard Spilsbury have now been presented to Scotland Yard. The reports have been the subject of a conference between Detective-Superintendent Brown and Divisional Detective-Inspector Hedges, and today the legal experts of the Home Office were consulted. The reports of the analyst and the pathologist show that there was doubt as to whether Mr Duff's death was actually due to natural causes. It is within the power of the coroner, in view of further evidence, to apply to the High Court for power to set aside the original verdict and ask permission to hold a second inquest. Equally, the Home Office may apply to the High Court to have the first verdict set aside and a second inquest held by another coroner. What steps will be taken will depend on the view held by the Home Office legal experts who are now considering the question.'

Next day's *Daily News* expected:

'that the Home Office will apply to the High Court within the next few days for permission to hold a second inquest on the late Mr Edmund Creighton Duff. The Croydon Borough Coroner . . . said yesterday that he had received no instructions concerning a further inquest.'

The *Daily Mail* was rather more specific:

'Consultations have taken place between Home Office officials, who, it is understood, have been in touch with Sir William Joynson-Hicks, the Home Secretary.'

The *Daily Mail* also reported that a number of abusive anonymous letters had been received by members of the Sidney family. They came from various parts of the country, and some of them offered highly libellous solutions to the mystery.

It was the *Daily Mail*, too, that, on May 30th, provided a completely fresh item of information:

'New inquiries are being made by the police . . . the latest investigations are being made concerning the cause of the deaths of Margaret Kathleen Duff, aged 7, who died in 1919, and Suzanne Duff, aged 2, who died in 1924.'

These were Grace Duff's daughters. Margaret Kathleen's death had been certified as due to rheumatoid arthritis and colectomy for intestinal obstruction. Suzanne had died, according to the death certificate issued by Dr Elwell, of cerebral tuberculous meningitis.

May came to an end with the question of whether or not there was to be a second inquest on the exhumed remains of Edmund Duff still hanging in the balance.

VI

The inquest on Vera Sidney sat for the sixth time on Saturday, June 1st.

Mrs Gwendoline Mary Stafford Greenwell bustled to the witness-chair.

She was the wife of Lieutenant-Colonel Herbert Maitland Greenwell, 4th Durham Light Infantry, retired, and she lived at 2 Grosvenor Road, Newcastle-upon-Tyne. Mrs Violet Emilia Sidney was the wife of her eldest brother.

Mrs Greenwell had been staying at Ford's Hotel, Manchester Square, in London, on February 13th, 1929, and went to lunch on that day with her sister-in-law, Mrs Sidney, at 29 Birdhurst Rise. She had written to Mrs Sidney a few days before — probably on the previous Friday (February 8th) — suggesting that she should come down and lunch with her.

She could not remember whether or not Mrs Duff went inside Number 29 with her when she took her there from the station, but said that if she did, it was only just into the hall.

Asked how much soup she had taken, Mrs Greenwell replied, 'It might have been six spoonfuls.'

She did not notice any unusual taste, but immediately she had swallowed a few spoonfuls she felt that she did not want any more, or want to eat anything else.

She did not think that she had told Mrs Duff on the way up from the station that she had had influenza, for the simple reason that she had not had it. She had, however, had a nasty cough the week before her visit, and she might have mentioned that. But the day she went to Croydon she was feeling quite well.

On the way back to the railway station Mrs Duff suggested to her that it would be a good thing if she stayed with her that night if she were not well enough to return to London, but she had replied that she would rather go back to her hotel. She did so, catching the 4.25 train, and was ill in bed until the following Tuesday. She was attended by a Dr Caithness, and explained to him what her symptoms were, saying that she thought that it was some soup that she had taken which had upset her. He did not tell her what she was suffering from. She herself was quite certain that she had had something which had poisoned her.

Mrs Greenwell was succeeded by Mrs Dorothy Winifred Gent, of 170 Frant Road, Thornton Heath, who was employed as a daily domestic by Mr Thomas Sidney. She had been in that situation for about a year.

She recalled Mr Sidney's coming home ill from Scotland a few months ago, and remembered that on the Ash Wednesday following his return, Miss Vera Sidney called at the house around 12.30 p.m., and stayed with him for about ten minutes. Miss Sidney had asked for some hot water to unfreeze her car, and waited in the hall while Mrs Gent fetched it for her. She did not on that occasion see Mr Sidney. About fifteen minutes later, Miss Sidney returned the can at the back-door, saying, 'Returned with thanks,' and it was then that she went in to see Mr Sidney, who was sitting in the drawing-room in his dressing-gown, as he was still unwell.

VII

Sitting Seven. Thursday, June 6th, 1929.

Mr Fearnley-Whittingstall was not present, his place being taken by Mr William Dumville Smythe, his instructing solicitor.

Mrs Kathleen Noakes underwent a further session of interrogation, and the story of the soup was taken up again.

She said that on Sunday, February 10th, she had left a saucepan of soup for Miss Vera's supper on the gas-stove when she went out at 3 p.m.

The coroner made a careful note. Then, regarding the attack of vomiting on the night of Monday, February 11th, asked if she was sure that she had not been sick *before* she had had any soup. 'Mrs Duff has said that Miss Vera told her that you had been sick before you had the soup.'

'No, sir, I was not. I am quite sure.' She was adamant.

'It is a coincidence that after your having been there about 180 nights, the only night that you take the soup is the one on which there was something wrong with it apparently,' observed the coroner.

Dr Jackson next inquired if she could remember whether Mrs Duff came to Number 29 on the afternoon of Tuesday, February 12th.

'I think she came in the evening, after tea. I'm not quite certain at what time.'

She was definite that Mrs Duff had not called at the house on the Wednesday prior to bringing Mrs Greenwell to lunch.

Before serving the soup at Wednesday's lunch Mrs Noakes tasted it to see if it was properly seasoned, but did not notice any unusual flavour. A lot of soup was left over, and she put it in a basin and took it to the pantry in the cellar. Later, she was told, by either Mrs or Miss Sidney, to throw it away. She did so.

The coroner: 'Did you think that there was poison in that soup at the time when you threw it away?'

'I had no idea. I thought our sickness was through the old saucepan.'

After the lunch party on the Wednesday, Miss Vera had come out to the kitchen to inspect the saucepan. It was an old one and she said that she thought that her sickness was due to it.

The last time that Mrs Noakes saw Miss Vera alive was on the Thursday (February 14th), when she 'peeped in' her bedroom before going out on her half day, and she wept as she gave her evidence about the events of that evening, tears rolling down her cheeks.

The coroner asked her if she gave notice to leave that Thursday night. She replied that all that she had said was that she was not feeling at all well, and that if she did not feel better she would have to go away for a few days. She did not give notice that evening. 'I will swear that,' she added.

Thomas Sidney, who was sitting at one side of the court with Mrs Duff, exclaimed angrily, 'My mother is a liar then?'

'You must not interrupt,' frowned the coroner. 'You will have an opportunity to make a statement, Mr Sidney. If you interrupt any more you will have to leave the court.'

At that, Tom Sidney got up and walked out.

A little later the coroner's officer and Inspector Hedges also left the court. They returned a few minutes afterwards with Mr Sidney, who turned to the coroner and said, 'I apologise for interrupting, sir.'

'It is all right, Mr Sidney. You quite appreciate I cannot have interruption of the witnesses. You will have an opportunity of saying all you want to. I will call you again later. I have sent for you now because I am particularly anxious that you shall hear the answers to questions I am going to put.'

The air cleared, Dr Jackson resumed his questioning of Mrs Noakes.

She spoke now of the occasion when the coroner's officer — Mr Clarke — called on her at nine o'clock one morning, a few days after Mrs Sidney's death. He had asked her about any

The Carved-Angel Headstone. The Open Grave. Queen's Road Cemetery, Croydon. The Exhumation of Edmund.

Mr Shakespeare's hearse delivers the exhumed body of Edmund Duff to the Mayday Road Mortuary. Tom Sidney (with umbrella) follows at funeral pace.

Major Edmund Creighton Duff.
'Tanned, vital, lusty, as of old.'

Grace Duff. His wife. Charismatic Mother of Mary,
John and baby Suzanne.

Brother Tom. Genial Entertainer.
The one that got away.

The Weeping Widow of Birdhurst Rise with Auntie
Gwen — who came bearing a pineapple and was
poisoned with soup.

deaths which had occurred in the family prior to that of Mrs Sidney, and she had then told him about Miss Vera's death.

'Mr Sidney came into the kitchen after Mr Clarke had gone and said, "One of us ought to have been here, as he would ask you questions, as the dead cannot speak, but they can make it very uncomfortable for those that are living."'

Detective-Inspector Reginald Morrish testified that he had accompanied Mr Thomas Sidney, in a motor-car, from his residence to Queen's Road Cemetery at about 1 a.m. on March 22nd, 1929, and that he conversed with him in the car on the way to the exhumation. Mr Sidney had been informed that the bodies were to be exhumed that day. Arsenic was mentioned and Sidney remarked, 'If they've found it in Mother there's no reason why they shouldn't find it in Vera.' He also said, 'Thank God I was indoors for a week with the 'flu at that time.'

Cross-examined by Mr Fearnley-Whittingstall, who had arrived at the court late in the afternoon, Morrish claimed that he had gathered from the general trend of Sidney's conversation that he thought that arsenic had been found, and that the symptoms preceding his mother's death were exactly the same as those preceding his sister's.

Fearnley-Whittingstall was not going to let it go at that.

'If you had had two mysterious deaths in a family, and you had had two interviews with the police, and there were going to be two exhumations, would you not thank God you had been in bed that week?'

'Do you wish me to answer that?' There was a note of defiance in Morrish's voice.

'Certainly.'

'I should certainly say that as an innocent man I should not care whether I was in bed or not.'

'Do you agree with me that even an innocent man welcomes some proof of his innocence?'

'I certainly do.'

Tom Sidney was given the chance to comment on Morrish's account of what was said.

'Very possibly I said every word. I was highly strung up that night. I do not deny a word of it. I couldn't swear one way or the other. I wasn't used to getting up in the middle of the night to see my mother and sister exhumed. It was rather an unusual experience.'

He went on to explain that he knew that arsenic had been found in his mother, and that he had thought it very likely that it would be found in Vera also, because the day after Vera died Dr Binning had visited him at his home and said that had he not known the family he would have suspected arsenical poisoning in Vera's case.

Regarding his inference that arsenic might be found in Vera's body, he said, 'I didn't suspect it at any time until I saw my sister's body in the mortuary — until the coffin lid was off.'

The coroner suggested that Mr Sidney had rather contradicted himself, pointing out that he had spoken of the possibility of arsenic in Vera's case on the way to the exhumation, and yet had just said that he did not suspect arsenical poisoning until he was in the mortuary.

'I am not a medical man,' retorted Sidney.

'There is no question of medical knowledge. It is a question of what was in your mind. Was there anything in the appearance of the body which caused you to think that her last illness was due to arsenic poisoning?'

'Not only the body, but somebody mentioned arsenic in the mortuary. The body was well-preserved.'

'Do you know who it was in the mortuary who mentioned arsenic?'

'I do know, but I would rather not say, because I don't think I was meant to hear. It was whispered all around. It got all round the place almost at once.'

'Do you know anything of the preservative effect of arsenic on bodies?'

'I have read a certain amount.'

'Where have you read it, Mr Sidney?'

'I don't know the exact titles of the books, but I've read a good many medical books in my time, and I have read books on poisoning. I have also read a good many of the arsenical poisoning cases of the last few years. I'm sure that it is general knowledge that bodies are preserved by arsenic.'

Sidney was anxious that it should be understood that he did not actually recollect making the remark in the car on the way to the exhumation — "Thank God I was indoors for a week with the 'flu at that time."

'I strongly suspect that all these statements are highly coloured. With all due respect to Inspector Morrish and Inspector Hedges, they try to build up their theories. I should do it myself if I were in their place.'

Dr Jackson let that pass without comment.

'Did you wish Inspector Morrish to believe that you had been indoors for a week prior to Vera's death?'

'No, sir. I'm quite sure I didn't care whether he knew or not.'

'You are not disposed to agree with Mr Whittingstall's suggestion that an innocent man welcomes some proof of his innocence?'

'I should not mind being charged with the murder of my mother and sister. I should sleep quite soundly at nights because I should know quite well what would be the result. I should have the experience of going into a gaol, and it would be very useful to me in my lectures afterwards. I expect I should get my expenses back in writing-up for the press. If I were a guilty person I should be very, very careful in speaking to the police at all.'

'As it was such a matter of indifference to you as to what the inspector thought or believed, why did you say "Thank God"?'

'I think when we have passed the hour of midnight perhaps we get more devout sometimes.'

He again insisted that he did not, however, recollect passing the remark at all. He was simply making conversation in the car and was perhaps speaking loosely.

'If,' observed the coroner, 'you really did say "Thank God", that is not quite the sort of expression of a man who was speaking very loosely and not attaching much importance to what he was saying.'

Tom Sidney bridled: 'It is an expression you use a dozen times a day — "Thank God it is not raining. Thank God it is fine." I shall say "Thank God" when this inquest is over, anyway!'

But there were to be two more sittings before Tom Sidney could say 'Thank God'.

VIII

In adjourning the seventh sitting of the inquest on Vera Sidney until June 22nd, the coroner had remarked, 'For reasons I cannot go into fully, it is impossible to close the case down at the moment.'

Turning the pages of the contemporary newspapers, those reasons into which Dr Jackson could not go are abundantly obvious. In a case already rich in sensational developments, almost every day seemed to bring forth more.

Thus, the *Daily Express* of June 1st had announced:

'A fourth exhumation is likely to take place in the Croydon Death Mystery. Certain suspicious circumstances surrounding the death of an unmarried woman who lived at Croydon have been brought to the notice of the coroner and the police.'

The woman was Miss Anna Maria Kelvey, who had lived for some time as a paying guest with Mr and Mrs Duff. She had died, aged seventy-six, at Hurst View, on January 12th, 1927. Her

death had been certified as a result of arterio-sclerosis and cerebral haemorrhage. The death certificate was signed by Dr
Elwell.

In her will Miss Kelvey left £407. Her bequests included £25
each to Grace's children, John and Mary Duff, and £50 to Dr
Elwell. She was buried in Queen's Road Cemetery, only a few
yards from the Duff family grave.

In the heel of it, Miss Kelvey was not, in fact, exhumed.
Neither was Kathleen Margaret, nor Suzanne Duff. Probably the
police felt that they already had enough bodies on their hands
as it was. If the exhumation of three was not sufficient to
bring the crimes home to the culprit, to have six was more likely
to prove an embarrassment than an assistance. Anyway, on
June 13th, Scotland Yard issued an official statement that no
further exhumations were being contemplated.

The *Daily Express* of June 12th told its readers:

'An application will be made shortly to the High Court in
respect of Mr Edmund Duff, asking for authority to hold a
new inquest . . . Every scrap of evidence has been laid before
Sir Archibald Bodkin, Director of Public Prosecutions. He
has held numerous consultations with the police and with the
experts in his own office. . . . Almost every day during the past
six weeks the Croydon case has been the subject of a conference at Scotland Yard.'

Said Grace Duff to a *Daily Mail* reporter who called on her
on the night of June 12th:

'Of course the police are nice straightforward people and
they have to find out the truth. To do that they have had to
make every possible kind of inquiry, and while it is exceedingly unfortunate for the family, they have got to do
their duty. I suppose they will find out the truth, and the
sooner the better for all concerned.'

Two days later, in the evening papers of June 14th, came
the really big news.

Arsenic had been found in the body of Edmund Duff.

IX

The coroner, taking his seat at the eighth sitting on Saturday,
June 22nd, announced, 'Mr Sidney has been ill. He hasn't
a temperature, but he has lost his voice, and the doctor says
although he's fit to attend, he's scarcely able to speak. . . .
Therefore I propose to let him write his answers to questions.'

But Tom Sidney indicated that he would rather whisper his replies, and sat face to face with Dr Jackson, a yard of green-baize-covered table separating them, and answered questions in a low, hoarse whisper, the coroner repeating his replies aloud.

Dr Jackson handed a small black pocket-diary to Sidney, who identified it as Vera's diary for 1929.

'Did Vera express a wish that this diary should be destroyed after her death?'

'I was told that by Mrs Duff.'

Grace Duff, who was sitting at the back of the court, called out, 'It was written on a piece of paper with her will. The banker, Tom and myself found it together. It was just a little slip on which was written, "Please burn my diaries unread at my death."'

The coroner turned to Tom Sidney. 'Do you remember this slip of paper?'

'No, I don't remember seeing it. I first knew that Vera wanted the diary burnt when Mrs Duff told me so.'

Mr Sidney was catechised about the remark which Mrs Noakes alleged that he had made to her when the coroner's officer had left after seeing her at the time of Mrs Sidney's death.

He had no recollection whatsoever of telling her: 'One of us ought to have been here, as he would ask you questions, as the dead cannot speak, but they can make it very uncomfortable for those that are living', but, if he did say it, he might have had in mind suspicions of Vera's having been poisoned. He had several reasons for thinking of poison in Vera's case. There was what Dr Binning had said. There was also his aunt's illness. 'I thought the officer would have seen some member of the family before questioning Mrs Noakes. I was chiefly cross with myself for not being there to receive the coroner's officer.'

He further said that he did not know about Mrs Greenwell's visit to his mother's house on February 13th until half an hour before she came. That was when Vera called at his house and told him.

A letter was handed to Mr Sidney. He identified it as one which he had written to Mr Charles Edward Lawrence, the Honorary Secretary of the Savage Club, Adelphi Terrace, Strand, London, on November 20th, 1928.[1]

Sidney smiled and passed the letter to his counsel, who glanced at it and passed it back to the coroner.

Dr Jackson then read it out:

[1] Tom Sidney had applied for admittance to this club on August 31st, 1928. He was elected a member on November 8th, 1928.

'Dear Mr Lawrence,

Many thanks for your letter. I was going to call in and see you to explain matters, but have been laid up with a cold.

I'm very sorry things have turned out as they have, but I fear it will be some time before I can look my creditors in the face. But I trust I shall have the privilege of joining the club one day in the future.'

'Was it a fact you could not look your creditors in the face at that time?'

'I had none. I found that the club was going to cost me a good deal more than I had anticipated, and I wrote this letter as an excuse for having my election withdrawn for the time being.'

Sidney told the coroner that he did not know whether Vera was taking any medicine during her last illness, neither could he throw any light on how she came to take the arsenic found in her body, nor how it came into the soup.

Asked if there might have been arsenic in the house, he replied, 'Possibly. I don't know. My only reason for thinking that was that during the war my mother was very nervous and said that if the Germans came over she would take poison.'

Fearnley-Whittingstall then put it to his client, apropos his letter to Mr Lawrence: 'This club is fairly well known for internal hospitality, and a month's probation showed you that you had bitten off more than you could chew — or swallow?'

Amid laughter, Tom Sidney agreed. It was a little human touch which, in that austere atmosphere, suddenly made him seem a warm, fallible creature of circumstance.

When the hearing resumed after lunch, Grace Duff was summoned back to give additional evidence.

She gave the court a résumé of her financial position.

'My relations allowed me £25 a month, and helped me as well. My mother contributed £50 a year, which went to help make up this £25 a month, and helped me additionally. Vera also gave me odd sums, and was very keen on sending my boy to a boarding-school at Bath. She offered to help towards the fees for the first two terms. I do not know that I should have accepted this offer. I had a National Health Insurance widow's and children's pension of twenty-one shillings a week, and a grant of a pound a week for five years from the Colonial Office. The tenant of my top-floor flat paid me a pound a week, and I was negotiating letting my downstairs flat when my sister died. I was going to let it at three pounds a week, with partial board. I had roughly £460 a year coming in apart from odd sums.'

She could, she said, always have raised several hundreds of pounds on her house, which she had bought out of the insurance payment on the life of her husband. The lease had fifty-five years to run.

Quoting from Vera's diary, the coroner read the entry for Sunday, February 10th:

'Grace came in before supper and stayed until 8.'

He also read out the entry for Tuesday, February 12th.

'Grace came in about seven and had a chat. I did not do any eating during the day, only tea and Oxo.'

That, Dr Jackson emphasised, was important, because, if Mrs Noakes was right, she made the soup on Tuesday morning and it was taken for lunch on the Wednesday. If the diary was right, Vera did not take any soup on Tuesday.

Referring to Mrs Greenwell's visit on February 13th, Mrs Duff was insistent that she came to know of the proposed visit two or three days before it took place, when either her mother or Vera told her. She accompanied Mrs Greenwell to the house, but stayed only a few minutes talking in the hall and then came away. She did not know that Mrs Noakes was in the habit of leaving the back door ajar.

Sir Bernard Spilsbury then read slowly, in his low, clear voice, a supplementary report which he had written giving his conclusions as to the cause of Vera Sidney's last illness and death.

'The cause of the death of Vera Sidney was, in my opinion, syncope due to acute arsenical poisoning, as is shown by the presence of approximately one-and-a-half grains of arsenic in the body, collected from analysis of the organs.

The symptoms of the last illness are characteristic of acute arsenical poisoning. The empty condition of the stomach and intestines, the inflammation of the lower part of the intestines, the unusual degree of preservation of the body, are also characteristics of acute arsenical poisoning, while the marked fatty degeneration which I found in the heart, liver and kidneys, are also accounted for by arsenical poisoning.

The official medicinal dose of arsenic is up to one-sixteenth of a degree, that is to say the so-called maximum dose which is prescribed. Arsenic is not a cumulative poison, that is to say it does not tend to collect in the body when taken medicinally for a period of time, and a course of medicinal doses extending over some period would not cause symptoms of acute poisoning, nor result in the finding of any but a very small amount of arsenic in the body if death occurred shortly after the last dose.

I am of opinion that the least possible fatal dose of

arsenic was not taken less than twenty-four hours before Miss Vera Sidney died.

I base this opinion upon the empty condition of the stomach and intestines, and the small proportion of arsenic found in them.

There was a large amount of arsenic in the liver and muscles.

The history of her illness points to taking the fatal dose shortly before the attack of vomiting on Wednesday afternoon, February 13th.

The fact that Mrs Greenwell was taken ill with similar symptoms about the same time, gives me the opinion that the poison was present in some article of food taken at lunch on that day.

From the rapid onset of the symptoms, I am of opinion that the food containing the poison was probably liquid rather than solid. The fatty degeneration of the heart, liver and kidneys could not have resulted from a poisonous dose taken within thirty-six hours of death.

The illness of Miss Vera Sidney on Monday night, February 11th, and on the following day, was similar, but less severe than that on the Wednesday and Thursday. That illness is consistent with a poisonous dose of arsenic taken on Monday evening.

The fact that Mrs Noakes and the cat were sick after taking the soup served on Monday, points, in my opinion, to the presence of arsenic in the soup.

If Vera Sidney had the poisonous dose of arsenic on Monday evening, the organs would still have been damaged by that dose when the second dose was taken on Wednesday, and the fatty degeneration would be explained. If the heart had been damaged by the poisonous dose of arsenic on Monday, the exhaustion after exercise on Wednesday morning, and the conditions of dilation and of pulselessness found on Wednesday evening after the second dose of arsenic had been taken, was fully accounted for. A rising temperature is a symptom found with acute arsenical poisoning, even higher than in this case of 102 degrees.

Arsenic was not likely to be found in the finger and toe nails if the only poison taken was within thirty-six hours of death. It might be accounted for if the first poisonous dose was taken on Monday evening, three clear days before death.

If the arsenic had been taken in medicinal doses for an appreciable time, I should have expected that the hair would have contained more than a slight trace of arsenic. This trace does not exclude the possibility of a previous administration of a poisonous dose if the effects passed off quickly.'

Dr Jackson made a brave effort to summarise it all for the jury.

'What you say amounts to this: that she took a dose which was in fact fatal on Wednesday, February 13th. That she had taken a poisonous dose on the Monday evening, and that you cannot say whether she had taken any arsenic before that period, with the reservation that you do not think she had taken arsenic over any extended period of time.'

Sir Bernard nodded his assent.

Adjourning the inquest until July 20th, the coroner said that he hoped then to finish it.

X

Exactly a week after that adjournment, the *Star* of June 29th announced that the authorities were considering a second exhumation of the body of Edmund Duff.

This drew an angry letter from his widow, published in *The Times* of July 2nd. In it, she protested that surely, as his widow and the mother of his children, she had the right to ask that before his grave was again disturbed a public inquest should be held to establish if such a course was really necessary. She did not think that in a Christian country the body of a good and decent citizen should be subjected to such cruel and casual treatment simply because two or three Home Office experts disagreed, presumably about the decimal quantities of drugs found in his corpse more than twelve months after his death. Even savages respect their dead.

That evening's papers carried the news that a statement had been issued by Scotland Yard declaring that there was no ground for the suggestion that any further exhumation of Edmund Duff would be required.

It was also announced that the Attorney-General, Sir William Jowitt, K.C., had that day moved for a writ of certiorari and an order for a further inquest to be held on the body of Edmund Creighton Duff.

The application, made in accordance with the provisions of the Coroners Act 1887 as amended by the Coroners Amendment Act 1926, was heard in the King's Bench Division of the High Court before the Lord Chief Justice[1] and Mr Justice

---

[1] Gordon Hewart (1870—1943), Lord Chief Justice of England 1922—1940.

Talbot. Their Lordships granted the Attorney-General's application.

The following day — July 3rd — Dr Jackson stated that he would open the second inquest on Edmund Creighton Duff at the Queen's Road Homes, Croydon, on July 5th, 1929.

XI

Although it had originally been arranged to hold the ninth sitting of the inquest on Vera Sidney on July 20th, it was not until Monday, July 29th, that the court met for the last time to conclude the inquiry that had dragged on for four months.

Having charged the jury that it was now their duty to find when and where Vera Sidney died and what was the cause of her death, the coroner began his summing-up at 11.17 a.m.

The evidence suggested that the arsenic was taken in the soup. The jury might think that they could say that the arsenic was in the soup consumed at Wednesday's lunch.

The next question to decide was whether the soup used on the Monday night was added to the fresh soup; or whether a fresh dose of poison was put in Wednesday's soup. There were points in the evidence to suggest that a fresh dose of poison had been added.

'Apart from the evidence that arsenic was taken in the soup, there is no direct evidence as to how, or by whom, it was administered.

'What are the circumstances? Here is Miss Sidney, a cheerful, affectionate woman, perfectly sane according to the evidence, though it is true she had often been tired lately — her sister said she was probably overdoing things. She had no other known cause for worry or anxiety. She had not been noticed to be suffering from depression of spirits. On the contrary, she apparently enjoyed life. She was devoted to her mother, with whom she lived, and on terms of the greatest affection with her sister, her brother and her family. She was comfortably off financially. She had never been known to threaten to take her own life, and we know of no reason why she should do so.

'If this is suicide, is she likely to have put the poison in the soup that she must have known Mrs Greenwell would be likely to take? She must, in all probability, have known some days before that Mrs Greenwell was coming to lunch that day. It does not look like suicide, but that is a question for the jury to say.

'Did arsenic get into the soup accidentally? There is no evidence of any arsenic being on the premises, except for a few specks of powdered rust in the old, empty weed-killer tin found in the shed in Mrs Sidney's garden.'

With regard to the ingredients of the soup, it hardly seemed likely, in the circumstances, for arsenic to have got into the soup accidentally, although that was not impossible. The most that one could say was that one could not see easily how it could have happened.

'The gravest suggestion is that Miss Sidney was poisoned by someone else.

'It was Mrs Noakes who prepared the food and brought it into the dining-room, and there is not any evidence that anybody else handled the soup before it was served. But it may have been doctored beforehand without her knowledge.

'Who could have had access to that soup? The whole of the household and, possibly, someone from outside. You may consider what would be the risk to an outsider. It would be more risk to such a one than to a member of the household, but perfectly possible to a cunning murderer. It would have to be someone who knew the ways of the household, and where the food was kept.

'Mrs Noakes seemed to have been attached to Miss Vera Sidney. She had given notice to leave, but was staying on to oblige her mistress. You will ask yourselves why should she poison the soup? There is no evidence that she did.

'Vera was devoted to Mrs Sidney, and Mrs Sidney was passionately fond of Vera, who was the only member of the family living with her. She took a life interest in £2,000 under Vera's will[1]. Would she be likely to weigh that for a moment against the loss she would sustain in other ways by her daughter's death? She, of course, had ample opportunity to administer the poison, but there is not the slightest evidence of administration. And you must bear in mind that she died by the same poison some days later.'

There were nieces and nephews, the children of Mr Thomas Sidney and Mrs Grace Duff, who often visited the house. Mr Sidney's children were so young — the elder was only five years old at that time — that the jury would no doubt rule them out. Mrs Duff's children, John and Mary, were older, but the jury would ask themselves why either of them should poison their aunt's food. There was not the slightest evidence that either did.

'As for the sister-in-law, Mrs Margaret Sidney, there is no evidence to show that she was not on good terms with her sister-in-law.

'Then there is the sister, Mrs Duff. What are the terms on which she and her sister were? The one outstanding fact with

[1] The coroner made a slip here. See page 52.

regard to the Sidney family is the mutual affection of the
various members. Their brother has told you that Mrs Duff
and Vera were very affectionate, always interested in each other's
affairs and deeply interested in each other's welfare, and others
have confirmed that they were on affectionate terms. Of course
people may pretend to be affectionate and harbour wicked
thoughts, but sooner or later it is noticed. In this case there is
nothing to show that Mrs Duff had any ill-feeling, or reason for
ill-feeling, against her sister. Did she stand to gain any benefit by
her sister's death? Vera left her £2,000 by her will, and £200 to
her son, John.'

Mrs Duff had said that she did not know that Vera had
made a will, and did not know that she would benefit under it.
Against the pecuniary benefit she would expect to gain by
Vera's death, the jury must set off the pecuniary loss she might
be expected to incur by it. Vera was helping Mrs Duff financially, and had offered to pay the fees for her son, John, for his
first two terms at a boarding-school. If Mrs Duff came into
money under Vera's will, her relatives, of course, would not
allow her so much. So her total income might be no larger, and
the net result of the calculation hardly seemed to establish a
motive in any way adequate for the commission of such an
atrocious crime.

'If she had wanted to poison Vera, would she be likely
deliberately to incur the increased risk of detection entailed by
poisoning her when Mrs Greenwell was coming to lunch? She
would have had unlimited opportunity without choosing that
day.

'Now we come to the brother. Like Mrs Duff, he was not
an inmate of the house, but one who would naturally be found
there. He was on intimate terms with the family, and there is
nothing to show that he had any reason for ill-feelings against
Vera.'

The coroner dealt with the benefits Tom Sidney might have
had from his sister's will, and asked, 'Can you think that that
provides an adequate motive for poisoning his sister's soup?'

He reminded the jury that Mr Sidney had a form of arsenic
in his possession, but that he had made no secret of this to the
police when they were prosecuting their inquiries. Moreover,
there was no evidence that Mr Sidney was in the house on the
day of Vera's death, or for some days before.

'In this case also, there is not a tittle of evidence of administration.

'There is no one else.

'I think it is right to tell you that there is no evidence, in my
judgment, which singles out one member of the family as the
poisoner. Several members were present, and if that is a fair

observation on all the evidence which you have heard, you will ask yourselves, "Are we justified, guided only by the evidence before us, in imputing the death of Vera to any particular individual?" You must be guided by evidence, and not by guess-work or surmise.'

The jury retired at one minute past twelve.

They were absent for seventeen minutes.

Dead silence fell on the court as they walked back from their room.

Coroner: 'Are you all agreed on your verdict?'

Foreman: 'Yes. We find that death occurred at 12.20 a.m. at 29 Birdhurst Rise on February 15th, 1929, and we are of the opinion that Vera Sidney was murdered by arsenic, wilfully administered by some person or persons unknown.'

So ended the second of the three inquests.

But there was still one more to go.

6

INQUEST ON EDMUND

I

Public excitement ran high on Friday, July 5th, 1929, when the second inquest on Edmund Creighton Duff was opened.

Some time before the proceedings started little groups of chattering women crowded the grounds at the front of the Queen's Road Homes. There was a stir of interest as Inspector Hedges drove up in a police-car, and the crowd watched, fascinated, as several baskets of exhibits were carried into the court.

Grace Duff, smartly dressed in a black coat, broad-brimmed black hat, and wearing a brown fur, paced up and down the lawn with her brother, Tom, and their counsel. Then, leaving Tom Sidney and Fearnley-Whittingstall talking together, she wandered nonchalantly off on her own to pick some daisies, seemingly unconscious of all the eyes that were fixed on her.

It was five minutes to eleven, twenty-five minutes late, when the coroner took his seat and the jury was sworn.

At the previous inquests on Violet and Vera Sidney the police had not been legally represented. Now, however, in accordance with directions received from the Secretary of State, Mr Henry Delacombe Roome, assisted by Mr William Bentley Purchase and instructed by Mr Elliot Francis Barker, of Messrs Wontner & Sons, appeared in the interests of the Commissioner of Police.

Having outlined the events leading up to Duff's death, and the results of the first inquiry of the previous year, Dr Jackson explained to the jury that a new inquest had been ordered by the High Court in consequence of fresh evidence disclosed by Dr Roche Lynch's examination of the exhumed remains of Edmund Duff.

First witness at the second inquest was Mr Samuel John Clarke, of 18 Tanfield Road, Croydon, the coroner's officer. The death of Mr Duff was reported to him on April 28th, 1928, when he went to Number 16 South Park Hill Road with the coroner, and saw Mrs Duff.

On May, 2nd, 1928, he again visited Mrs Duff's home. He searched the house, and she pointed out to him a gallon tin of Noble's liquid weed-killer in her cellar. It was not sealed, but there was a cork in it which was difficult to remove.

Clarke went on to say that Duff's brain, liver, spleen, kidneys, heart and stomach were sent for examination to Mr Candy, the analyst at the London Hospital Medical College. During this part of his evidence Mrs Duff sat with bowed head, holding a handkerchief to her eyes.

Questioned by Mr Roome, Clarke stated that he did not remove the tin of liquid weed-killer, but used a tin funnel to extract a sample from it. The tin was full, and if any had been taken out of it previously it was only a very little.

John Henry Baker, mortuary attendant at the Mayday Hospital Mortuary, gave formal evidence of receiving Mr Duff's body on April 28th, 1928, and of assisting Dr Brontë in the post-mortem examination the following day. While he was giving these details, Mrs Duff left the courtroom and walked up and down on the lawn outside, talking to Fearnley-Whittingstall.

Baker was sure that Duff's organs had been placed in jars and sealed before the only other body in the mortuary that day was opened.

Dr Elwell, the next witness, deposed that he first became acquainted with Mr Duff, his wife and family about December 1920, and that they were patients of his from that time onwards. He had attended Mr Duff professionally five times since 1920, but only for slight ailments. He had never at any time prescribed or administered arsenic to Duff, nor, so far as he knew, was he suffering from any illness for which arsenic would be likely to be prescribed or taken.

'At about 7 p.m. on April 26th, 1928, Mrs Duff telephoned and said, "Edmund has come home and is not feeling well, and he wants you to come round and see him."

'I asked Mrs Duff what was the matter with him, and I heard Mr Duff say at the other end of the telephone, "Tell him I've got bubonic plague." He said this in a joking voice.

'When I saw him, Mr Duff complained to me of feeling rotten. I examined his throat. It was quite clean, but slightly red. I examined his chest, heart, lungs and abdomen through his clothes, but found no tenderness, nor anything abnormal there. There was no complaint of vomiting or of nausea on my first visit. Knowing Duff to be a person who would readily lie up with an illness, I did not think very seriously of his illness at the time.

'The next I heard of the deceased was on the afternoon of April 27th, when I heard that I had been sent for when I was out, and that Dr Binning had gone to see him.

'Later that day, Dr Binning rang me up and told me that Mr Duff had been very sick, and that he had not discovered anything on examining the patient to account for it.

'I saw deceased later that afternoon. He was in bed, rather collapsed. He complained of feeling very sick, but did not actually vomit while I was there. I advised him to take large draughts of sodium bicarbonate and water to wash his stomach out. I had formed no idea then as to the cause of his sickness.

'My next, and last, visit was late that evening. Mrs Duff rang me up and asked me to come round quickly. I did so, and found deceased very collapsed. Dr Binning arrived soon after me.

'The mode of death was syncope, that is heart failure. I was puzzled as to the cause of his illness. I thought he had had some form of food poisoning, and I therefore reported the death to the coroner.'

The coroner had been listening carefully to Dr Elwell's description of the course of Duff's last illness. 'Do you remember after Mrs Duff brought in the tea hearing her say, "He's not going to die is he?" '

Elwell did remember that remark. Mrs Duff had appeared to be very anxious and very distressed about her husband. So much so that, without saying a word to each other, he and Dr Binning went on applying artificial respiration for at least twenty minutes after Duff's death, in order to lessen the shock and give Mrs Duff time to realise what had happened. He then told Mrs Duff that he did not know what her husband had died from, that he was unable to give a death certificate, and that he would have to report the death to the coroner. She did not raise the slightest objection. The impression that he formed was that her one idea was to find out the cause of death, and she did not seem unduly disturbed or worried at the prospect of an investigation.

Adjourning the inquest until Thursday, July 11th, the coroner mentioned that there was a lot of pathological and other evidence to be taken, and that he hoped to sit on the Thursday, Friday and Saturday.

II

Immediately he had taken his seat at the opening of the second sitting of Thursday, July 11th, Dr Jackson said that before calling any further evidence he wished to bring to the notice of the jury the fact that he had had a report from Dr Roche Lynch as to the results of the examination of the organs of Mr Duff, submitted to him by Sir Bernard Spilsbury.

'Put quite roughly, the result is as follows: Dr Lynch states first of all that he has found arsenic to be present in every tissue he has examined. The larynx, thyroid, spinal cord and membranes have not been examined. This is not to say that arsenic is not there. He has estimated the amount present, and calculates there is a total of 0·815 grains, calculated as arsenious oxide, or, roughly, four-fifths of a grain, present in the organs on which he based his calculations.'

Colonel Charles De Vertus Duff, a lawn-tennis coach of 184 Cromwell Road, Earls Court, the youngest brother of Edmund Duff, then gave evidence. He was a retired colonel (Reserve) of the South African Brigade, his elder brother[1] resided in the South of France, and he also had four sisters living. Since his return to this country — in 1919, shortly after the Armistice — he used to meet his brother, Edmund, five or six times a year, sometimes in the City, and sometimes at his house.

Edmund was a very active man for his age. He remembered seeing him vault over a sofa to sit beside his wife only a few months before his death. He was in robust health when last he saw him.

He had never known his brother to take arsenic medicinally, but everybody who had lived abroad or in the colonies, like his brother or himself, doctored themselves.

Edmund had suffered from malaria a great deal, and arsenic was given for malaria. As to calomel, it was a favourite medicine in the tropics, and although he didn't happen to know if his brother used to take it, he felt certain that he did occasionally. It was usual to take epsom-salts after calomel.

Edmund had always been perfectly sane, and for the last twenty years of his life had been a cheerful man generally, although when younger he was very self-centred. He was extremely happy in his home life, and he and his wife were devoted to each other. He had never known them to quarrel. He knew of no financial loss that he had sustained — 'He never had any large amount of capital to lose.' He had heard that Mrs Duff had inherited a little money, which she and her husband had invested and lost, but he did not know any of the details.

And . . . yes . . . his brother was probably a jealous man, but he had never heard that Grace had given him the slightest cause for jealousy.

Colonel Duff finished his evidence by saying that his brother had been only a moderate drinker, very strong mentally and physically, and that he had never heard him threaten to take his own life, and did not think that he was the sort of man who would be likely to do so.

Dr Elwell, recalled, described the death of Edmund Duff. He and Dr Binning had been giving her husband artificial respiration for some time before he told Mrs Duff, 'I'm afraid he's gone.' She replied, 'Oh, he can't really have gone.' She

[1] J. George J. Duff.

appeared frightfully distressed, and knelt down beside her husband's corpse and kissed it.

Listening to Dr Elwell giving this evidence, Mrs Duff wiped tears from her eyes several times.

Donald Arthur Smith, of 151 Aurelia Road, West Croydon, assistant mortuary attendant at the Mayday Hospital Mortuary, swore that nobody besides himself and Mr Baker had access to the cupboard, used for storing organs for analytical examination, in which the jars containing Mr Duff's organs were put in April 1928.

The court then adjourned for lunch.

Tom Sidney was in good caustic form when the afternoon session opened.

Giving his occupation as an entertainer, he qualified it with the afterthought,'Well, I was up to five months ago, and may be again if these inquests finish before my old age.'

He had known Edmund Duff for about a month before his marriage to Grace. He and his brother-in-law had always been good friends and had never quarrelled. Their homes were about fifteen seconds' walk apart, but Duff seldom visited his house. He went to the Duffs' about once a fortnight on average. The Duffs were happily married. Edmund was a very good husband and Grace a good wife. They were extremely fond of each other and he had never known any serious quarrel between them.

He had, however, known Edmund to be very angry with his wife. It was just before he went to Hampshire on his fishing trip — two or three days before. The incident took place in the Duffs' house. He, Edmund and Grace were in the sitting-room, talking. Grace said something to her husband, asking him to get something or other, and he just jumped up in a frightful temper. He didn't say anything, but he was shaking with rage. Then he shouted, 'All right, then,' and stamped out of the room. 'Poor old Eds, this trip will do him good,' said Grace. He was away about a minute, and when he came back again he was perfectly placid.

'From your knowledge of Mr Duff, would you say that was a most unusual incident?'

Tom Sidney hesitated for a fraction of a second before telling Dr Jackson, 'No, I understand it was not. My mother told me after his death that he had lost his temper with my sister several times. But he was usually good-tempered.'

Grace Duff had just returned to the court, and Tom nodded in her direction. 'My sister can substantiate that.'

Grace responded right on cue. 'Certainly. He was a *very* good-tempered man.'

The last witness of the day was 24-year-old Miss Amy Clarke. She was now a waitress at the Dewdrop Inn, Steyning Avenue,

Peacehaven, Sussex, but had formerly been employed as a
domestic servant by Mrs Duff. She had worked for her for
eight months, leaving her service in September 1928. She had
been at Hurst View about three months when Mr Duff died.
The Master had seemed a very healthy man. He was cheerful
and she did not ever see him suffer from any fits of depression.
He lived quite happily with his wife and family. Mr and Mrs
Duff appeared to be very fond of each other. She never saw him
angry with his wife. If fact, she had seldom known a more
devoted family. She thought that he looked well when he
returned from Hampshire, but he did not say how he felt. She
cooked and prepared his supper on the night of his return.
When she brought his supper in Mrs Duff said to her, 'Don't
you think Mr Duff looks well?' With the meal she took in a
small bottle of ale. The stopper of the bottle was sealed when
she put it on the table. She left the house between 7.20 and
7.30 p.m. At that time she had not the faintest idea that
there was anything wrong with Mr Duff.

The coroner: 'Would you have noticed had the seal been
broken?'

'Yes, I think so.'

That concluded the day's hearing.

III

Miss Amy Clarke came back to the witness-chair when the
third sitting of the inquest on Edmund Duff resumed at 10.30
a.m. on Friday, July 12th.

She was questioned about the events of the morning of
Mr Duff's death.

She arrived at the house at half-past seven. She did not see
Mr Duff alive again. Mrs Duff was with her husband a great
deal that day. Miss Clarke did not recall any visitors other than
the doctors coming to the house that Friday. She had not
known Mr Duff to take medicine before his return from
Hampshire. She had on no occasion seen calomel or arsenic in
any form in the house. One of the reasons why she left Mrs
Duff's service was because her mistress told her that she could
not afford to keep her on, and that she was going to have a
maid for afternoons only.

Mr Roome's questioning elicited the fact that it was usual for
Mr Duff to have his supper on a tray. Mr and Mrs Duff did not
have their evening meal together, as Mrs Duff did not take
supper. The last meal Mrs Duff usually had was tea, sometimes
with the children in the dining-room, sometimes alone in the
drawing-room. During the week, breakfast was the only meal

that Mr Duff took with his family, but he would have breakfast, lunch and tea with them on a Sunday. Generally, they all
went out on Saturday afternoons. On Sundays Mr Duff drank
beer with his lunch.

Mr Roome lifted a small bottle of Bass in a paper bag from the
table in front of the coroner. It was a very warm, sunny day
and, smilingly, Roome observed, 'It is very tempting, sir, on a
day like this!' (laughter).

Then, turning to Miss Clarke, he held up the bottle: 'Was
it a bottle like this?'

'Yes.'

Fingering the unbroken label band around the stopper,
Roome pointed to it, 'You always took it in in this condition?'

'Yes.'

Mr Duff would invariably open the bottle and pour out the
beer himself. She had never seen anyone pour it for him. The
beer was purchased from an off-licence in the Selsdon Road,
just opposite the Swan. Half a dozen small bottles were delivered
at a time and were kept on the larder floor, or on a lowish shelf
away from the window.

When she came in at 7.30 a.m. on the Friday (April 28th), she
saw Mr Duff's supper tray in the kitchen. There was an empty
beer-bottle on the tray and a used glass beside it. She washed
the glass and the bottle was sent back to the shop which
supplied the household's beer.

A juror wanted to know what had happened to the rest of
the beer.

'What happened, was that there was no poison found in the
body, and it was no good analysing anything else at the time,'
rejoined the coroner.

At the close of Miss Clarke's evidence Tom Sidney was asked
by Dr Jackson to step back to clarify some points.

'I understand from Colonel Charles Duff that Mrs Duff came
into some money between the day of her marriage and her
husband's death. Do you know about that?'

Sidney knew that Mrs Duff had received £5,000, and that the
money was invested and lost. He did not know by whom the
money was invested. He had had nothing to do with that
investment, though he thought that part of it went to buy a
house, and he had a vague recollection that the unfortunate
investment was connected with oil.

The coroner held up a green-and-white striped tin with the
word 'Poison' on the lid.

'Is this the one that you had in your possession before
Edmund Duff died?'

Sidney nodded. Yes — and he had used it for several years. It
had been in the tool-shed in his garden ever since he bought it in

September 1927.

Mr Roome inquired of him if the tin which he had bought in September 1927 was the first tin of weed-killer that he had purchased after going to South Park Hill Road. Sidney thought that he had had one previously. He went to America for about six months at the beginning of 1926, and when he returned the gardener told him that there was a tin of weed-killer in the shed. It might have been bought by the tenants to whom he let the house while he was away.

'What made you buy a tin of weed-killer in September 1927?'

'I expect that when I got back from the tour the weeds were very thick and I bought it to kill them.'

Roome wondered if before buying the weed-killer in September 1927, he had satisfied himself that there was none in the garden shed.

'I am certain I should. I am not a Scotsman, but I don't throw money away.' He added that from September 1927 to April 1928 he was away, touring the provinces, about two days a week.

IV

The court met for the third consecutive day on Saturday, July 13th, when the fourth sitting of the inquest on Edmund Duff was held.

At 10.30 a.m. Thomas Sidney took his seat in the witness-chair again, and Mr Roome opened up with a burst of quick-fire questions.

'Was anyone except yourself aware that you had a tin of Eureka weed-killer in the shed in your garden?'

'Yes.'

'Who would know?'

'Anybody who went into the shed would know.'

'Between September 1927, when you bought it, and April 1928, when Mr Duff died, was your shed locked or open?'

'It was open. The key was kept in the lock.'

'When did you start keeping it locked?'

'One day when I saw my little boy trying to unlock it and I realised he was tall enough to reach the key.'

'Was that after Mr Duff died?'

'It was early this year — in January, before my sister's death.'

'Did many people walk about your garden?'

'Very few.'

'What about Mr and Mrs Duff who lived so near?'

'They very seldom came. I don't remember one instance of

them coming in the twelve months previous to his death.'

As a rule, he rehearsed for his entertainments every morning. In the afternoon he was usually in the West End. He agreed that Mrs Duff might have called then. He had no recollection of her having called in the evening.

'As far as you know, did Mrs Duff know you had any weed-killer?'

'No.'

When he handed the tin of weed-killer over to the police it was about three-quarters full. He had only used it in the garden on one occasion and was unable to say whether any of the weed-killer had been extracted after he had used it.

Mr Fearnley-Whittingstall questioned Sidney about the quarrel which he had said that he witnessed between Mrs Duff and her husband shortly before Duff's departure for Hampshire. He was inclined to think now that it was not really a quarrel, and that there was nothing in it, except that he happened to remember it. 'I would even go so far as to say that the anger might easily have come towards myself, and not towards Mrs Duff.'

'What makes you think it might have been towards you?'

'Well . . . one thing occurs to me. I very often went in there in the evening and played over my latest compositions, such as they were, and he hated music like poison.'

This remark produced a ripple of much-needed laughter, which was, however, rapidly subdued by the coroner's scandalised frowns.

Perhaps to underline the propriety of his attitude, Dr Jackson, betraying not a flicker of humour, repeated the words. 'You say he hated music like poison?' 'Well, *my* music,' said Sidney.

And this time not even a succession of quite ferocious frownings could suppress the laughter.

Answering a juror, Sidney said that his sister, Vera, and Mr Duff were 'great pals', and that he thought that Mrs Duff loved her husband very deeply. 'With regard to my mother, I say frankly I think she disliked him.'

Dr Jackson inquired how long Mrs Sidney had disliked her son-in-law. Sidney thought that it had been for several years. The coroner could not see that there was any reason for her disliking him, and when a juror asked why it was so, Sidney replied, 'I think there were a variety of reasons. First, I think she liked the good things of life and liked her children to be well-off. Mr Duff had lost the £5,000, had given up his job in Nigeria for a pension and his circumstances had been reduced. Also, I think she thought he had too many children, for every addition to the family caused a great deal of worry.'

Dr Jackson: 'Did your mother ever blame Mr Duff for the loss of the £5,000?'

'She blamed Mr Duff for many things. Most of the mis-fortunes of the Duff family were credited by my mother to Mr Duff.'

The friend who had been Duff's host on his last fishing holiday — Mr Harold Stanley Whitfield Edwardes, of Armsley, Godshill Woods, Fordingbridge, Hampshire — had come along to give evidence.

Mr Edwardes was a retired political officer in the Nigerian Civil Service. He and Mr Duff had been stationed together at Bida, in Nigeria, for a short time in 1905. That was when they first met and, although they kept up a correspondence, it was not until 1914 that they saw each other again. He then served as Duff's second-in-command for about four months in Ilorin Province, and they became great friends.

When Duff arrived for his holiday on Monday, April 23rd, 1928, he was quite well and cheerful and seemed very glad to be making the visit. He spent most of the Tuesday fishing. There was a hot sun, he wore no hat and would have had the sun on the back of his head most of the day.

The following morning (Wednesday), Duff said, 'I think I have a touch of fever,' which Edwardes understood to mean malaria, from which he knew that Duff had suffered in Nigeria. That day Duff did no fishing, but played tennis instead.

On the Thursday (April 26th), Edwardes and his wife went shopping in Salisbury, and on their return found Duff quietly reading in the library. He looked a little puffy about the face, but ate a good lunch. After the meal, Edwardes drove him to Breamore station, where he caught the 2.45 p.m. train. Duff then seemed quite cheerful and keen to pay another visit to Fordingbridge in the future.

The next thing that Edwardes heard was on the Saturday morning, when Mrs Duff telephoned and asked if they were all well, as her husband had died and food poisoning was suspected.

Then came the medical evidence.

First of all, Sir Bernard Spilsbury.

On May 18th, 1929, he had made a post-mortem examination of Edmund Duff in the presence of Dr Brontë and Dr Binning.

The body bore marks of the incisions and cavities caused by a previous post-mortem and most of the organs were missing. In the absence of so many organs it was impossible to state the cause of death on the post-mortem examination alone.

The history of the last illness pointed to some form of acute gastro-intestinal irritation, and this was corroborated by the empty condition of the parts of the intestines remaining in the body, and the reddening of their inner surfaces. The remarkable feature of the examination was the degree of preservation of the body, in view of the fact that death had occurred more than a year previously.

The coroner intimated that Sir Bernard would be recalled after Dr Roche Lynch had given evidence.

Dr Gerald Roche Lynch then presented the result of his examination of the organs which he had received from Spilsbury. He mentioned that, in addition to them, he had had samples of soil from the grave and sawdust from the coffin.

A quantity of arsenic was present in every tissue removed from the body which he had examined. The larynx, thyroid, spinal cord and membranes had not been examined.

He gave the following figures for the arsenic which he had found, stating that they were obtained by calculation based on the portions analysed:

Large intestine	·014 grain
Small intestine	·004 grain
Pancreas	·002 grain
Bladder	·001 grain
Fluid from the chest	·005 grain
Toe-nails	·0001 grain
Finger-nails	·0001 grain

In the case of the following organs, he had calculated the amount of arsenic on the assumption that the tissues were of average weight for a normal man:

Lungs	·016 grain
Brain	·027 grain
Muscle	·654 grain
Bone	·049 grain

The total amount of arsenic in the weight of tissue received — and in other cases for the average weights — found by analysis, was ·815 of a grain,[1] calculated as arsenious oxide.

Mr Duff, he thought, would weigh eleven stone, but he had for the purpose of his calculation deliberately lowered the weight, so as not to get too high an estimate.

In one ounce of skin he found 0·0005 grain of arsenious oxide.

In one ounce of hair, 0·002 grain of arsenious oxide.

In one ounce of shroud, 0·001 grain of arsenious oxide.

In one ounce of the sawdust, 0·001 grain of arsenious oxide.

In one ounce of the soil, 0·00005 grain of arsenious oxide.

Taking into consideration the results of his analysis, the fact that certain organs — liver, kidneys, heart, stomach and contents

---

[1] The author is aware that the figures given above add up to ·7722, but ·815 is the final figure supplied by the analyst.

— were not available for analysis, and that some of these usually contained considerable quantities of arsenic in cases of poisoning by this substance, and also the evidence at the original inquest, Lynch was of the opinion that Mr Duff died of acute arsenical poisoning. He was further of the opinion that he must have taken a very considerable quantity, probably amounting to several grains, for he had suffered severe vomiting and diarrhoea, which must have eliminated a considerable quantity.

Mr Roome: 'On the assumption that the only food taken by Mr Duff after his return home was supper, between seven and eight o'clock, in your opinion, was his condition consistent with arsenic having been administered to him at that meal?'

'I think it quite possible.'

Mr Fearnley-Whittingstall wanted to know: 'How can you say he could not have taken arsenic in any quantity before this last dose or doses?'

'By the intensely small amount found in the skin and nails.'

Hard on the heels of Roche Lynch, came Dr Brontë.

He described the condition of the organs at his original post-mortem examination of April 29th, 1928.

The wall of the stomach was normal and showed no evidence of poison. He removed the liver, spleen, heart, kidneys, intestines, stomach and part of the lungs. These he placed in a large stone jar, which he tied up, labelled and sealed. He gave the jar into the custody of the mortuary keeper, telling him to keep it under lock and key until he heard from the coroner.

Dr Jackson observed that the food poisoning examination had proved negative.

'Yes,' agreed Brontë. Then, hastily, 'I should like to say that I had written in my carbon copy of the report of the post-mortem examination "A.S." That means arsenic.'

'That shows the possibility of arsenic was in your mind?'

'Yes.'

It was a not very adroit effort at face-saving.

Brontë went on to say that on the same occasion he had made a post-mortem examination of the body of a woman named Rose Ellen Walker. This examination was conducted first, and on a separate table from that on which he examined Mr Duff. He kept the two cases absolutely separate.

'If,' asked the coroner, 'a piece of trachea got into the stone jar you sealed and labelled, how can you account for it?'

Brontë wrinkled a puzzled brow. 'The only possible explanation is that someone must have opened the jar and put it in after I sealed it up.'

Not exactly plausible. Even he must have realized how hollow *that* rang.

'Could that be done without breaking the seal?'

Dr Jackson was being — having to be — merciless.

'I don't see how it was possible . . .'

And neither, to judge by his expression, did the coroner.

He tried another tack.

'Were there, Dr Brontë, any other parts of any other body on the table when you made your post-mortem examination on Mr Duff?'

Brontë was not going to fall for that one.

'I am perfectly certain there were not.' He saw a chance of restoring a little of his lost face. 'I should never allow such a thing.'

Brontë confirmed that he was present at Sir Bernard Spilsbury's examination of the exhumed body of Edmund Duff, and stated that he had now formed the opinion that Duff died from acute arsenical poisoning. He agreed that at the original inquest he had expressed the opinion that death was from natural causes.

This brought Fearnley-Whittingstall smartly to his feet.

'What made you change your mind, Dr Brontë?'

'The report of the analysis of Dr Roche Lynch, and Sir Bernard Spilsbury's report.'

Open confession is good for the soul.

His face glistening with sweat, Dr Brontë stepped down.

The last of the medical witnesses was Mr Hugh Charles Herbert Candy, lecturer in chemistry at the London Hospital Medical College, Mile End Road.

On May 3rd, 1928, he had received a large stone jar containing organs. It was sealed and labelled "Edmund C. Duff". He broke the seal and opened the jar in the presence of his assistant, and later put a note in his book to the effect that, besides the other organs, he had found lung and trachea in the jar. 'I want to be perfectly fair. It is very hard to remember what happened twelve months ago, and I may have used the word "trachea" loosely for an attachment to the lung. It might have been a piece of bronchial tube.'

He described the tests which he had performed.

'I made an aqueous extract of portions of all the organs in the jar. I tested that aqueous extract for arsenic and found none. I then extracted some of the same portions of organs with alcohol, and then took one of these portions of an organ and destroyed the organic matter by what is called "Kjeldahlising" it, and then tested the solution so obtained by the Gutzeit test, which is a modification of Marsh's test. I found no arsenic. That is to say, I did not get any stain. I do not know which particular organ it was which I took for this latter test.'

He was, he pointed out, conducting his analysis in a very different atmosphere from that which obtained now. He was not only testing for arsenic, but for all poisons. He was content with one negative result then, but he did not know that he would be now.

Mr Roome was quick to pounce on this.

'Had you known then as much as you know now, you would have conducted the analysis more thoroughly?'

'I should certainly have taken another sample. Yes, I admit that.'

Instantly, Fearnley-Whittingstall is up again.

'You did go through the recognised official tests for arsenic?'

'Yes,' says Candy.

'And you did not find any?'

'No.'

'Do you agree that it is difficult to miss?'

'It depends on the quantity. It was not difficult to miss if you had two parts in a million.'

But Fearnley-Whittingstall is persistent.

'Is it not useless for anyone, after your very careful examination, to say that there was arsenic in those parts you mention and formally reported on on oath?'

Candy is nothing if not honest. 'I cannot possibly say that. I am not a superman.'

And he tells the coroner: 'It would be quite possible for arsenic to be present in appreciable quantity in the organs from which I made the aqueous extract, and yet for my test of that extract to fail to disclose the presence of any arsenic. Apart from my tests of the aqueous extracts, there was only one organ which I tested for arsenic. There might be a considerable variation as regards richness in arsenic between those different organs. I think my failure to find arsenic may have been entirely accounted for by my happening to select an organ which was poorer in arsenic than any of the others.'

V

The proceedings of the fifth sitting of Tuesday, July 16th, were held in the recreation room of the Nurses' Institute at the Mayday Road Hospital, instead of at the Queen's Road Homes, where all the previous hearings had taken place. It was a rather more cheerful setting than the Workhouse boardroom, although there was something incongruous about its chintzy atmosphere, the walls hung with willow pattern plates, the piano and loudspeaker immediately behind the coroner's chair proclaiming the room's more usual public function as a dance-hall.

Dr Binning, who had attended Mr Duff prior to his last illness, and had seen him frequently for a year or two before he died, took up the story.

His first visit to Duff on the day of his death (April 27th, 1928), was at about midday. He gave the patient a somewhat casual examination.

Dr Binning and Dr Jackson were old acquaintances.

The coroner smiled benignly at him. 'I know, Dr Binning, that you are not a casual man as a rule; why do you say "casual" examination?'

'I didn't think he was seriously ill. I think he was always a man to make the most of small things. I thought he was doing so on this occasion.'

The next visit which Binning paid was between six and eight o'clock in the evening, when he found Duff's condition very much altered and realized at once that he was seriously ill. The doctor had then thought that he was probably suffering from ptomaine poisoning, and asked Duff what he had had to eat. 'He informed me that his last meal, the previous evening, had been chicken and potatoes, and he also said he had had two bottles of beer.'

The coroner was anxious to discover if Duff had said anything about having gone to a railway station refreshment-room at Salisbury on his journey home from Fordingbridge.

Binning could not remember, but he did remember Duff's saying that he had had some fish to eat while he was away.

Mr Roome: 'Did you hear Amy Clarke, the servant at the house, give evidence that she took in only one bottle of beer, and that there was only one bottle of beer on the tray to be washed up the next morning? Are you still quite certain that Mr Duff told you he had two bottles of beer?'

Binning was immovable on that point. 'I am quite certain.'

He was next cross-examined by Fearnley-Whittingstall, who suggested that if Mr Duff had taken arsenic between Binning's first visit in the morning and his second visit between 6 and 8 p.m., a great deal of arsenic would have been found in the body with death coming so shortly afterwards.

'Not necessarily,' objected Binning, 'because of the elimination which took place.'

He did agree, however, that there would be no difference in the symptoms of acute arsenical poisoning, whether the arsenic was taken at a particular hour, or twenty-four hours earlier.

Fearnley-Whittingstall picked up a book lying on the table in front of him and read out from it: 'The symptoms [of arsenical poisoning] may remit for a time and then recur. This should not be considered as due to further administration of the poison.'

He turned to Dr Binning. 'Do you agree with that?'

'Yes, I do, — considerable remissions. A doctor visiting a patient during one of those remissions would have no ground for suspecting arsenic poisoning.'

Binning thought it quite possible that calomel, taken by a person with whom it did not agree, would cause vomiting and diarrhoea. He could not remember whether he ordered the calomel, or if he had it with him, but he thought that it was already in the house.

'Would the calomel, kept in a bottle not properly stoppered, and even in plain, uncoloured glass, become oxidised into mercuric chloride?' asked Fearnley-Whittingstall.

'Very slightly,' was Binning's answer.

Now came the moment that everybody had been awaiting with the keenest interest. Wearing a mourning dress, relieved by a white lace collar, Grace Duff walked solemnly to the witness-chair.

Her married life, she testified, had been very happy. Mr Duff was a good husband, always fond of her, and she was very fond of him. Her eyes filled with tears and she hung her head momentarily. Apart from measles, Mr Duff had had no bad sickness for some years prior to his fatal illness, though he had had black-water fever and malaria — twice — in Nigeria.

She could not remember what her husband had had for supper on the night of his return from Fordingbridge. Chicken, beer and potatoes, she thought. The beer was Bass, and was brought in in a screw-stoppered bottle which, as was always the custom, stood in a big pewter mug. He poured out his beer himself. She did not notice whether the seal over the stopper was intact.

'Going from my knowledge of my husband, he would probably have noticed it if it had not been. He was very careful and fastidious and he did not like his beer flat.'

She did not see the supper things again after she came downstairs. Her husband ate only a little of the chicken, and she and the children finished it the next day.

Mrs Duff smiled when she was asked if she could explain how it was that the servant had said that she took in only one bottle of beer, whereas Dr Binning had given evidence that Mr Duff had told him that he had had two bottles.

'I should say he snaffled it when he took the tray back to the kitchen. I have no actual knowledge of it, but he might do it. It would be quite in keeping, as he would know that there were some extra bottles owing to his having been away.'

Dr Jackson: 'Was Amy Clarke peculiarly observant?'

'Well, she was very smart and intelligent in some ways, and was rather observant. She was a little bit hard of hearing. She impressed me by her powers of observation.'

At six o'clock, after she had been three hours under examination, Mrs Duff showed that she was feeling the effects of her ordeal, and Dr Jackson directed that the hearing should be suspended for a few minutes.

During the interval she was provided with a large pot of tea and a cup. 'I feel much better for that,' she told a friend, 'but it is really disgusting that I should be having all this tea to myself.' She then filled another cup and, turning to the women sitting in the public seats just behind her, offered it to them. The tea was gratefully accepted.

Mrs Duff was still giving evidence when the coroner adjourned the inquest until the following Saturday when, he said, it would be resumed at the Queen's Road Homes.

VI

Sixth sitting. Saturday, July 20th, 1929.

Mrs Duff returned to the witness-chair.

By now, after twenty-one sittings, the triple inquest proceedings really were becoming like a game of musical (witness) chairs. The order in which their occupants appeared changed, was shuffled, but — a sprinkling of rare and fleeting newcomers apart — the players remained virtually the same. It seemed to have become, in more senses than one, a family affair.

The coroner asked if her husband's life had been insured.

She said that it had, by two policies, both with South African companies. One policy was for approximately £1,000, and the other for approximately £500. Her husband had settled both of these policies on her by deed of gift before their marriage. At the time of his death there was a charge of between £300 and £400 in favour of his bankers, Messrs Grindlay & Co., on one of these policies. He had left a will appointing her his sole executrix and devising all his property to her, but the will was never proved, as he left no property. After paying the funeral expenses, general charges and debts on the estate, there was nothing left. He was drawing a Colonial Office pension of £30 a month and that ceased entirely at his death. She wrote to the Colonial Office asking for an allowance. They replied that they could not grant it, but later, after Spicer Brothers took the matter up on her behalf, she received a widow's and children's allowance of one pound per week for a term of five years. The first instalment of this was paid early in 1929, nearly a year after her husband's death.

Coroner: 'Did you gain or lose financially by your husband's death?'

Mrs Duff: (With tears welling in her eyes) 'I lost everything. But for my relations, I don't know what I should have done.'

She was most insistent that her husband was, on the whole,

a cheerful man, although inclined to get depressed when he was unwell. He was very cheerful immediately before his last illness, and she had never heard him threaten to take his life. She was sure that he would never have done so.

The coroner went closely into the question of the beer.

She told him that it was kept in the larder, and that the entrance to the larder was through a passage which led from the kitchen to the front-door. It was situated in an extraordinary little angle, and the door opened at the end of the passage. The side-door of the house was next to the larder door. The larder door opened from the passage and was very near the side-door of the house. The side-door was kept unlocked during the day, and there was free access from the road to that side-door.

'I think,' said Mrs Duff, 'that access to our house was pretty easy.'

She then elaborated as to why it was that she and her husband had occupied separate bedrooms all their married life.

'We started off doing it apparently because he used to snore, and read at night. I don't know why we did it, but we sort of arranged it from the start. He had always been accustomed to have a room to himself. He also used to smoke in bed, and thought that I shouldn't like it, and he used to get up early in the morning to typewrite articles.'

The coroner wrote it all down.

'Was your husband on good terms with your sister, Vera?'

'Yes, they were quite friendly.'

'Your brother told us that your mother disliked your husband. What would you say to that?'

Grace gave a little half-smile. 'I think mothers-in-law often have that feeling about their sons-in-law.'

Very neat. But too vague, too generalised, for the pertinacious Dr Jackson.

'I should like to have your own view as to the reason why your mother was not so friendly as she might be to your husband. If this is a matter you do not wish to make public I will clear the court.'

'There was no reason why she shouldn't like him — except that she thought he was extravagant.'

'There was no stronger reason?'

'I don't think their tastes were very congenial. He was a very much out-of-doors man, and I don't think they had a subject on which they were congenial. They didn't quarrel at all.'

Mrs Duff identified the tin of Noble's liquid weed-killer. It had been kept in the cellar of her house, and she thought that her husband had bought it some months before his death. It had been lying about in the back-yard for several months. Then the small tin cap came off. 'The tin was lying on its side and I

thought it might leak and asked my husband to take it into
the cellar.'

'Do you know whether it had ever been opened before the
coroner's officer opened it in your presence?'

'I am sure it had never been opened.'

In answer to further questions, Mrs Duff 'seemed to remember'
that the tin cap was somewhere about when the coroner's
officer called. After he had gone, the tin was left where it was
until she moved into her present house, about the beginning of
August 1928. 'I had forgotten all about it, but the men must have
brought it when I moved, and I suddenly saw it there. My
sister, Vera, was with me at the time. I said, "I think I'll pour
this away," but Vera said, "What a wicked waste; give it to
Mother's gardener," and I did so.'

Her husband was, admittedly, a jealous man, but she had never
given him cause to be seriously jealous, nor had they ever had a
serious quarrel.

Dr Jackson referred to the occasion, spoken of by her brother,
when her husband was angry shortly before he left for his
holiday.

She had no recollection of it. Edmund would 'bubble with
annoyance' sometimes when her brother used to come in and
play his compositions on the piano while he was writing his
articles.

Mr Roome took up the questioning.

She told him that her husband was popular among men and
usually cheerful and congenial.

'So far as you know, had he got an enemy in the world?'

'I don't know, but if he was killed he must have had an
enemy.'

'If he had an enemy it was a secret enemy?'

'Yes.'

And then Mr Roome put his foot in it.

He was asking her about her finances. . . .

'As things have happened, you are not, in fact, worse off in
consequence of your husband's death?'

'*Not worse off* ?' She almost spat the words out.

'I mean financially,' interjected Mr Roome hastily.

'As things have happened, yes. But things may not always
remain the same. But I don't think you can compare the two
conditions. In one case I was absolutely irresponsible because
my husband was keeping me, and in the other I have the burden
of everything. You can't judge financially only . . .' She hung
her head, suddenly crumpled into an utterly abject, pathetic
figure. 'I should say the difference is between a happily married
woman and a miserable widow with no one to look after me.'

Mr Roome switched rapidly to the subject of the weed-

killer. Mrs Duff recalled that, on one occasion, when her
husband put some down on the paths, their cat had fits and
died. He bought two tins of weed-killer within three weeks,
and one was used up. That tin was thrown in the dust-bin.

During the afternoon the atmosphere in the court became
very oppressive, and Fearnley-Whittingstall took off his jacket —
an example followed by Tom Sidney and several others. Jugs
of water and glasses were supplied to all parts of the room.

Fearnley-Whittingstall asked Mrs Duff: 'Did Mr Duff tell
Dr Elwell that he felt ill when he was away?'

'I think that whatever poison might have been had, he took
it away with him, and had a little while he was away, and some
more when he came home. This is the only thing I can think
of. I don't mean purposely. I mean he took it without knowing
he was taking poison. During the last few months I have
tried to think of a thousand solutions.'

And that was the end of Mrs Duff's examination.

Sir Bernard Spilsbury, summoned back by the coroner,
stated it as his opinion that Duff died from acute arsenical
poisoning, and that if liquid arsenical weed-killer or soluble
solid arsenical weed-killer had been used on Duff's grave, or in
the cemetery near his grave, it in no way affected his opinion as
to the cause of death.

The coroner required Spilsbury to give his reasons.

'The result of the post-mortem examination,' he said. 'The
very inflamed condition of the intestines, together with the
condition of the body and the remarkable preservation. That
suspicion is confirmed by the results of the analysis made by
Dr Roche Lynch and by the history of the last illness.'

In his opinion, the arsenic was taken by mouth. The changes
in the intestines in conjunction with the history of very severe
vomiting, led him to that conclusion. He thought it quite clear
that Duff was suffering from acute arsenical poisoning at about
7 a.m. on April 27th, when he vomited the tea. It was possible
that solid arsenic taken the night before might not have produced
vomiting until the following morning. But if he had nausea when
he went to bed the night before, and if he suffered from
vomiting during the night, then he must have had a poisonous
dose of arsenic *before* he went to bed, probably with the
evening meal, or shortly afterwards, and it was more likely to
have been in liquid than in solid form.

Spilsbury found it impossible to say from the evidence
whether Duff took more than one dose; nor could he say
with any certainty how much arsenic must have been present
in the body at death.

'It is clear that there must have been substantially more than
was estimated by Dr Roche Lynch (·815 grain) from the parts

of the body which he analysed. With such a large amount in the muscles as was found here — about two-thirds of a grain — the liver would certainly have contained a substantial amount, and there would have been more in the organs missing from my examination. So there would have been well over a grain of arsenic if these organs had also been available.'

The coroner: 'Does it follow that he must have taken considerably more than a grain?'

'Very considerably more. He must have had two or three grains at least, and possibly more.'

Sir Bernard was in no doubt that the most likely vehicle for the arsenic to have been taken in was the beer.

Examined by Mr Roome, he thought that there were no indications from the symptoms which Mr Duff had when at Fordingbridge, that he was suffering from arsenical poisoning. The symptoms were those of a feverish chill. On the assumption that Duff vomited for the first time after he had gone to bed on the night of his return home, the most likely time that he would have taken the fatal dose of arsenic was at, or shortly after, his evening meal.

Beer would disguise the taste of liquid arsenic.

Fearnley-Whittingstall then cross-examined Spilsbury.

'When you said it was possible solid arsenic taken the night before might not have produced violent vomiting until 7 a.m. the next morning, what did you mean by "the night before"?'

'I meant some time before he went to bed, or about the time he went to bed.'

'If Mr Duff vomited violently in the early night, would that, according to your theory, antedate the taking of the poison by a corresponding time?'

'No, because of the intervention of the evening meal, which would have delayed the action of the poison.'

'If a man out East had taken arsenic in the form of a medicine for malaria, would that increase his physical tolerance for it?'

'Not if he took it for malaria only. If he had taken the medicine for illness it would have no such effect.'

'Has it happened before that beer has shown itself as containing arsenic, and lost lives?'

'Yes, in cases of chronic arsenical poisoning.'

'In the case of bottled beer it is not inconceivable that if any arsenic had got into it, it might be there in some quantity?'

'I think it is inconceivable that it would have got in in the process of manufacture. A very large number of bottles are filled from one brew.'

'Let us take the bottle, then. If by chance white arsenic was put into the bottle you could get acute arsenical poisoning from it?'

'Any form of arsenic put into the beer would cause acute arsenical poisoning.'

Coroner: 'The question is how should it get into the beer?'

'I don't know. The theory has been put by Sir Bernard Spilsbury, and I am asking questions on it.'

Counsel asked whether arsenic would not make the beer flat.

Sir Bernard considered. Some forms of arsenic might, but white arsenic would not. He readily conceded that cases were known where the symptoms of acute arsenical poisoning had been delayed for twelve hours.

'Taking that into consideration, is it fair to say that there is a good deal of conjecture as to the time when you say the fatal dose was taken?'

'No, I do not think there is. I have allowed a substantial margin in the times I have given. We know what food he had after he came home, and that is an important factor in these cases.'

But the tenacious Fearnley-Whittingstall kept hammering away at the eminent pathologist, and in the end succeeded in wringing from him a somewhat grudging modification of his earlier dogmatism. On reflection, the facts were so vague that it was impossible to speak very positively as to whether Duff took a poisonous dose after his return home. He still thought that he did, but, within certain limits of time, he might have taken it before his return. The poison could have been in some whisky which he took away with him on his holiday, and of which he had a little left when he returned.

Mrs Duff contributed the information that, 'The flask was given to him full of whisky, and that makes me wonder whether it was poisoned.'

And Fearnley-Whittingstall explained to the court, 'It was one of the flasks that one buys at railway stations.'

VII

The *Daily Express* of July 22nd contained an interesting pen-sketch of the proceedings of the previous Saturday's (July 20th) sixth sitting of the Edmund Duff inquest. It was written by Hannen Swaffer.

'"I'm going to the Croydon inquest," I said to Herbert Marshall, the actor, meeting him on Victoria Station on Saturday.

"Oh, that's the greatest drama in London," he said.

"Yes," I replied, "and one of the longest runs."

The little that I saw of the production was dull, uninspired and boring. The actors and actresses were obviously overcome by the heat. It had been going on too long. Even the work-house inmates in the gardens outside took no notice, but went on dozing in the sun. It was the one excitement that had come into their lives for years, but now even they were bored.

"Yes, it is a long hearing," Thomas Sidney said to me . . . "My last job was at the Connaught Rooms two or three nights before my sister's death. I am missing all my dates now."

Now, if a dramatist made a play of the great Sidney inquest, what characters would he select?

Would he choose the coroner, who, . . . has sat for nearly 150 hours, or six complete days, writing, writing, writing, perhaps 160,000 words of evidence.

"I can't keep pace with you," said the coroner impatiently on Saturday, addressing Sir Bernard Spilsbury. "I'm writing it down in longhand. I can't start until you have finished, or I have to cross it all out."

If I were a dramatist in search of characters for a great inquest play, I should revel in Mr Fearnley-Whittingstall. Here is a character. He is only 26! He is over six feet tall. He has the appearance of an undergraduate, and yet he shows the skill and the persistence of a great cross-examiner. He fought Ramsay MacDonald at the last election. He is obviously marked out for high legal distinction. Yet he looks languid. He has an acquittal in a murder case to his credit, and another good murder case in his record before that. He is strangely young for such experience and he looks it. Yet his name is too long to get into a newspaper headline or on a poster. Publicity helps barristers, you know, just as it makes actors.

The members of the three juries, more than thirty tired-looking men, sit on deck-chairs in the sun in the workhouse grounds outside when there is a respite. Some of their businesses are neglected. They cannot take a holiday . . . . Some of them would make interesting characters in a play, especially the one who never moves.

Which of the other leading actors would best help the drama of a great inquest plot?

Among the witnesses are a half-blind gardener, deaf and hesitant, an undertaker's assistant, always in careful mourn-ing with a red-brick sunburned face. Then there are the precise Treasury manner of Mr H.D. Roome, called in late by the police; the meticulous coroner, analytical, persistent; two detectives, one like a farmer, who always wears a rose; and three servants, a little flustered now and then.

I was the only one who, on Saturday, noticed the four tins of weed-killer. The others had seen them so often that they were just part of the scenery, like the inkpot, or the coroner's pile of notes. Weed-killer always fascinates me. "Keeps gravel" was all I could read on half of the label on the largest tin. "Brightens the", I read underneath. The rest was hidden except that, lower down, there was a black hand pointing to the word "Poison". The tins have been on the table for weeks. They bring them every day in a motor-car, and then take them home again.

Another motor-car brought Mr Roome's tea. He and his assistants and two women had it in the garden. Mrs Fearnley-Whittingstall, her lemon silk dress heightening her blondness, smoked a cigarette. Her husband wanted a break once. He walked out of court, getting a cigarette ready while he walked. It is free and easy now. Every one knows everybody else. They will be using first names soon.

Mrs Grace Duff had finished her evidence when I arrived. She was sitting with her arms on the table, leaning forward, her bright, black-blue eyes eager, interested, almost staring sometimes. She wanted to ask a question once. Otherwise, she just leaned forward. Now and then she has gone outside and picked daisies in the workhouse grounds, or looked at the fountain, or walked about in the sweltering heat. When the horrors of the post-mortem detail have become too gruesome she has withdrawn and gone into the lobby, where you can see the currant rolls ready for the inmates' tea or watch the old people reading away the end of their lives.

For weeks Croydon stayed away. Even on Saturday some dressed-up street entertainers with an organ drew a larger crowd outside. Now, however, there is a queue sometimes — women of course — and two policemen wait in case there is a crowd. Women sat at the gates all the afternoon on Saturday, hoping that there was a chance to see, although they knew that there was none.'

The newspapers of the following day — July 23rd — made great play of the fact that Tom Sidney, Mrs Duff, Dr Jackson and Inspector Hedges had all been receiving anonymous letters, some containing threats. 'Poison Pen in Arsenic Mystery', was the inevitable line.

The *Daily Mail* of July 24th carried a large photograph of Mrs Duff's younger son, Alastair, entered by his mother in their Beautiful Children competition — '£1,320 is offered in prizes.'

Mrs Duff's elder son, 15-year-old John, figured in the *Daily Mail* of July 25th, where it was stated that he was returning to London from his school in the country, as he might be called as a witness at the next day's resumed inquest.

VIII

There was a larger crowd than usual when the coroner
entered the court on Friday, July 26th, 1929, to open the
seventh sitting. Hundreds of people, most of them women,
scrambled for the available accommodation, and as many people
as had gained admittance to the public seats in the court stood
at the gates trying, unsuccessfully, to argue their way past the
police.

Sir Trevor Bigham, Assistant Commissioner of the Criminal
Investigation Department of Scotland Yard, occupied a seat
near the coroner, and Superintendent Brown of the Yard was
also present.

John Duff, the schoolboy son of Mrs Duff, had been subpoenaed to attend the proceedings and was the first witness. A
sturdy, full-faced and rather good-looking boy in a grey flannel
suit and a straw-hat banded with the colours of his school, he
went quietly to the witness-chair and took the oath.

He told of the night of his father's return from holiday.

'I went to kiss him, but he didn't want me to. He said, "Go
away. I think I've got the 'flu." '

John remembered seeing a bottle of beer standing by his
father's tankard, but did not notice whether or not the paper
seal over the stopper was broken, nor did he see the beer
poured out. He had gone to bed before his father started to
eat his supper. About a quarter of an hour after he had left
the drawing-room, and when he was coming out of the bathroom, he heard the voice of Dr Elwell, who was then leaving the
house. He slept right through the night and did not hear anything. He saw his father for the first time on the next day,
between ten and eleven o'clock in the morning.

'I went to his bedroom. He was in bed. I sat in there for a
very few minutes. I was out in the garden most of the day.
Before lunch I was in my room, and I heard him come out of
his bedroom to the bathroom, and I saw him standing there.
He went back into his bedroom and slammed the door.'

John Duff never saw his father alive again. Early next
morning his mother came to his room and told him that his
father was dead.

The boy answered the coroner as he would answer his headmaster. He did not hesitate or flinch when Dr Jackson,
biting his lips, asked the unavoidable question, 'Have you any
idea how your father came to be poisoned?'

'No,' said John steadily.

'Do you think your sister, Mary, has?'

'No.'

While these questions were being put to her boy, Mrs Duff stared out of the window. Her left hand played with his straw-hat.

Neither Mr Roome nor Mr Fearnley-Whittingstall had any questions, and when John had finished his evidence his mother looked towards him and her eyes filled with tears. She watched him as he stood up to sign his deposition, and when he returned again to his seat beside her she patted him on the shoulder.

A few minutes later Mrs Duff herself was being examined again.

Coroner: 'Did you know before your husband died that your brother, Tom, had weed-killer in his possession?'

Mrs Duff: 'No.'

Fearnley-Whittingstall tackled her about the flask of whisky which she had said was in her husband's possession before he went off on his fishing holiday.

'He was packing his bag, and I noticed a new flask of whisky being tucked away among the contents. I asked him who gave it to him. Was it a friend? He smiled and remarked, "Ah Ha!" "Oh," I said, "then perhaps you have bought it yourself," and he grinned, and said, "He He!".'

Mrs Duff joined in the laughter which this explanation caused. She added, 'That was the whole conversation. I thought he had bought it himself until all this happened, and then I wondered.'

When she had finished her evidence she asked Dr Jackson if she might leave, as her baby, Alastair, was in hospital with tonsilitis, and she wanted to go to see him. The coroner gave her his permission.

After Mrs Duff and her son had left the court, Mrs Margaret Neilson McConnell Sidney, Tom Sidney's wife, deposed that, on the night of Edmund Duff's death, she and her sister-in-law, Vera, had been to the Croydon Theatre. Passing the Duffs' house on the way home between 10.30 and 11 p.m., they saw Dr Binning's car outside. Vera said, 'I wonder if Edmund is worse? I'll just go in and see.' That remark was the first inkling that Mrs Margaret Sidney had that her brother-in-law was ill. Vera went in. She came out a few minutes later and said, 'It's all most funny. Grace is downstairs very worried and depressed, and says that Edmund is very bad indeed. But when I went upstairs, I found Dr Binning quite cheerful. He said he had just got Edmund to bed, as Grace was worn out, and Edmund had been making a fuss about nothing.'

At seven o'clock the next morning Margaret Sidney found

Vera sitting on her bed, and asked, 'What are you doing here so bright and early?'

Vera replied, 'It's not cheerful news. Edmund has died.'

The coroner: 'Did any member of the family appear to be upset or annoyed at the prospect of an inquest?'

'Well, I think Mrs Sidney, my mother-in-law, was rather annoyed, and thought the doctor should have prevented the inquest. That was at first. I don't think she was annoyed later on.'

Margaret Sidney had been given to understand that old Mrs Sidney thought that it was an unpleasant thing to have an inquest in the family, and also unnecessary.

She told Mr Roome how, on the day following Duff's death, she went round at 8.30 a.m. to see Grace Duff. 'She was greatly distressed, and the only thing I could think of to give her any comfort was to say, "After all, he was spared a long illness." Grace said, "Yes, but he did suffer."'

Mrs Sidney had to admit that her mother-in-law and Vera were always rather worried about Mrs Duff's financial affairs. Old Mrs Sidney was extremely careful herself and she seemed to be convinced that the Duffs did not know how to economise. Margaret Sidney, however, did not think that they could have managed very much better than they did. Mr and Mrs Duff and their children had struck her as one of the happiest and most united families she had ever known.

Questioned by Mr Fearnley-Whittingstall about the conversation between Vera and Dr Binning, Mrs Sidney was disposed to agree that it might have been the doctor's tactful way of getting rid of Vera.

Percy Warren, manager of Thorpe and Company, wine and spirit merchants, of 131 South End, Croydon, said that on April 19th and 21st, 1928, he supplied six bottles of beer, in half-pint, screw-stoppered bottles, to Mrs Duff. His boy had special instructions not to deliver bottles with the paper seal broken.

In the course of Mr Warren's evidence several bottles of beer were produced. Each had a paper band sealing the screw-stopper. The coroner examined them minutely, and observed, 'With a damp towel it would be child's play to remove one of these stoppers and replace the band without damaging it.'

Dr Jackson told the court that he would adjourn the inquest for a further eleven days.

'I hope then we shall finish it,' he remarked.

IX

In the interval between the adjournment of the seventh sitting of the inquest on Edmund Duff, on July 26th, and its resumption on August 6th, 1929, the inquests on Violet and Vera Sidney were concluded.

Commented the *Daily Mail* of July 30th:

'One of the three inquests, so long in progress, closed yesterday with the verdict by the jury that Miss Vera Sidney "was murdered by arsenic, wilfully administered by some person or persons unknown."

In these Croydon deaths there are many strange coincidences, . . . (but) the coincidences point nowhere at all. The real criminal is as yet undiscovered, and perhaps will never be discovered. This is a grim and disagreeable thought. Some person is at large who has a diabolical propensity for putting arsenic into other people's food.'

The *Daily News* observed:

'The first of the Croydon arsenic inquests ended yesterday without throwing any fresh light upon one of the most baffling cases upon record. Indeed, as this inquiry has proceeded, the mystery seems simply to have deepened . . . . It is impossible to remember, difficult even to imagine, the parallel of a case like this which, beginning with one death under ambiguous circumstances, now revolves about three successful attempts at arsenical poisoning on three different occasions. Reading the accounts of the long-drawn-out inquiry day by day, it has seemed to be like the development of the nightmare of a detective story, with periodical fresh disclosures of a murder, but with little hint of purpose and less of clue.'

The *Star* thought it,

'quite likely that the police have a theory, a shrewd suspicion as to the identity of the murderer.'

but pointed out:

'They cannot be blamed for proceeding with the utmost circumspection or for hesitating to indicate a suspicion until they can support it with evidence which would convict the guilty person.'

Referring to the finding of the inquest on Vera Sidney, Grace Duff told reporters:

'It was the only possible verdict from the evidence given. Sooner or later the whole truth must come out.'

She was asked what she thought would happen in the other cases:—

'I don't know, but they are a little different from this one, and I couldn't say whether the same verdict might be expected in those cases. The truth, however, must be found out. There have been three cases, and they cannot be allowed to rest without the truth being discovered no matter how long it takes.'

Her plans for the future were vague, but she would probably go for a holiday after August 6th when the inquest on her husband was expected to finish.

'I am tired. I need a rest. I want a holiday, peace and quiet, and I hope to take my boy with me, if his health permits.'

This last, was a reference to two-year-old Alastair, who had been taken ill with tonsillitis on July 23rd, and had had an operation on July 27th. The child was making a satisfactory recovery.

'But there is always the danger, though, of a recurrence of his illness. The operation, we understand, was wonderfully successful. He was in a state of coma when it began. I truly hope that all will now go well. It would have been the end of me if my darling had died.'

The *Daily Express* of August 2nd, commenting on the murder-suicide verdict at the conclusion of the inquest on Mrs Violet Emilia Sidney, asked:

'Will the Croydon arsenic mystery go down to history as the greatest unsolved poison case in the annals of crime? . . . The verdict of "Murder by some person or persons unknown" in the case of Miss Vera Sidney, followed by the "Murder or suicide" verdict at Wednesday's inquest on Mrs Violet Emilia Sidney, has only added to the baffling quality of the tragedy. . . . Crime experts are divided in their opinions about the possibility of the crime being solved. "It is too premature to say yet whether the police will solve the mystery," said Sir Arthur Conan Doyle to a *Daily Express* representative. "The police may be searching for one little

link in a chain of evidence which may lead to a conviction.
We do not know just how much the police know. Anything
may happen. A crisis may come tomorrow or the next day.
Who can say?" '

The *Star* of August 3rd chronicled the jurors' woes at what
had already proved a record series of inquests — 25 sittings
spread over five months, and still one more sitting to come.

'A number of the jurors are commercial travellers or men in
small businesses of their own. Their enforced absence from
work has caused them losses far greater than can be made
good by the nominal fee allowed to jurymen. One juror had
to travel from Exmouth, where he is on holiday with his
family, to attend the final hearing of the inquest on Mrs
Sidney. Eleven married men investigated Miss Sidney's death,
and they all live in Alton Road, Waddon. They sat all hours
of the day, on Saturday afternoons, and late into the evening.
A *Star* representative today learned something of the trials
of a juryman's wife in such circumstances. He was told of
spoiled dinners, disorganised homes, delayed or cancelled
holidays and broken appointments for the cinema. Nearly
all the 22 jurymen at the inquest on Mrs Sidney and Mr Duff
(which is still unfinished) were taken from Alton Road or its
immediate neighbour, Waddon Park Avenue.'

The coroner had his troubles, too. Threatening letters, whose
arrival Mrs Jackson withheld from her husband, and the attempt
of a mysterious half-caste to enter the house when she was
alone, were among the unpleasant experiences which Dr Jackson's
wife endured. For some time she kept them secret from her
husband for fear of upsetting him, but eventually the police
were informed, and a night-and-day police guard was mounted
at the Jacksons' house — Sunnycroft, 34 Pollard's Hill West,
Norbury.
The *Daily News* of August 5th reported that the police guard
was still being maintained. But Dr Jackson's ordeal was nearly
over, for the following day was to see the end of the last
of the inquests.

X

The court conducting the inquisition on the death of
Edmund Creighton Duff met for the eighth and last time at
10.30 a.m. on Tuesday, August 6th, 1929.
A queue of women, some of whom had been there since

half-past eight in the morning, waited in pouring rain outside the Queen's Road Homes. The boardroom was crowded with members of the public, the majority of them women, and all the witnesses, more than twenty of them, were present. There was an air of excitement and expectancy.

Mrs Duff, wearing a black coat and a white blouse with black buttons, entered the courtroom. She left her son, John, who had accompanied her, and went across to the witness-chair.

The coroner presumed that she had read over her depositions. She replied that she had.

Dr Jackson then asked if she could tell the jury why her husband had taken the flask of whisky with him to Fordingbridge.

She was afraid that she did not know. He did not usually take whisky with him when he went fishing, and she did not think that he very often had whisky. He might have drunk some there, or saved it till he got home.

'You knew your husband much better than anyone else here. What do you think was the probability?'

Mrs Duff considered. 'He might have saved it till he came home. I really can't say. I should think he thought he might like a nip. After he came home he said that he had finished it during the night.'

Mr Bentley Purchase, for the Commissioner of Police, asked who unpacked Duff's things when he returned home on the night of April 26th.

Mrs Duff explained that they were not unpacked, because her husband was so ill. She did not see the whisky flask that night. She saw it subsequently, but there was nothing on it to indicate where it had come from. 'It looked like one of those little station ones. My husband had bought them before from the station.'

Sir Bernard Spilsbury was then recalled.

Reverting to his original view, he repeated that he felt sure that Duff could not have had the arsenic before he arrived home; that he was then suffering from nothing more than a feverish chill; that he probably took the poison with his evening meal and that it was most likely administered in the beer.

At that time Sir Bernard Spilsbury's status in the courts was Olympian. In matters morbidly anatomical and forensically problematical, his was a divine afflatus only one celestial notch below that of the Almighty. And that was a diagnosis, moreover, with which Sir Bernard found himself able to express satisfactory concurrence.

It needed an advocate of confidence and courage to tangle with this medico-legal paragon. Fearnley-Whittingstall was, justifiably, lacking in neither of these attributes. He faced Sir Bernard with equanimity, and launched upon a fierce cross-examination.

'Do you in the capacity of a pathologist or a doctor put forward the statement that of the three articles the beer was most likely to contain arsenic?'

'Neither.'

Fearnley-Whittingstall raised his eyebrows. 'It is not a medical fact you are giving us?'

'Scarcely.'

'It is simply what you think, without any evidence on the data you have read?'

'It is based on the times; on the assumption that he complained of dizziness followed by vomiting during the night. The arsenic must have been taken before he went to bed.'

'But why was the arsenic in liquid form?'

'If taken in solid form the interval before the arsenic symptoms would probably have been longer. The interval was now about two hours.'

'But if he arrived home at seven and went to bed after ten that would be three hours, and we do not know when the sickness started.'

'I think it was rather less than three hours.'

'I merely want to find out why it is even probable — if you don't know when the symptoms of real sickness first started — to be able to distinguish between liquid and solid when the two were taken together. How can you say it was even probable, one or the other?'

'It is on the assumption that the sickness started that night shortly after he went to bed.'

'What do you call a symptom — sickness or feeling sick?'

'Nausea followed by sickness.'

'We do not know how soon after it was followed by sickness.'

'No.'

'So, not knowing that, how do you gauge the interval, and so date that to the taking?'

'All these answers have been based on the assumption that he had sickness during the night.'

But Fearnley-Whittingstall was determined to pin Spilsbury down.

'How soon during the night? You see it is coming down to rather a fine point when you are distinguishing between taking arsenic in food and the taking of arsenic in liquid, especially when liquid is taken with the food, which would aid its swiftness.'

Undeterred, Spilsbury repeated that it was merely a matter of probability.

'I still don't follow how you can even say probably one

way or the other,' insisted Fearnley-Whittingstall, 'when you don't know when the man was first sick, whether it was in the beer, potatoes or chicken, all taken at the same time.'

Spilsbury: 'If you eliminate sickness during the night it is impossible. If sickness occurred during the night it is much more probable it was taken in liquid form. If it were taken in solid form sickness would probably have been delayed for a longer time.'

Fearnley-Whittingstall: 'How much longer?'

Spilsbury: 'It is impossible to give any period. It would be the length of time to allow solid food to be fairly completely digested.'

Fearnley-Whittingstall: 'Would not the taking of liquid loosen the arsenic if it were in solid food?'

Spilsbury: 'In potatoes or chicken it would have been extremely difficult to administer arsenic. These foods would have to be fairly fully digested before the arsenic was liberated.'

Fearnley-Whittingstall: 'Would that take three hours?'

Spilsbury: 'More than that to liberate arsenic. I think probably four hours before the early symptoms occurred.'

Fearnley-Whittingstall: 'Let us suppose that it took four hours to digest food. Let us suppose that nausea was a repercussion of the slight feverish chill . . . '

Spilsbury: 'I do not suppose that.'

Fearnley-Whittingstall was asking what would have happened if the arsenic had been taken in the chicken, when Spilsbury interrupted him with 'I do not see . . . '

'Sir Bernard Spilsbury, I am asking you if the arsenic was in the chicken would you say Mr Duff would have felt sick by the time he went up to bed?'

'I think probably not.'

'If it was in the chicken would you assume that the complaint of sickness at the time of going to bed was due to arsenic?'

'If it stands alone, no.'

Fearnley-Whittingstall said that on the thesis that he was putting forward it did not matter if it stood alone or in a thousand. In these circumstances, could Sir Bernard say that the feeling of sickness was due to fever?

'Yes, if there is no arsenic to account for it, certainly.'

Fearnley-Whittingstall then suggested that Spilsbury assume that he had not heard that any liquid was taken with the supper, but merely chicken and potatoes. 'What then would you say about this feeling of sickness on going up to bed?'

Sir Bernard's answer was that without evidence of vomiting or feeling sick, it was impossible to say whether it was arsenic or a feverish chill.

'So,' said Fearnley-Whittingstall triumphantly, 'when you say either arsenic or a feverish chill, do you mean that arsenic taken with the chicken might produce these symptoms of nausea on going to bed?'

It was an extremely adroit piece of manoeuvring, but Sir Bernard was too experienced a witness to be caught.

'Arsenic taken previously,' he replied.

Still Fearnley-Whittingstall would not let go.

'If it was taken previously he would have been sick immediately after supper according to you. Therefore we cannot have that.'

If the arsenic was contained in the chicken, Fearnley-Whittingstall pointed out, Sir Bernard's argument was rendered worthless.

Spilsbury: 'I have said that the arsenic was more likely to be in the beer.'

Fearnley-Whittingstall: 'Why should it be so much more likely? It would be a fifty-fifty chance of its being fever.'

Spilsbury: 'It is not a fifty-fifty chance.'

Fearnley-Whittingstall: 'What would happen if I took arsenic? After the first mouthful should I be sick if I took a subsequent course of food?'

Spilsbury: 'It would continue to mix with the food.'

Fearnley-Whittingstall: 'When arsenic symptoms are delayed it is because the stomach is not inflamed. And when the stomach is inflamed by arsenic, sickness follows?'

Spilsbury: 'Yes.'

Fearnley-Whittingstall: 'Supposing there were symptoms of arsenic, in this case having been taken before supper, the taking of supper would not produce immediate vomiting?'

Spilsbury: 'No. We have not dealt with the cause of the delayed symptoms.'

Fearnley-Whittingstall: 'Then this argument you have produced again falls to the ground.'

Spilsbury: 'It is based entirely on the assumption that the arsenic was taken in liquid form.'

Fearnley-Whittingstall: 'I am assuming delayed symptoms. In the middle of that delayed time, if he had a feverish chill and felt sick, would you put the sickness down to the chill?'

Spilsbury: 'Only in the absence of the arsenic should I do so.'

Fearnley-Whittingstall: 'If a stomach is not irritated by arsenic it cannot make me sick?'

Spilsbury: 'Yes, it could. (Laughter) I am afraid we are at cross purposes. I should expect a period of delay if the arsenic were taken in solid form mixed with a suitable food, and after a large meal the period of delay might extend four, five or six hours.'

It had been a brilliant piece of advocacy, but at the end of it all Sir Bernard told the coroner that he was still definite in his opinion that it was highly probable that the arsenic was taken after Duff returned home.

The ground gained on July 20th was lost.

Sir Bernard Spilsbury was like that.

During the luncheon adjournment spectators who had secured admission in the morning immediately lined up again outside the grounds and waited in the heavy rain for readmission.

The coroner embarked upon his summing-up at 2.52 p.m.

'It is true,' he began, 'that at the first inquest the examination of the body was made by an experienced pathologist, and a critical analysis of certain parts of the body by a skilled chemist, and the presence of arsenic in the body was not then detected. But I think it must be concluded in view of the evidence now before us, that an error was made by someone at some stage of that earlier investigation.

'Mr Candy and Sir Bernard Spilsbury have suggested a possible explanation for the negative result then obtained. Whether or not that be a true explanation, you will doubtless have been satisfied by the evidence of Sir Bernard Spilsbury and Dr Roche Lynch that death was due to acute arsenical poisoning.

'You will remember that Dr Roche Lynch found arsenic in all the organs and tissues he examined, and there were several organs not available for examination, and he estimated that 0·815 of a grain of arsenic, calculated as arsenious oxide, was present in the organs and tissues examined.

'Sir Bernard has told you that there would have been well over one grain of arsenic if all the organs had been available, and that deceased must have taken between two and three grains at least, and probably more.

'There is no direct evidence how the arsenic was administered, in what vehicle, or by whom, or with what intent. We don't know what compound of arsenic was taken, nor can we be certain from the evidence that it was taken in liquid or solid form.

'As to the time when it was taken, it is difficult to speak with any certainty. It would appear to be very probable that a poisonous dose was taken after the deceased returned home in the evening of April 26th and probably with his supper soon afterwards. There is no evidence that Mr Duff took more than one dose, or that he took arsenic on the day of his death.

'You may think that the beer was the most likely vehicle. The arsenic might have been taken in the whisky, but there is no evidence to show that he had taken any whisky after he returned home and before the symptoms of acute arsenical poisoning commenced. If the arsenic was in the flask, is it not likely that he would have exhibited symptoms of poisoning during his holiday? There is no evidence that he did.

'You may think that the arsenic was in the chicken, but other members of the household subsequently partook of it without ill effects. You may think it was in the potatoes, but there is no evidence to show that, nor any to show that he took any cheese.'

The coroner said that there was nothing to indicate that Duff's previous indisposition when on holiday, and upon reaching home, was due to arsenical poisoning. It was a feverish chill, such as a man who had lived in the tropics would be liable to get.

Mr Duff was a man living on good terms with his family. Apart from the evidence that his mother-in-law disliked him, he seemed to be on good terms with all his relatives. There was no history of suicide or violence in the family and there had been no threats to kill. Mr Duff seemed to have been in terror of death before he died. It did not look like suicide.

'There is no evidence that he had any solid arsenic in his possession which he might have taken in mistake for epsom-salts or calomel. True, there was a tin of weed-killer, but there is no evidence that it was moved, or that its contents had been touched.'

Suicide or accident, said the coroner, was an explanation which the jury might find it very hard to accept.

There was no evidence that arsenic was given through the criminal carelessness of someone else.

The grave question which the jury had then to consider was whether Mr Duff was poisoned by somebody else — murdered.

On the evening that Mr Duff returned from his holiday, the maid-servant, Amy Clarke, had brought him his supper, which she had prepared. There was no evidence that anybody else handled the food that night except the girl.

'It is possible that the food or drink might have been doctored beforehand without her knowledge.

'Who had access to the beer and the food? The whole of the household, and possibly someone from outside. Amy Clarke has told you that the front-door was sometimes left open when the children were in and out. Dr Elwell, when he called at eight in the evening, said the front-door was open and he walked in. Miss Clarke also said that the side-door was kept open all day, and that anybody could obtain access without difficulty. Mrs Duff confirms that there was easy access from outside. She says her house was spoken of as "the house with the ever-open door".'

The jury might consider the risks to an outsider going to the house and doctoring the beer, or more probably substituting an already doctored bottle for the one in the larder. There would be no difficulty in doctoring the bottle, as the paper band could easily be removed and gummed back on again without leaving any trace. But there was not a scintilla of evidence that any outsider had doctored the bottle.

'Amy Clarke you have seen and heard. She seemed a decent, straightforward young woman, and there is not a scrap of evidence of motive in her case, nor of administration.

'There are the children, John, aged fourteen, and Mary, twelve. You have seen and heard John, and you will ask yourselves why on earth he or his sister should have doctored their father's food or drink. And there is no evidence whatever that they have done it.'

Dr Jackson then referred to Mrs Duff.

'What are the terms on which she and her husband lived? One outstanding fact of the family is their mutual affection. What does Mr Duff's own brother say, speaking of the deceased? He says that he was very happy in his home life, very fond of his wife, and she was as devoted to him as he was to her. He had never known him quarrel with his wife or complain of her, or she of him.

'Mr Duff's old friend, Mr Edwardes, said they seemed happy in their married life. Mr Duff always spoke in affectionate and endearing terms of his wife. The day before his death he spoke also of his children, and brought photographs of his wife and children on his last visit to him.

'The servant said he lived quite happily with his wife and family, and she never heard any quarrels, and had never known a more united family. I don't think I need say any more than that. In this case there is nothing to show that Mrs Duff had any ill-feeling or reason for ill-feeling against her husband. What could she expect to gain financially by his death? His Colonial Office pension of something over £360 a year ceased on his death, as did his earnings of about £182 a year from his employment in the City, and also his earnings from his writings. That being about £542 a year gone, without counting the earnings from his writings.

'You have seen this woman, you have heard her, and heard of her from those best qualified to judge. She had in one sense an opportunity to poison, but I tell you I have heard no evidence which would explain from the point of view of motive any such act, and she appears to be, though perhaps emotional, a frank and truthful witness, and you must remember the conditions under which she appeared before you. It is also for me to tell you that there is not a tittle of evidence of administration.'

The coroner then dealt with Mr Thomas Sidney. He was not an inmate of the house, but he would naturally be found there. He had arsenic in his possession in the form of Eureka weed-killer, and it was conceivable that he could have got access to the beer or food in the absence of his sister, or the servant, or the children.

'But I only mention this as a possibility, and there is not a scrap of evidence that he did. You will ask yourselves: Why should he? He is happily married with children, on good terms with Duff and his wife. There is no evidence that he was in pecuniary difficulties, and if he had been, Duff's death would not only not benefit him, but might possibly throw on his shoulders the support of his sister and her children.'

Mrs Margaret Sidney was on friendly terms with Mr Duff, and his death would have been more likely to involve her in financial loss than gain. Moreover, there was no evidence of administration.

Regarding Mrs Violet Emilia Sidney, the jury had been told that she frankly disliked Mr Duff, and a reason had been suggested.

'But God only knows why she should poison her son-in-law for reasons such as these. There is no evidence that she had a fatal dose of arsenic in her possession. There is only the old rusty tin, practically empty, and not a tittle of evidence of administration.'

The sister-in-law, Vera, was devoted to her sister, and to Mr Duff, and no reason was known why she should have poisoned him. Neither was there any evidence of administration, nor of the fact that she had the means. Both she and her mother were to die within a year from the same poison.

'I think there is no one else, unless it be Dr Elwell, and in his case there is no evidence whatever of motive or administration.'

Referring to all three deaths in the Sidney family, the coroner remarked, 'There is, in my opinion, no evidence which singles out any one member of the family as the poisoner. Several members were present and would have access to the vehicles by which the poison was administered. Are we justified in attributing the death of Mr Duff to any particular individual? If you do, it must almost certainly follow that the same individual poisoned all three persons.'

At 3.22 p.m. the jury retired.

Twenty minutes later they filed back into the court.

The foreman delivered their verdict.

'We find that Edmund Creighton Duff met his death on April 27th, 1928, from acute arsenical poisoning, wilfully administered by some person or persons unknown.'

So ended the second inquest on Edmund Duff.

XI

Now came the closing minutes of the lengthy inquisition on the greatest poisoning mystery of modern times.

The court broke up.

The jury departed.

The large boardroom of the old Croydon Poor Law Institution was nearly empty.

Dr Jackson pulled out his pipe and started to smoke.

Tom Sidney lit a cigarette.

Mrs Duff went across and sat down beside the coroner. For some time they chatted. Then Dr Jackson rose, removed his pipe from his mouth and gave Mrs Duff a hearty handshake. She shook hands, too, with her solicitor and the youthful Mr Fearnley-Whittingstall.

Then, affectionately arm-in-arm with her son, John, she walked out of the building, down the drive, and passed obliviously through a small knot of curious women who were waiting at the gateway.

The long trial by inquest was over.

PART THREE

PURSUANCE OF ONE

INVESTIGATION AND
REINVESTIGATION

7

THE SIDNEYS AND THE DUFFS

I

The story of the Sidney family opened for me beside a memorial wall-tablet in the Collegiate Church of St Mary, in Stafford.

On the tablet I read the following inscription:

> To record the Memory of
> William Sidney, late of this town,
> Who died October 13th, 1822, aged 54 years,
> And of Ann his wife, who died,
> July 7th, 1838, aged 61 years.
> In their lives they were esteemed.
> In their deaths they were deplored.
> This tablet was erected in the year 1858
> by their third son Thomas Sidney
> Late Lord Mayor of London and formerly
> a representative of this borough in Parliament.

William Sidney had a good tailoring and woollen-drapery business in Gaol Square, Stafford, and it was here, on January 5th, 1805, that his son, Thomas, was born. The house still stands — although Gaol Square has since been renamed Gaolgate Street — and an inscription on the wall records his birth there. It was this Thomas Sidney who was the founder of the not inconsiderable Sidney family fortune.

Concerning his early life the records are not so complete as one might wish.

In 1817 he left school and went to serve an apprenticeship with a grocer in Rugeley, from where he used to walk home every Sunday so that he could spend the day with his family. He was, even then, an ambitious lad, and told his fellow-apprentices that he would never stop until he was Lord Mayor of London. His apprenticeship ended, he went into the grocery business in Leeds. It was some time during the latter part of the 1820s that he arrived in London, where, with a couple of partners, he opened premises in Ludgate Hill, and rapidly made a fortune, mainly from the sale of fine quality China tea. When he retired he was the head of a large wholesale business in the tea trade, with establishments in Leeds, Liverpool, and several other provincial towns, as well as in London.

By 1843, Thomas Sidney had already attained to a position of such consequence in the community that he was elected a common councillor of the Corporation of London, representing Farringdon Without. The following year he was made an alderman for the City of London, and appointed sheriff of London and Middlesex. He entered the wider field of politics in 1847, becoming a Member of Parliament, sitting as Liberal-Conservative Free-Trader for Stafford from 1847 until 1852. He was unsuccessful at Leeds in 1852, Worcester in 1857, and Stafford in 1859, but represented Stafford again, as a Liberal, from 1860 to 1863.

Meanwhile, in 1849 he was elected Master of the Girdlers' Company and, four years later, he made good his boyhood vow. From 1853 to 1854 Thomas Sidney was Lord Mayor of London.

By now a man of considerable substance, he bought, on the death of its owner, Lord Truro, in 1855, Bowes Manor, a magnificent house standing in twenty-five acres of its own grounds at Southgate, in Middlesex.

Thomas Sidney married twice. His first wife, Sarah, daughter of William Hall, of Renton, Dumbartonshire, whom he married in 1831, bore him a daughter, Ellen, who subsequently married the Reverend Sir Edward Graham Moon. Sarah Sidney died in 1857, and in January 1860 Thomas Sidney married Eleanour Mary, the daughter of William Ward, of Beaumont Chase, Belton, Rutland. They had eight children.[1] The name 'Stafford' was given to each as a tribute to their father's birthplace, which was always to remain very dear to him.

He remembered Stafford in other ways, too. In 1857 he gave £700 to the town, in order that twenty aged widows and widowers might have their hearts gladdened on his birthday. The Sidney Charity still operates. And during the general distress of 1860, he sent two hundred guineas to Stafford, to be distributed among the poor.

To the end of his life he was very hospitable on all occasions to any inhabitants of Stafford who came to London, and if they called on him they could always be sure of a hearty welcome.

His native town gratefully erected a fountain in the centre of

---

[1] Florence Mary Stafford Sidney, *b.* October 27th, 1860. *d.* 1868.
Augusta Sarah Stafford Sidney, *b.* January 18th, 1862. *d.* 1931.
Thomas Stafford Sidney, *b.* September 29th, 1863. *d.* 1917.
Eleanour Kathleen Stafford Sidney, *b.* October 1st, 1865. *d.* 1930.
William Stafford Sidney, *b.* January 11th, 1867. *d.* 1950.
Gertrude·Amy Stafford Sidney, *b.* December 8th, 1868. *d.* 1956.
Gwendoline Mary Stafford Sidney, *b.* July 5th, 1870. *d.* 1957.
Herbert Stafford Sidney, *b.* August 13th, 1871. *d.* 1903.

Gaol Square to his memory. It bore his shield, which displayed thirteen oak-trees surmounted by a porcupine, together with the Sidney family motto, *Gratias deo agere*, and the square was for many years popularly known as Sidney Square.

Resigning his aldermancy in 1875, Thomas Sidney continued to live quietly at Bowes Manor. He died at his seaside house — 94 Marina, St Leonards-on-Sea — on March 10th, 1889. He was buried at St Michael-at-Bowes, Southgate, which church he had built, and where two stained glass windows have been erected to his memory at the western end of the church.

He left £129,175, in addition to property at Walton-on-Thames, Esher, Sunbury-on-Thames, Beddington, Fetcham, Leyton, Brighton and Liverpool. His widow survived until 1905.

II

It is with old Thomas Sidney's eldest son, Thomas Stafford Sidney (the father of Grace, Vera and Tom), that we are concerned.

Born at Bowes Manor, on September 29th, 1863, he was educated at Harrow and Trinity Hall, Cambridge, and admitted a student of the Middle Temple on November 14th, 1882.

It was during his years as a law student that Thomas Stafford Sidney began to pay attention to Miss Violet Emilia Lendy, the daughter of Major Auguste Frederic Lendy and Sophia Lendy (née Bulley).

Major Lendy was a distinguished, but not very well-to-do, military man, who rented Sunbury House, at Sunbury-on-Thames, from old Thomas Sidney. Born, it appears, in or near Geneva in 1826, he was at one time a captain of the French Army Staff, but came to England as military tutor to the Orléans princes. About 1853, he set up a private military college at Sunbury House, where he was for many years one of the ablest and most successful of the army crammers. From 1859 to 1879 he held a commission in the 4th Royal Middlesex Militia, retiring with the honorary rank of major. Apart from being an expert on the art of fortification of the period prior to the introduction of the polygonal system, and the author of eight treatises on warlike subjects, he was a keen horticulturist and well known as an amateur breeder of orchids.

His daughter, Violet, was born at Sunbury on August 13th, 1859. She and Thomas Stafford Sidney were married at Holy Trinity Church, Eastbourne, on October 14th, 1884. He was then just twenty-one, a not very prepossessing-looking man with a heavy moustache and thick glasses. She was four years older and extremely pretty. They settled at Carlton Lodge, a

charming house on the fringe of the Bowes Manor estate at
Southgate, and, on June 17th, 1885, Thomas Stafford Sidney
was called to the Bar of the Middle Temple.

Their first child, Grace, was born at Carlton Lodge on
August 27th, 1886. In 1888, Sidney received his M.A., and on
February 16th of that year, his second daughter, Vera, was
born. On June 26th, 1889, Violet was delivered of her third
and last child, a son, Thomas.

At this time Sidney was practising as a barrister on the
South-Eastern Circuit, Surrey and South London Sessions, and
was in Chambers at Essex Court. But when, in March 1889, old
Thomas Sidney died, his son inherited £25,000, and the urgent
necessity to obtain briefs was removed. In October 1889, his
father-in-law, Major Lendy, died.

After five years, the marriage between Thomas and Violet
was beginning to show ugly cracks. As Violet herself was later
to admit, she had never really been in love with Sidney. In fact,
she was in love with her cousin, Georges Dagron, a young
French doctor, practising in Paris. He came over to this country
only once, but they corresponded for years and used to write
poems to each other in French.[1] He died in 1928. Neither had
Violet's father ever cared much for his son-in-law, but it was a
'good' marriage and, as Major Lendy had put it, 'Beggars can't
be choosers.'

It may be that Thomas Stafford Sidney became aware of a
basic coldness in his wife as the days of their emotionally sterile
marriage lengthened, or it may have been that she objected to
his incessant womanising. Whatever the reason, the gulf between
them widened, and in 1891 he left Violet and went off with a
Miss Blanche Adams, the sister of his younger brother, William's,
wife, Maud. The pair left England and went to India, but not
before there had been a very unpleasant scene, Violet turning up
unexpectedly at her errant husband's chambers, and chasing him
round the table with a knife. Miss Adams died in India, having
first given birth to a son, Richard John Hamilton Sidney, at
Ootacamund, on June 23rd, 1893.

In 1894 Sidney was made Advocate of the High Court of
Madras, and he remained in India for the next seven years,
practising law and also engaging in occasional journalism. It was
during this period that he first encountered and struck up a
friendship with a man named Edmund Creighton Duff.

Between 1901 and 1903, Sidney served as District Commissioner at Lagos, West Africa. He also spent some time as
Chief Justice in Northern Nigeria, and it was here that he met
up with Duff again.

---

[1] Violet Emilia Sidney did, in fact, publish two volumes of poems.

From 1904 to 1909 Sidney appears to have been living in England once more, and practising from chambers at 1 Plowden Buildings. In 1909, however, he was appointed Attorney-General of the Leeward Islands, and went to reside at St John's, Antigua. In 1911 he took silk.

Six years later, in 1917, Thomas Stafford Sidney returned from the Leewards on sick-leave. He arrived at Liverpool aboard S.S. *Philadelphia* on September 3rd. During the homeward voyage he became very violent, and was taken straight from the landing-stage to a private lunatic asylum — Tuebrook Villa, Green Lane, Liverpool — and there, on November 15th, 1917, he died, insane.[1] He was buried at Anfield Cemetery, Liverpool, on November 19th, his brother, William, who since Sidney's defection had looked after Violet, and acted *in loco patris* to Grace, Vera and Tom, journeying up to Liverpool to see to the funeral arrangements.

Thomas Stafford Sidney left £4,132. Of this sum he bequeathed £2,000 to his son, Richard John Hamilton Sidney. Everything else of which he died possessed, real and personal, he left in a will, dated March 23rd, 1914, to a Mrs Edith Emily Martin (née Penchoen), of Montserrat, who had been his companion-housekeeper. There was no mention in his will of his legal wife, Violet Emilia, or of the three children she had borne him.

III

After her husband's departure in 1891, Violet Emilia Sidney and her children stayed on at Carlton Lodge, Southgate. It was not until the autumn of 1897 that Mrs Sidney, with 11-year-old Grace, 9-year-old Vera and 8-year-old Tom, moved to a house named Garlton, number 15 The Ridgeway, Enfield, Middlesex. The family was to remain there for the next sixteen years.

Mrs Sidney was by no means wealthy but, with the help of an allowance contributed by her husband's relatives, she managed to live comfortably and bring her children up quite well. Grace was sent to a boarding-school at Eastbourne, and Vera to one at Folkestone. Tom went first to a boarding-school, kept by a school-friend of his Aunt Amy's,[2] near Wellingborough, and afterwards to Cheltenham College.

In 1913 Mrs Sidney left Enfield and moved to a much nicer house, Glenville, Hersham Road, Walton-on-Thames. She remained there until 1917 when, wishing to be more con-

---

[1] As the result of a brain tumour.

[2] Gertrude Amy Stafford Sidney.

veniently situated for London, she went to what was to be the
last of her homes, number 29 Birdhurst Rise, Croydon.

When the First World War broke out, Tom, who was by
then working as a professional concert entertainer, was on tour
in Australia with his close friend, the singer, Peter Dawson. He
immediately returned to England and joined the army. Vera
trained as a hospital nurse and masseuse.

At the end of the war Vera gave up regular work in order to
remain at home with her mother. She continued to attend the
occasional massage case locally, but the fact that she, Grace and
Tom had, on their father's death in 1917, each received a
reversionary legacy of £5,000 from old Thomas Sidney's will,
meant that Vera did not need to work.

After his demobilisation, Tom went back into the entertainment business. In the course of a trip to America in 1921, he
met, in New York,[1] a young American girl, Margaret Neilson
McConnell, a graduate of Tulane University. They married in
New Orleans on February 28th, 1922. He brought his bride
back to England with him and, after living with his mother at
Birdhurst Rise for a while, they bought their own house, Pauliva,
6 South Park Hill Road, Croydon, in September 1923. A son,
Cedric, had been born to them in New Orleans on May 31st,
1923, and on June 14th, 1925, Margaret Sidney gave birth
to a daughter, Virginia.

IV

A child whose destiny was to be tragically interwoven with
that of the Sidney family was born in Mandla, in the Jubbulpore
district of India, on April 24th, 1869. His name was Edmund
Creighton Duff[2].

His father, Jekyl Chalmers Duff, was, at the time of Edmund's
birth, District Superintendent of Police at Mandla. Duff senior,
the only son of Daniel George Duff, late of the East India
Company, and Anne Duff (née Hayter), had been born in India
on December 17th, 1834. He was educated in England, at Rugby,
and by private tutors, returning afterwards to India to join his
father, then a lieutenant-colonel in command of a regiment of
the Bombay Army.

When the Mutiny broke out, Jekyl Chalmers Duff enlisted in

[1] They actually met as the boat, bringing them both to England,
where she was coming on holiday, was leaving New York Harbour.

[2] The tracing of this simple fact proved unexpectedly difficult, for
there was no record of Edmund Duff's birth at Somerset House.
Eventually, I succeeded in finding a copy of his birth certificate at the
India Office.

the Bengal Yeomanry Cavalry, and served with it from September 1857 to January 20th, 1859, chiefly in Gorakhpur and Oudh, and was slightly wounded by rebels in the course of the fighting. His regiment was brigaded with the force under General Rowcroft, and was favourably mentioned on various occasions. On January 21st, 1859, he was commissioned lieutenant in the 6th Bengal Military Police Battalion, and served from 1861 until 1889 as District Superintendent of Police, Central Provinces.

At St Thomas' Church, Howrah, near Calcutta, Jekyl Chalmers Duff, described as a bachelor living at Bhandara, married, on December 30th, 1863, 20-year-old Harriette Elizabeth Lincke, spinster, the daughter of John Gottlieb Lincke, of Ballabhpur, Nadia.

Their son, Edmund, was baptised by the Reverend W. B. Drawbridge, Senior Chaplain, at Mandla on January 29th, 1871. His younger brother, Charles — born on October 4th, 1870 — was baptised at the same time. There would appear to have been at least six more children of the marriage — a third, elder, brother[1], and five sisters.[2]

In the *India List* of 1877, Jekyl Chalmers Duff is listed as District Superintendent 4th-class. This means that although he was a gazetted officer of the Indian Police, he did not attain to particularly high rank, District Superintendent 5th-class being the lowest in the scale. Apart from the fact that during a big-game hunting expedition he was mauled by a tiger and lost an arm, Duff's life in India seems to have been relatively uneventful. On his retirement, in 1889, he went to Australia, and lived for many years at Warrnambool, in Victoria.

We get a last glimpse of him in 1912. Following the death of her father, the Duke of Fife, on January 29th, 1912, Her Highness Princess Alexandra of Fife became Duchess of Fife in her own right but, according to the *Daily Mail* of January 31st, the Fife earldom (of 1759) descended in the Irish peerage to Jekyl Chalmers Duff.

On February 1st, 1912, a *Daily Mail* representative interviewed Duff at his home in Blessington Street, St Kilda, Melbourne. Duff said that his great-grandfather was the Honourable George Duff, deputy-sheriff of Elgin. He died at Elgin in 1818. He had married a Miss Frances Dalziel, by whom he had had a son, the Reverend George Duff, D.D., who, in turn, married a Miss Ogilvie. Their son, Daniel George Duff, was Jekyl Chalmers

---

[1] J. George J. Duff.

[2] One of Edmund Duff's sisters was a Mrs Lilian Annie Hopkins of Maripasa, Park Street, Portarlington, Victoria, Australia. In May 1929 she wrote to Inspector Hedges. She had read in the newspapers accounts of the case, and asked Hedges to forward official details to her.

Duff's father.

A member of the Fife family living in London denied, however, that there ever was a Reverend George Duff, son of George Duff, or any Daniel Duff in the line of descent. The George Duff who appeared in their family tree was the fifth son of the first Earl Fife. He had four children — James, George, Jane and Frances. James was a lunatic from birth. George was a major in the army, and died unmarried in 1828. Jane and Frances both died unmarried. 'It may be,' he added, 'that Mr Jekyl Chalmers Duff is the descendant of another branch of the family.' An official of the College of Heralds examined the relevant pedigrees and agreed that, if proved, they would be an absolute answer to any claim which Jekyl Chalmers Duff might make. And there the matter ended.

It has proved possible to discover very little about the first thirty years of Edmund Creighton Duff's life. It seems fairly certain that he spent them in India, and that after leaving school he was employed in tea, coffee and rubber plantation work.

In 1900, Duff, then aged 31, enlisted as a volunteer in the Boer War, serving mainly as a trooper, but, it is said, attaining commissioned rank and retiring in 1902 as a major. After leaving the army he joined the Colonial Service, being appointed one of thirteen Assistant Residents in the northern region of Nigeria on November 1st, 1902. He was subsequently promoted Resident 3rd-class on August 2nd, 1905, and Resident 2nd-class on October 1st, 1908. He was to remain at that level until his retirement, eleven years later.

According to the testimony of those who knew him in his Colonial Service days, Duff was an average, steady officer of somewhat limited intellectual capacity. He was 'no flyer', and had gone as far as he ever would in the service at the time of his retirement. As a Resident 2nd-class he would have district officers below him, but his status was inferior to that of a Resident 1st-class, and his salary scale would have ranged no higher than £600 — £700 per annum.

It was while on leave in England from August 19th to December 8th, 1909, that Duff first met Grace Sidney. He was introduced to her by her father, with whom he was going down to the Brighton races one day. Thomas Stafford Sidney was afterwards to say that he deeply regretted having effected the introduction, for he was not at all happy when his daughter married a man only six years younger than himself.

Duff's next tour of duty in Africa lasted nearly eighteen months, and throughout that time he and Grace Sidney wrote to each other frequently. He returned to England on leave on May 29th, 1911, and took lodgings at 12 Shirley Road, Enfield.

On June 20th, 1911, he and Grace were married at St Mary Magdalene's Church, Enfield. Grace was then twenty-five, her husband forty-two.

V

When, on November 6th, 1911, Duff's home-leave ended, he was posted to Kano. His bride of four months remained behind at Garlton with her mother, and here, on July 8th, 1912, her first child, Margaret Kathleen, was born.

Duff came home again on December 15th, 1912, to attend a Colonial Office course, and was able to spend Christmas with his wife and baby daughter, and when, on April 14th, 1913, he had to return to Africa, he took Grace with him.

Between May 1913 and February 1914, the Duffs were on tour together in Ilorin. During that time Grace became pregnant again, and Duff went down with a series of tropical diseases. Towards the end of February Grace returned alone to England and went to stay with her mother at Glenville, Hersham Road, Walton-on-Thames. There, on March 25th, 1914, she gave birth to a son, John Edmund Sidney. She was joined at Glenville by her husband in April, he having been sent home on sick-leave with severe dysentery. He was not fit enough to return to Nigeria until the September.

The Duffs' third child, Grace Mary, was born at Glenville on June 2nd, 1915. Following the birth of her second daughter, Grace Duff went for a time to Bournemouth, before moving, in August, to a house which she had taken at 9 St Matthew's Avenue, Surbiton. Her husband returned on leave from Africa on November 27th, and was able to remain with her at Surbiton until April 5th, 1916.

The following year, because of his knowledge of German and French and his great interest in agricultural schemes, he was selected to take temporary charge of the British sphere of the Cameroons.

He next returned to England on June 28th, 1917. Grace and the children were then living at 27 Upper Bridge Road, Redhill.

He should have gone back to Africa at the end of August, but requested, and was granted, an extension of leave on half-pay. His leave was further extended at the end of September, in view of the fact that his wife's father had returned from the Leewards a sick man, and a specialist had given him only three weeks to live. As it turned out, Thomas Stafford Sidney did not, in fact, die until the November, and Duff was ordered to catch a boat back to Nigeria on October 17th.

This was Duff's final tour of duty abroad. It lasted sixteen months. He arrived back in England on February 11th, 1919, and joined his family in a house which they had rented, called Chalmers, at 29 Park Hill Road, East Croydon. Once again when his leave was up he was granted an extension until August 6th, on the grounds of ill-health.

Meanwhile, however, on July 27th, 1919, Duff wrote to the Colonial Secretary asking to be allowed to resign his appointment as Resident 2nd-class, Nigeria, and retire on pension. The reason that he gave for wishing to retire was the critical state of health of his seven-year-old daughter, Margaret Kathleen, who was suffering from Still's disease and who had just undergone a colectomy at the hands of Sir Arbuthnot Lane. Margaret Kathleen Duff died on September 21st, 1919. The causes of her death were given as rheumatoid arthritis and colectomy for intestinal obstruction. The certificate was signed by Dr F. Gayner.

The following year Edmund Duff obtained a temporary job with the Ministry of Pensions and he, his wife and their two surviving children moved first to Holmwood, Sutton, and then to Dorset House, Sevenoaks.

Towards the end of 1920 the Duffs returned to Croydon. They rented apartments at 96 Avondale Road, South Croydon, and then, about July 1921, bought The Limes, 16 Park Hill Road, East Croydon. And there, on July 15th, a third daughter, Suzanne Violet Amy, was born.

Financially things were not going too well, and on January 19th, 1922, Duff wrote to the Colonial Office to ask if he could have an advance on his pension. He is troubled, he explains, by pressing bills as a result of his wife's confinement and long illness, and refers to what he calls his 'bitter needs.' Regretfully, the Colonial Office was unable to help.

On March 16th, 1924, two-year-old Suzanne Violet Amy died. Her death, certified by Dr R. G. Elwell, was attributed to cerebral tuberculous meningitis.

Duff had scarcely time to recover from his grief before another blow fell. On May 5th, 1925, he had to leave the Ministry of Pensions, owing to what was euphemistically styled 'retrenchment'

For a while things looked rather black. The only money coming into The Limes was the Colonial Office pension and a small weekly sum from the Duffs' paying guest, an elderly spinster, Miss Anna Maria Kelvey. Then Duff got a job as a clerk with Spicer Brothers.[1]

[1] One of the family, Irene Spicer, was a close friend of Grace Duff's and it was through her that Edmund was offered a position with the firm.

It is hardly surprising that a man of Edmund Duff's background and experience should have found clerking in the City very little to his taste and, at the beginning of 1926, he wrote hopefully to the Colonial Office asking for employment on either the West or East coast of Africa. In his letter, dated January 20th, he says, 'I am in robust health,' and adds that he is a good linguist, 'Very fluent in French and German. Fair at Portuguese. Some Spanish, Dutch and Hindustani.' He points out that he also knows the local Nigerian tribal dialects of Hausa and Yoruba. But it was no good. The Colonial Office thanked him for his letter, but regretted . . .

Later in 1926, the Duffs moved from East to South Croydon. They sold The Limes and rented Hurst View, 16 South Park Hill Road, for £105 per annum. Here, on January 12th, 1927, Miss Kelvey, who had accompanied them to the new house, died. Her death was certified by Dr R.G. Elwell as the result of arteriosclerosis and cerebral haemorrhage.

Three months later, on April 2nd, 1927, the Duffs' fifth and last child, Alastair Michael, was born at Hurst View. And a little over one year after that, also at Hurst View, Edmund Creighton Duff was murdered.

8

THE MIND OF INSPECTOR HEDGES

I

At eleven o'clock on the morning of May 2nd, 1928, the telephone rang in the office of Divisional Detective-Inspector Hedges at Croydon Police Station. The caller was Dr Beecher Jackson, the Croydon coroner. He had, he said, a matter of very great importance which he was anxious to discuss, and he asked Hedges if he could come along to see him right away.

Within the hour, Hedges was sitting with the coroner in his private room at the Coroner's Court. Dr Jackson handed him a letter which, he said, he had received from Dr Elwell. The letter, dated April 28th, 1928, was a long one. It reported the death of a patient, Edmund Duff, in circumstances which puzzled the doctor.

'My opinion,' the doctor had written, 'is that the case was one of ptomaine poisoning — but enquiry revealed that no one in the house where he was staying had been ill at all — I am unable to give a certificate without further examination.'

The Inspector read the letter through and gave it back to Dr Jackson. The coroner told him that he had, in fact, already been in communication with Dr Holden, the Medical Officer of Health for Croydon, who had had the contents of the stomach analysed. He had just received the result. It was negative. Dr Brontë had also been asked to carry out a post-mortem examination. He had done so, but had been unable to make up his mind as to the cause of death, and Dr Jackson considered it necessary to hold an inquest. He proposed to open it later that day, and thought that it would be as well if the Inspector were to be present at his court.

Hedges asked if there were any suspicious circumstances. The coroner replied that there were none so far as he could see, but that he intended to send some portions of the intestines to an analyst, and felt that it was his duty to bring the case to the attention of the police. Hedges knew Dr Jackson well, knew what a cautious, conscientious man he was, and decided that he ought to make a few enquiries.

So, that afternoon, he paid a visit to Miss Amy Clarke, the Duffs' daily maid, at her home at 46 Sydenham Road North, West Croydon. She told him that Edmund Duff, his wife and children were all very devoted to each other.

The picture she painted of life at Hurst View w
one, and she left him in no doubt that Edmund I
had been a terrible blow to his wife and family.

This impression was amply confirmed when, late
day, he attended at the Queen's Road Homes, where ʋɪ ɟackson
opened the inquest, and heard the widow, Mrs Grace Duff, give
her evidence. Her obvious sincerity and distress affected him
deeply. She struck him as a decent, straightforward woman, and
he felt extremely sorry for her in her sad and sudden bereavement.

The proceedings of that first sitting did not last long, and
after Dr Jackson had adjourned the inquest until June 1st,
when, he said, the court would have the results of the various
medical investigations, Hedges paid his second visit that
Wednesday to the coroner's room. It was then that he asked
Dr Jackson point-blank whether he had any suspicion against
any individual in the matter of Duff's death. The coroner
replied that he had not, but confided that what was greatly
troubling him was the fact that nothing had been found in the
stomach of the deceased to account for his death, and that
Dr Brontë had failed to trace any mark of violence, or any sign
of disease. In order to safeguard himself, he would like the
police to take a full statement from Mr Edwardes of Fordingbridge, the friend with whom Duff had been staying.

Inspector Hedges accordingly got in touch with his superiors
at Scotland Yard, and requested that the Chief Constable of the
Hampshire County Constabulary at Winchester should be asked
to look into the matter. And, on May 8th, Superintendent
S. J. Jacobs, of the Ringwood Division, went to see Mr Edwardes.

The statement which Superintendent Jacobs elicited, and in
due course forwarded, threw no further light on the enigma of
Duff's death. Neither for that matter did any of the numerous
pathological examinations and chemical analyses which were
carried out during the ensuing month.

The inquest was resumed at 10.20 a.m. on June 1st.

This time, after the hearing of the evidence of the doctors, a
verdict was reached — 'Death from natural causes'.

And that, or so Inspector Hedges thought, was an end to the
matter.

In fact, within less than twelve months he was to think more,
much more, of the mysterious death of Edmund Creighton
Duff.

II

In 1929 Fred Hedges was fifty-three years old. A big, burly, heavy-featured man, clean-shaven, with greying hair and a ruddy complexion, there was a bucolic air about him, something that irrisistibly suggested tweeds and gaiters and the farmyard. Indeed, he looked much more like a farmer than a policeman, although if anyone were ever sufficiently tactless to remark this to his face, he did not like it at all. On one occasion, when he was wearing a vaguely rustic tweed suit, an acquaintance jocularly told him that it made him look like a farmer. He was so put out that he promptly gave the suit away.

The son of a builder, he was born in Putney on October 2nd, 1875, and, on October 26th, 1896, three weeks after his twenty-first birthday, he enlisted in the Metropolitan Police at Peckham, where he spent the first three years of his service as a uniformed constable. In those days parts of Peckham were considered fairly tough and Hedges always remembered the first arrest that he made there. It was following a street fight and, as he was good-naturedly helping one of the combatants on with his coat and trying to persuade him to move along quietly, he was rewarded for his trouble with the worst punch on the nose he was ever to receive throughout the whole course of his career.

After four years in the Force, he married, in 1900, Kate Dawes, a young woman from Hedley, in Hampshire, who subsequently bore him two children, a son, Leslie, and a daughter, Muriel. In the March of that year, the satisfactory record of the way in which he had discharged his duties on the beat having favourably impressed his superiors, he was recommended for the CID, and served as a detective-constable, first in Peckham, and subsequently in Camberwell.

In 1914 he was selected for service at Scotland Yard, where he remained for four years. It was during this period that, largely because of the initiative which he displayed, the possession of cocaine was brought within the Defence of the Realm Regulations. Hedges had found some peculiar white powder secreted on the person of a woman whom he had arrested on suspicion, and had had searched. He submitted this powder for identification by an analytical chemist. It was cocaine. The case was heard at Bow Street in May 1916, and it was as a direct result of Hedges' discovery that a new and special branch was established at Scotland Yard to deal with the problem of cocaine running.

Upgraded to detective-sergeant first-class, he left the Yard in 1918, being posted first to Vine Street, and then to Kennington Lane. Further promotion to the rank of detective-inspector came on May 26th, 1919, when he was transferred to Croydon, where, two years later, he was appointed divisional detective-inspector and placed in charge of the newly formed Z Division. He was to remain there for the last eleven years of his police service.

As a type, Hedges was almost a cliche. But that is to say no more than that he was true to type — and the best type of police-officer at that. He was an exceedingly clever detective, whose bluff exterior and somewhat slow-seeming and cumbersome manner masked a sharp and energetic brain. There may have been an air of the farmyard about him, but there was no straw in his hair. Academically, he was not perhaps outstanding. He was not great on what used to be called 'book-learning,' but he had an inborn shrewdness, almost a cunning, which, allied to a natural gift of psychological acuity, made him an unexpectedly formidable adversary. There was, too, a cliché streak of the bulldog in his make-up, an obstinate tenacity which kept him plodding doggedly on long after most people would have given up.

And never was that invincible determination of his more rigorously tested than in the investigation of the Sidney-Duff poisoning case.

Day after day, night after night, for five wearisome months between March and August 1929, he worked unsparingly away, following up every tiny clue, exploring every conceivable — and sometimes inconceivable — possibility, weighing in the balance every theory, no matter how remote and unlikely. He interviewed dozens of witnesses, cross-questioning them, taking statements, laboriously checking and double checking. Then back to his office to write lengthy and subtly-argued reports that ran into many thousands of words, and the composition of which often occupied him far into the night. He criss-crossed Croydon interminably in his quest for a solution, travelled to Fordingbridge, Bath and various far-flung parts of London. He was present at all twenty-six sittings of the protracted series of inquests, attended conferences at Scotland Yard, the office of the Director of Public Prosecutions, the Home Office, the chambers of counsel and the offices of their instructing solicitors. He arranged and supervised all three exhumations. He held long and frequent consultations with the doctors, the forensic experts and the coroner. Nothing was too much trouble, no line of enquiry too tenuous to be pursued, no stone that could be turned was left unturned. His private life suffered. His wife and family saw precious little of him at their home in Trafford Road, Thornton Heath. He was often short of sleep. If ever a man deserved to succeed, that man was Fred Hedges.

III

On the evening of March 6th, 1929, Inspector Hedges was working late, clearing up some arrears of paper work in the CID office at Croydon Police Station. He was just thinking of going home when, shortly before seven o'clock, his telephone rang. It was Dr Jackson. The coroner told him that he would like to see him at once, and, accompanied by his colleague, Detective-Inspector Reginald Morrish, he hurried over to the Queen's Road Homes.

There, Dr Jackson explained that he had sent for him urgently because he was very worried regarding the death the previous evening of a Mrs Violet Emilia Sidney. The facts as reported to him struck the coroner as very suspicious, and he wanted Hedges to make a full investigation. He went on to say that since the death of Edmund Duff, followed by that of his sister-in-law, Vera Sidney, Dr Elwell and his partner, Dr Binning, had been extremely cautious in their professional dealings with the Sidney-Duff family and, on hearing of the illness of Violet Emilia Sidney, they were careful to secure all the material possible in order to elucidate the matter should that illness prove fatal. Now it *had* proved fatal and, although Hedges would, of course, have to proceed warily and with tact, this third and latest death must certainly be looked into.

Never a man to let the grass grow under his feet, Hedges decided to go along to 29 Birdhurst Rise there and then. He took with him Inspector Morrish and the coroner's officer, ex-Police-Sergeant Samuel John Clarke. Since the death of old Mrs Sidney, the servant no longer slept at Number 29, and the house was unoccupied. So the three officers had first to call at Tom Sidney's home in nearby South Park Hill Road in order to get the key. At Number 29 they began to set in motion the purely routine measures normally observed in the investigation of cases of suspicious deaths. The obvious implication of Mrs Sidney's very sudden demise was that, if it were not the result of natural causes, it might well be due to her having taken poison and, with this possibility in mind, they proceeded to search the place from cellar to attic, taking possession of all the various unlabelled bottles and so on which they could find, so that they could be subjected to toxicological analysis. Carefully labelled, these were given into the charge of Mr Clarke, whose responsibility it would be to deliver them to the analyst.

At this stage Hedges was not by any means certain that Mrs Sidney had died from poisoning at all. It was no more than a possibility. And even if it eventually turned out that she had, there would still remain the very difficult task of discovering whether the poison had been taken accidentally, suicidally, or administered to her criminally.

By the time they had completed their search at Number 29 it was getting on for half-past nine, but Hedges told the others that he thought they should all make their way to Dr Binning's surgery at 1 Birdhurst Road, in order to collect the various objects which the doctor had removed from his patient's home — her bottle of Metatone, one dish containing pudding, a chicken bone, some brown bread and butter, a quantity of milk in a bottle, two jars of vomit and a jar of stool. These, too, were delivered into Mr Clarke's safekeeping, before subsequent conveyance, on the coroner's instructions, to Dr Ryffel, of Guy's Hospital, for chemical examination.

At ten o'clock the following morning Hedges and Morrish were back at Number 29, where they took possession of a wine glass, which Hedges found on the dining-room sideboard, and which was believed to have been used by Mrs Sidney when taking her last dose of medicine, and interviewed Mrs Kathleen Noakes, Mrs Sidney's cook-general. Her position was, to say the least of it, an awkward one. She was the only person to come out of that house alive. She was, too, the person who had handled all the food and drink there.

Naturally, Hedges questioned her very closely. She answered all his questions with a readiness and candour which impressed him strongly in her favour. She was not, he thought, a particularly intelligent woman, but neither did she strike him as being in any way devious or dishonest. She seemed to have been fond of her mistress, and positively devoted to Vera Sidney. Indeed, she broke down and cried several times in the course of the interview when Vera's name was mentioned. Mrs Noakes frankly admitted that she had never been really happy at Number 29, but was hard put to it to give any definite reason for this, beyond the fact that she had felt lonely there. Her one grievance against the Sidneys was that during her service with them she had never had sufficient to eat. She said that at Christmas 1928 she had made up her mind to leave, but Vera Sidney had persuaded her to stay on. Hedges pressed her hard as to whether she had ever purchased any medicines or poisonous substances for herself or for the family. She replied most emphatically that she had not. There was not, he decided, any reason to doubt the truth of her statements, and by the time he had finished his interrogation he was completely satisfied that there was nothing so far to connect her with the deaths of either her mistress or her mistress' daughter.

Just before noon, he called on Dr Binning, from whom he took a routine statement regarding the deaths of Vera and Violet Emilia Sidney.

The Inspector had by now decided to proceed on the assump-

tion that Mrs Sidney *had* somehow received a fatal dose of
poison. In that event, he reasoned, it could have been an
accident. Perhaps the poison had got into the bottle of
Metatone, sent to her on Dr Elwell's prescription, as the result
of a mistake.

So his next visit that afternoon was to the George Street
premises of Mr Frederick Sandford Rose, the chemist who had
supplied the Metatone. Mr Rose gave him a full account of the
various medical preparations which he had despatched to both
Vera and Violet Emilia Sidney between February 13th and
March 5th, 1929, but it did not contribute anything of significance to the investigation.

The only other obvious people to be interrogated at this
stage were Mrs Sidney's two closest surviving relatives, her son,
Tom, and her daughter, Mrs Grace Duff. It was a ticklish position.
The Sidneys were a respected, and respectable, family, and
Hedges by all the pressures of his upbringing and environment
was loth to think that such gentlefolk would be likely to resort
to murder. And where was the motive? Nevertheless, the fact
remained that, in all probability, murder *had* been done, and
Hedges was nothing if not a conscientious police-officer. However distasteful, however unrewarding it might seem, he knew
where his duty lay. He had to start off by treating the two
remaining members of that stricken family as prime suspects.
He began that very evening with a frontal attack. He called at
the house of Tom Sidney.

The Inspector found him quite an amiable man, who
answered his questions freely. He appeared deeply distressed by
the death of his mother and, though he admitted having had in
his possession a supply of arsenical weed-killer and a quantity of
rat-poison, he assured the Inspector that he had never taken any
of either substance to his mother's house.

Hedges saw, too, Tom Sidney's wife, Margaret, who struck
him as a very refined woman. She said that her husband had
always been extremely devoted to his mother, and that he would
never have done anything to harm her. She and her husband
usually went to tea at Number 29 on Sundays, but on no
occasion had she ever taken any food to her mother-in-law's,
and certainly nothing in the nature of medicines or drugs.

Hedges spent a long time at the house, questioning them both
on every conceivable point, and when at last he left, he felt
reasonably certain that there was nothing whatsoever to raise a
finger of suspicion against either of them.

Finally, the Inspector made his way to the home of Mrs
Grace Duff, at 59 Birdhurst Rise. She, too, received him most
affably. She was, he observed, a somewhat highly strung
woman, displaying at times a markedly hysterical demeanour.

She seemed restless, too, now sitting on the floor, now curling herself up on a couch, as he questioned her. But, as in the case of her brother, her replies to his questions were frank and forthright and certainly did not disclose anything which led him to suspect that she was in any way concerned with bringing about her mother's death.

By March 13th, Hedges had learned from Dr Ryffel that, although his chemical analyses had not yet been completed, a large quantity of arsenic had been found both in Mrs Sidney's vomit and in the sediment remaining in her Metatone bottle. There seemed, said Ryffel, little doubt that Mrs Sidney had died as the result of taking a fatal dose.

This put a new complexion on the case. Now there *was* something definite to go on. The source of the arsenic *must* be traced.

Actually, anticipating Dr Ryffel's positive findings, Inspector Hedges had already put certain enquiries in train. He had ordered that the books of all the chemists in Croydon should be examined and, on March 8th, he had himself visited the shop of Samuel Atkinson Noble, chemist, of 12 Ye Market Place, Selsdon Road, South Croydon.

Mr Noble told him that he had known Major Duff quite well, and remembered having sold him two tins of arsenical weed-killer. Together they examined Noble's poisons register and found two relevant entries in it. The first recorded the purchase by E. C. Duff of a one-gallon tin of liquid arsenical weed-killer on September 24th, 1927. The second showed that Duff had purchased another one-gallon tin on October 15th, 1927.

The following day — March 9th — Hedges called again on Grace Duff, and asked her what had become of the tins of weed-killer which her husband had purchased. She said that so far as the first tin was concerned it had, presumably, all been used up by her husband in the garden. The second tin had remained, unopened, at Hurst View, where it was seen by the coroner's officer at the time of her husband's death. When she was about to move from Hurst View to her present address, she had given the tin to Mr Lane, her gardener.

That evening he went along to 17 Mansfield Road, South Croydon, where he saw Arthur Henry Lane, who confirmed that, after the death of Mr Duff, Mrs Duff had given him a tin of weed-killer to get it out of her way.

Still casting about for the source of the arsenic, on March 11th the Inspector collected from Mr Rose the 80-ounce stock-bottle of Metatone from which Mrs Sidney's prescription had been supplied. This, together with the wine glass removed from Number 29 on March 7th, he himself delivered to the coroner's officer at 3 p.m. the same day. He also had some further con-

versation with Mrs Noakes, who gave him a list of the various
shops from which Mrs Sidney habitually ordered her provisions.

During that first hectic week Hedges also collected, on March
9th, a second quantity of bottles, some apples and packets of
soup powder from Number 29 and additional foodstuffs from
Dr Binning. Further statements were taken from Mrs Noakes
(March 9th), Tom Sidney (March 9th), Grace Duff (March 9th),
Dr Elwell (March 11th) and Mrs Margaret Neilson McConnell
Sidney (March 12th), none of which added anything of signifi-
cance.

On March 13th, he saw Dr Jackson, who told him that he had
been in communication with the Director of Public Prosecutions, Sir Archibald Bodkin, and had discussed with him the
advisability of exhuming the body of Violet Emilia Sidney, and
also that of her daughter, Vera.

A week passed, and on the morning of March 20th, Dr
Jackson sent for Hedges and gave him a warrant signed by the
Secretary of State, authorising the exhumations.

The Inspector immediately got in touch with Sir Bernard
Spilsbury, and together they agreed that the exhumations
should take place at 2 a.m. on March 22nd.

Hedges then delivered the warrant to the Town Clerk of
Croydon, Dr Newnham, who telephoned to the superintendent
of the Queen's Road Cemetery, Mr John William Bird, and
instructed him to make the necessary arrangements.

Later that day, he made it his business to see Drs Brönte and
Binning, and asked them to attend at the Mayday Hospital
Mortuary to receive the bodies after the exhumation.

At 7 p.m., accompanied by Inspector Morrish, he visited
Mrs Duff at 59 Birdhurst Rise, where he thoroughly searched
the house and carried off a number of bottles which he found
there.

Then, around 9 p.m., Hedges, Morrish, and Clarke called on
Tom Sidney, and the Inspector asked him if he would attend
the exhumation in order to identify the bodies of his mother
and sister. At the same time, he took possession of a tin of
weed-killer and a packet of rat-poison belonging to Tom Sidney.

His last call that evening was to see Sydney Gardiner, assistant
to Messrs J. B. Shakespeare, undertakers, of 67 George Street,
Croydon. Gardiner had carried out the original funeral arrangements and was therefore in a position to identify both bodies.
He, too, was asked to attend the exhumations, Mr Clarke
requesting him to undertake the conveying of the corpses from
the cemetery to the nearby Mayday Road Mortuary.

In the early hours of the morning of March 22nd, Hedges, in
company with Inspector Morrish and Superintendent Brown of
the Yard, supervised the exhumation of the two women. After

Spilsbury had concluded his post-mortem examination of the body of Vera Sidney, he told Hedges that the condition of the corpse was compatible with death's having resulted from arsenical poisoning, and he took away with him a selection of organs, which he said he would deliver to the analyst himself.

Hedges was watching, too, when, at 1 p.m. on March 22nd, Brontë dissected out the body of Violet Emilia Sidney at the Mayday Road Mortuary. He saw that the condition of the corpse was precisely the same as that of Vera, and as scissors and scalpel snicked and sliced, and organs and portions of organs dropped with a soft plop into specimen jars, which would in due course be delivered for analysis to Dr Ryffel's laboratory, he felt pretty certain in his own mind that he knew what the outcome of that analysis would be.

The inquest on Vera Sidney was opened at six o'clock that evening, and at the conclusion of the brief, formal proceedings Inspector Hedges had a private chat with the coroner regarding the death of Edmund Duff. Dr Jackson told him that he had already conferred with Sir Archibald Bodkin and Sir Ernley Blackwell at the Home Office about the possibility of an exhumation, and that, although nothing had been decided as yet, it was his intention to pursue the matter further with Sir Archibald.

Before going home, Hedges slipped round to Birdhurst Road to have a quick word with Dr Binning. He told the doctor that he was anxious about Mrs Grace Duff. She was, he felt, a highly strung woman, and he was afraid that she might have a breakdown because of the severe strain to which she was being subjected. He thought that she should have some companion constantly with her. Binning agreed and said that he would make a point of seeing Tom Sidney and mentioning it to him. Then the conversation turned to the subject of the death of Duff, and Binning told the Inspector that he was convinced that if Duff's body were exhumed arsenic would be found in it. And, indeed, by now Hedges himself was perfectly sure that that would prove to be the case. He felt that Dr Jackson thought so, too. And hadn't Dr Brontë hinted strongly that, although in the face of Mr Candy's negative findings he had previously assigned chronic myocarditis as the cause of death, he, too, had come round to the view that arsenical poisoning might well have been the real cause?

As he headed homewards for Thornton Heath, Hedges began to speculate. Supposing Duff *were* exhumed. Supposing arsenic *were* found in his remains. That would definitely eliminate Mrs Noakes from his slender list of suspects. At the time of his death she had not been in any way connected with the Duff or Sidney families. That would leave Tom Sidney, Grace Duff, or

some person or persons at present unknown, as the possible
killer. Yes, the more he thought of it, the more certain one
thing became. He must press with every means at his disposal
for the raising of Edmund Duff.

IV

In the course of the last week of March and the first week in
April, copies of four medical reports were handed to Inspector
Hedges by Dr Jackson. These confirmed the presence of a
considerable amount of arsenic in connection with the death of
Violet Emilia Sidney and left Hedges in little doubt that Vera
Sidney had succumbed to the same substance. In view of this,
he determined now to cast his net wide in pursuit of any
ancillary medical data.

He began, on April 5th, with a visit to the home of Miss
Maggie Eveline Gillman, at 24 Avondale Road, Croydon. She
was the qualified nurse who had been called in by Dr Elwell at
6.15 on the evening of March 5th to attend Violet Emilia
Sidney.

Her statement was matter-of-fact and unenlightening.

'Mrs Sidney's room was the first-floor front. Mrs Duff was in
the room when Dr Elwell, the specialist and I entered. I did
nothing until Dr Binning came into the room. Then I assisted
him in the treatment of the patient. But her condition became
worse, and at about 7.15 p.m. she died. After the death I performed the last offices, washing her and laying her out. I left
the house at about 8.45 p.m. The only time that I spoke to the
servant in the house was when I required something. She seemed
quite calm and collected. I had no conversation with Mrs
Sidney, as she was partially unconscious. Neither did I have
any conversation with Mr Thomas Sidney or Mrs Grace Duff.'

The Inspector also requested the Sheffield police to interview
Miss Mary Keetley, of Clifton House, Cavendish Road, Sheffield.
She was the nurse called in by Dr Elwell on February 14th to
attend Vera Sidney.

Seen, on April 8th, by Superintendent F. Naylor, of the
Sheffield City Police CID, Miss Keetley stated: 'I am forty-six,
single, and for the past seventeen years I have been employed as
a nurse. I arrived at 29 Birdhurst Rise at about 11.20 a.m. on
February 14th, and remained there until 2.30 p.m. on
February 20th. I was not present when Miss Vera Sidney died,
as I had retired to bed about ten minutes before.' She also gave
details of the various injections which, acting under the doctors'
orders, she had given to her patient.

And, on April 10th, Hedges, together with Inspector Morrish, called at 8 Addiscombe Avenue, Croydon, to see Miss Daisy Geer, the second nurse, called in by Dr Elwell to act as night relief to Miss Keetley.

Her stay at Number 29 was, however, of so brief a duration that her evidence was of scant importance. She had arrived at 11.45 p.m. on February 14th, and was shown up to Vera Sidney's bedroom on the first floor, where she found the patient only partially conscious. 'She turned towards me, and I said to Dr Binning, "She looks strange." He replied, "I think she's going." And within half an hour she was dead. I washed her and laid her out. After I had attended to my duties I went to bed. When I got up at seven o'clock the next morning I went to call Mrs Noakes. I had to call her several times before she would get up. She seemed to be extremely drowsy and she said that she was tired. After Mrs Noakes was up, I went along with Mrs Duff to her house at 59 Birdhurst Rise, where she gave me some breakfast. I left Mrs Duff's at 8.30 a.m., and went home.'

In order to close all possible gaps, Hedges also secured statements from four outsiders who had visited members of the Sidney and Duff families.

He saw the first of these, Mrs Elsie Adelaide Anderson, wife of the Reverend Richard William Eric Anderson, the new curate of St Peter's Church, South Croydon, at her home, 18b Selsdon Road, South Croydon, on April 5th. She and her husband were newcomers to Croydon and, according to a statement made by Tom Sidney at the second sitting of the inquest on Violet Emilia Sidney on April 4th, Mrs Anderson had paid her first and only visit to his mother between 4 p.m. and 4.20 p.m. on March 4th.

'I was admitted to the house by the maid, and was shown into the drawing-room, in the front of the house, where I saw Mrs Sidney and her son. We conversed and I was given tea, not at a table, but sitting beside the fire. Tea was brought in by the maid, and our conversation was mainly about my husband and I having just come to the district. I think it was about 5.15 p.m. when I left. As I was going I said to Mrs Sidney, "You should be careful." I was referring to her taking care on account of the bitterly cold weather. She seemed to me to be looking fairly well for a person of her age. I have never met Mrs Duff, nor any members of Mr Thomas Sidney's family.'

It all sounded innocent enough, and it did not take Inspector Hedges long to decide that it was just as innocent an encounter as it seemed.

Then there was Frederick William Lodge, of 17 Churchill Road, South Croydon. He was a rat-catcher, employed by Croydon Corporation, and had visited Mrs Grace Duff at 59 Birdhurst Rise on November 30th, 1928.

On April 11th he told Hedges: 'I attended for the purpose of killing rats. I set a small quantity of poison in various places which could not be reached without first removing the floor boards. The entire amount of poison I used in the house would be no larger than a walnut. It was a well-known rat-poison called Exo. That was my one and only visit to the house.'

As far as Lodge was concerned, Hedges was satisfied that he had not taken sufficient phosphorus into the house to destroy human life.

Thirdly, there was Mrs Gwendoline Mary Stafford Greenwell, Mrs Sidney's sister-in-law and Vera Sidney's aunt. At Hedges' request Detective-Sergeant George Oswald Winterburn, of the Newcastle City Police, saw her at her home, 2 Grosvenor Road, Newcastle-upon-Tyne, on April 12th. She gave him a detailed account regarding the events of her visit of February 13th, 1929, to 29 Birdhurst Rise, but it added nothing to what Hedges already knew.

Finally, on April 26th, the Inspector saw Joseph Talbot Thornes, a plumber, of 56 Frith Road, Croydon. In the course of her evidence at the fifth sitting of the inquest on Violet Emilia Sidney on April 22nd, Mrs Grace Duff had mentioned that a plumber had been in her mother's house on March 4th.

Thornes, who was employed by Messrs. Baldwins Ltd, builders, of 19 Duppas Hill Lane, Croydon, said that he had gone to 29 Birdhurst Rise on March 4th in order to carry out some repairs to a burst water-pipe.

He told Hedges: 'I arrived there at about 10 a.m. that Monday, and was admitted to the house by a maid. She showed me upstairs, and Mrs Sidney followed us into the bathroom, where the burst was. I was engaged repairing the pipe until around 4.45 p.m. I was alone and did not have a labourer with me. I made frequent visits to the kitchen and scullery, but I certainly did not take any poisons of any kind into the house with me. The maid told me that she had lost a good friend by the death of Mrs Sidney's daughter, and she seemed deeply grieved about it. About 3.45 p.m. I saw Mr Thomas Sidney arrive at the house, and soon afterwards a lady came. I think she was the curate's wife. The maid gave me a cup of tea, and then I left.'

Thornes said that he had also been called to Number 29 on Sunday, February 17th, to attend to a burst pipe.

'This time the burst was along the corridor and was quite an easy job. I was there about half an hour. It was dinner-time and Mrs Sidney gave me a cup of tea and a biscuit. The next occasion I was at Mrs Sidney's was on February 20th. That was to attend to a burst pipe in the pantry. The job took me about four hours, and I had to go to various parts of the house. I know Mrs Duff very well. I have worked in her house at 59 Birdhurst Rise many times, but I have never taken anything of a poisonous nature there. I was at Mrs Duff's on the morning after the death of Miss Vera Sidney, and Mrs Duff seemed very upset, though she did not make any comment to me. I have only been to the residence of Mr Thomas Sidney once. That was a long time ago. I went there to fix a lavatory basin. I have never taken any poison there, either.'

Certain members of the Sidney family had cast aspersions on Mrs Noakes, and, on April 16th, Hedges decided to interview her again. He made a point of questioning her closely on the subject of her alleged sickness and that of the cat, and she confirmed that it was on the day before Mrs Greenwell came to lunch at Number 29 that she, Bingo and Vera Sidney were sick for the first time.

Mrs Noakes said that she had noticed that Mrs Greenwell looked very poorly when she arrived that day. She was also emphatic that Mrs Sidney never had any soup.

'The last time I remember Mrs Sidney's having soup was at Christmas (1928). The whole family were together for the last time that Christmas, and I remember they were all very happy and jolly. I cooked the dinner, and we began with soup, which I made. At this gathering were Mrs Sidney, Miss Vera, Mr Tom, and his wife and their two children, and Mrs Duff and her three children. To the best of my recollection they all had soup, with the exception of Mrs Duff's baby, Alastair. Neither Mr Tom nor his wife came to the house to lunch after the Christmas party, though I believe that they would come and stay to supper on Sundays, when I used to go out after the midday meal. I would lay everything on the dining-room table ready for them before I went out, and Mrs Sidney would prepare the meal herself.'

Mrs Noakes then went along with him to Tom Sidney's house, where Hedges asked him if he would let them into Number 29. He did so, and in the kitchen there Mrs Noakes showed the Inspector a large stain on the hearth-rug which, she said, was where the cat had been sick after she had given it the soup. She also showed him the tureen in which the soup had been served at luncheon on February 13th. He took possession of both objects and, later the same day, delivered them to Dr Ryffel at Guy's Hospital for chemical examination.[1]

That evening Tom Sidney got in touch with Inspector Hedges and handed him a sealed envelope in which, he said, was a portion of a torn envelope containing a small quantity of white powder. He had, he explained, found it in a kitchen

---

[1] On April 27th Ryffel reported that both hearth-rug and tureen were arsenic-free. Presumably both had been washed in the interval, anyway.

drawer at Number 29 immediately after Hedges had left with the hearth-rug and tureen. The Inspector was puzzled, as he himself had actually searched that particular drawer — it was one used by Mrs Noakes — on the occasion when he, Morrish and Clarke had visited the house on March 7th. However, he readily acceded to Tom Sidney's suggestion that it should be submitted to Dr Ryffel for analysis.

Two days later, on the morning of April 18th, Tom Sidney came up with another exhibit — a sheet of brown lining-paper which he had removed from Mrs Noakes' kitchen drawer. Again, he asked that it should be forwarded to Dr Ryffel. Again, Hedges was puzzled, as he felt satisfied that his own searches at Number 29 on March 6th and 7th had been extremely thorough. This, and the contents of the portion of torn envelope, were both subsequently reported by Dr Ryffel to be innocent of any traces of arsenic.

During his evidence at the third sitting of the inquest on Violet Emilia Sidney on April 12th, Tom Sidney mentioned that he had found an empty Eureka Weed-Killer tin in the tool-shed at Number 29. Hedges, who had seen this same tin in the shed on March 7th, when in company with Morrish and Clarke he had searched the house, had attached no importance to it. Dr Jackson, however, took a different view[1] and, on the instruction of the coroner, the Inspector went along on the evening of April 12th and took possession of the tin in question. It, too, was handed over to Dr Ryffel.

In the meantime, on April 10th, Hedges was given, by Dr Jackson, a copy of the anxiously awaited final report of Ryffel's analysis of the organs of Violet Emilia Sidney. It made it clear that she had indeed died of arsenical poisoning.

It was about this time that Inspector Hedges received an anonymous letter concerning a Miss Anna Maria Kelvey, who had died, aged seventy-six, at Hurst View, on January 12th, 1927. The writer pointed out that Dr Elwell and two of Mrs Duff's children had benefited under the will. Hedges promptly obtained a copy of Miss Kelvey's will. He also made enquiries as to the cause of the woman's death which, so far as he could discover, had been a natural one.

Morrish was despatched to the Trustee Department of Barclays Bank, at Lombard Street in the City, to make a copy of Vera Sidney's will which was lodged there, while Hedges himself made discreet enquiries as to the respective financial positions of Tom Sidney and Mrs Grace Duff prior to the deaths of their sister and mother.

Neglect no possibility.

[1] See page 51.

What about the children?

Ridiculous? Never mind.

Check.

On April 23rd, with Morrish, Hedges interviewed 15-year-old John Duff and his 13-year-old sister, Grace Mary, at 59 Birdhurst Rise.

John told him that for the past five years he had been attending a preparatory school, The Limes School, Melville Avenue, South Croydon — since Christmas as a weekly boarder. He said that at the moment he was recovering from an attack of chicken-pox, and would be going, as a boarder, to a new school, Monkton Combe School, near Bath, on May 3rd.

His last term at The Limes had finished on Tuesday, March 26th, and the previous week-end (March 23rd-24th) he had not come home as he usually did at week-ends, but stayed on at the school to take part in a rag, so that he had not been at home since Monday, March 18th. He had not, he said, seen his mother from Monday, February 25th, until the morning of Saturday, March 2nd. He had stayed at home that week-end and returned to school on Monday, March 4th.

John said that he had been in the habit of visiting his grandmother's on Sundays, or Saturday afternoons. He would go there alone as a rule, and she used to lend him books. On one of these occasions — he thought it was about a week before his grandmother died — he was admitted by Kate (Noakes), and he asked her where his grandmother was. She told him that she was in her bedroom. He went upstairs to the bedroom and saw a medicine-bottle standing on her chest of drawers. He had not been round to his grandmother's on Saturday, March 2nd, so it must have been on the Sunday, March 3rd, that he saw the bottle.

Hedges asked John if there was a laboratory at his school. The boy said that there was, but that as he did not study chemistry, he had never been up there. 'No-one is allowed to go there without permission, except with the master,' he added.

The Inspector then saw Grace Mary Duff. She told him that she was at Croham Hurst Girls' School, and that she came home every night. She had slept occasionally at her grandmother's before her Auntie Vera's death. She would sometimes go into her grandmother's bedroom, but could not remember ever having seen a medicine-bottle there. She said that she was interested in detective stories, and that that was why there was a notice on her bedroom door, 'The Lone Star Gang — Knock 3 Times.'

'My brother wrote up on his door, "Criminal Investigation Dept." It was only a joke. He was the crime investigator and I was the criminal.'

Mary said that she had not yet reached the class which took chemistry at her school, and that she was not really interested in it. She was much more interested in photography.

After leaving 59 Birdhurst Rise, the Inspector went straight round to The Limes School. There he saw the principal, Major Harold Gordon Atkinson, O.B.E., M.A.

Major Atkinson said that he had always found the boy Duff 'most truthful and clean living,' though he was 'temperamental and religiously inclined.' He was a good sportsman on the field and, though mischievous, certainly not wicked.

Still neglecting no possibility, Hedges questioned Major Atkinson about the school's chemical laboratory. Would John Duff have had the opportunity to go there? Were many poisons kept there?

The Major replied that young Duff was not interested in chemistry. Not only would he have had no occasion to use the laboratory, but he would not have been allowed to go in there. Yes, there were poisons there, and they were kept in an unlocked cupboard. Were any missing? Not so far as he knew, but they would go up there right away and check.

Major Atkinson found that a small bottle of arsenious oxide, which he remembered having in September 1928, was missing, and promised that he would immediately set enquiries afoot to discover what had become of it. There was a boy named Anthony Ashwin Harrison, who was studying to qualify as an analytical chemist, and went up to the Royal College of Science at South Kensington two days a week. It was possible that he might have taken the bottle.

Hedges shook hands with the Major, thanked him and left The Limes . . . wondering.

Any uneasy doubts he may have had were set at rest when, a few hours later, Major Atkinson telephoned and told him, 'I was mistaken, Mr Hedges. I've spoken to the lad, Harrison, and I now find that no arsenious oxide has been used since last September, and there was, in fact, none of the poison left.'

A couple of weeks later, on May 9th, Inspector Hedges saw Harrison himself.

'I never remember seeing any arsenious oxide at The Limes,' he told him. 'There was, I think, a small stock of arsenic trioxide in the poison cupboard. I know John Duff, but I've never seen him in the laboratory.'

Hedges also made 'certain enquiries' at Croham Hurst Girls' School. Just to make sure. He found that it would have been absolutely impossible for Mary Duff to have got into the laboratory there. What was more, the school's entire stock of poisons could be satisfactorily accounted for.

He was now completely satisfied that both the Duff children

were innocent.

Next, he turned his attention to the servants of the Sidneys and the Duffs. Could they perhaps throw a shaft or two of below-stairs illumination that would pick out a motive?

On April 23rd, he saw Mrs Ivy Walter, of 112 Crowley Crescent, Waddon. She was the separated wife of Horace Walter, a milk roundsman, and had one child. She told him that she had been employed by Mrs Duff as a daily help since January 7th, 1929, and had on several occasions been employed by Mrs Thomas Sidney, at 6 South Park Hill Road. Mrs Duff and Mrs Thomas Sidney had always been very nice to her, and beyond that there was really nothing that she could say.

The servant who had immediately preceded Mrs Walter in Mrs Duff's service was a Mrs Jennie Fleming. A widow, also with one child, she lived at 9 St Saviour's Road, West Croydon. He went to see her on April 26th.

She told him that she was employed by Mrs Duff for some two months, having first gone to her about three weeks before Vera Sidney's death. She liked Mrs Duff and had never noticed anything suspicious about her or her family.

Two days previously, on April 24th, he had sent Morrish to interview Miss Amy Clarke, who was now working as a domestic servant at Carter's Hotel, Albemarle Street, Piccadilly.

She had taken up a situation as domestic servant in the Duff household about three months before Edmund Duff died, and had remained there until September 1928, when, 'As there was too much put on me, I left.'

Miss Clarke was much more forthcoming than any of the other servants interviewed to date, and her statement provided Hedges with a very interesting glimpse of the life lived behind the walls of Hurst View.

'Mrs Duff used to sleep in the big front-room upstairs, and Mr Duff in a small room off the landing leading to the dressing-room at the front. His room was divided into two parts — one section in which he used to keep his fishing-tackle, and the other in which he slept. It was very small. He had a dressing-table and a small bedside table on which he used to put his matches and so on. He kept aspirins and Eno's fruit salts on the dressing-table. Mrs Duff never told me why she did not sleep with her husband, though she did once tell me that they had never slept together. I thought this queer when I first went there, as hers was a very large room and there would have been plenty of space for two beds as well as the baby's cot.

'After Mr Duff died, Mrs Duff was always out. She used to go up to Town a lot, and was often out to lunch. I had all the washing and cooking to do, and I had to look after the children as well. She was frequently out all day, not coming home until

half-past six or seven in the evening. She had a friend called
Irene. I don't know her surname.[1] She would have been about
thirty-six to forty years of age. I think she was an old school-
friend of Mrs Duff's. I know she was single, but I don't know
where she lived. Sometimes she came to the house, sometimes
they would meet outside. I know they used to go up West
together, because Mrs Duff would telephone from Town and
ask if the children were all right. They would meet three times
in a week, and then there would be a lapse of a few weeks
before they met again. Irene was very tall. She had grey hair
and was rather a nice looking woman, though her features
were sharp. She was always well dressed. She was not so lively
as Mrs Duff. She stayed at the house on one occasion before,
and once after, Mr Duff's death. I do not know any other
friends of Mrs Duff's. No men friends ever called at the house.

'Mr and Mrs Duff never quarrelled. Now and then there were
sharp words between them, but not a real quarrel. Mrs Duff
usually wanted her own way — and she got it. Mr Duff was of a
quiet disposition and seemed very devoted to his wife. He
would take her up a cup of tea to her room every morning, and
always kiss her as he left for business. She called him Eddie.
After he left, she used to bath the baby. Then she would get
ready and go out shopping with her mother, getting back in
time for lunch.

'I remember that at about eleven o'clock one morning — I
can't say if it was before or after the death of Mr Duff — I saw
a small packet of white powder on the dressing-table or wash-
stand in Mrs Duff's bedroom. There was no label on it. It could
have been a packet of teething powder for the baby. It was
about the same size as that.

'Mr and Mrs Duff used to go out together once or twice a
week. They would take the children with them and go to the
pictures in Croydon. Occasionally they would go up West
together without the children. Mrs Duff was always good to the
children and seemed to be extremely fond of them.'

Impressed by this remarkably detailed picture of life in the
Duff household, Hedges himself went to see Miss Clarke at
Carter's Hotel on May 7th, when she added a little more to her
previous statement.

'I left Mrs Duff's service on September 8th, 1928. On the
whole she was very good to me. Before her husband's death
Mrs Duff was rather extravagant to my way of thinking. I mean
as regards food and things like that, not clothes. She had plenty
of clothes, but she never seemed to buy much in the way of new

---

[1] Irene Spicer, a member of the Spicer's paper manufacturing
family.

ones. Mrs Duff always had her way as regards shopping, or going
to the pictures, or anything else. Sometimes Mr Duff wanted her
to do one thing and she wanted to do something else. It
usually ended up with his giving way to her. The night before
he went for his fishing holiday to Fordingbridge, Mr Duff
wanted to take his son, John, with him, but John wasn't well.
I forget exactly what was wrong with him. Well, anyway,
Mrs Duff was upset because John could not go and Mr Duff
proposed going off without him. I heard Mr and Mrs Duff
having sharp words in the drawing-room the day before he
went away. I could not hear properly as I was in the kitchen,
but I am sure that it was about this.'

He asked her about the children. John, she said, was a good
boy. Everybody was fond of him. He was not even as mischievous as most boys. He used to sit quietly at the bottom of
the garden for hours on end watching the trains go by. He had a
good disposition and he and his sister did not quarrel much.
Mary was a 'very morbid' and quiet girl. She did not speak
much. She was a nice girl, but rather backward in her education.
She could sketch well, but was not lively like other girls. She
seemed somewhat nervous in temperament, and used to sit still
for long periods of time saying nothing. She often went shopping
with her mother in the mornings. They were about together
quite a lot. On the whole, John seemed more open than his
sister. Vera Sidney used to visit Mrs Duff after Mr Duff's death
and would take her out for drives in her car. Old Mrs Sidney
was, however, the most frequent visitor of all.

Finally, on April 27th, Inspector Morrish had an interview
with Mrs Noakes, who was now living at 44 Scarbrook Road,
Croydon. The statement which she then made, and which
Morrish hurriedly imparted to Hedges, was a curious one.

'I now remember that on the day that Mrs Sidney died, after
Dr Elwell had been, and just before Mrs Sidney took her
medicine, I was taking in the things to get ready for Mrs
Sidney's lunch, when, to my surprise, *I saw Mr Tom standing in
the hall at 29 Birdhurst Rise with one of his children.* The
front-door was closed and, as I had not admitted him, I
wondered how he had got into the house.'

That, Hedges decided, was something that, if Mrs Noakes was
right, Mr Thomas Sidney was going to have quite a bit of
difficulty in explaining, for he had already given firm evidence
that he had never had a key to Number 29 until after his
mother's death. How, he wondered, would Tom Sidney cope
with it when the bombshell was exploded in Mrs Noakes'
evidence at the next inquest sitting on May 6th?

It was Mrs Noakes, too, who, at the fourth sitting of the
inquest on Violet Emilia Sidney, on April 17th, had brought to

light another significant fact which had not been previously known. Namely, that on the morning of the fatal March 5th, when Mrs Duff called to see her mother, she had been left alone in the dining-room where the Metatone bottle was kept.

Now, as April drew to a close, Inspector Hedges took stock of the situation. Two full months had gone by since Dr Jackson had asked him to investigate — and what had been accomplished?

On the negative side, plenty.

He had eliminated Mrs Noakes to his own satisfaction. He had taken full statements from the medical witnesses, doctors and nurses, and cleared all suspicion concerning them from his mind. By April 26th, he had checked up on all the people who had visited Number 29 prior to the deaths of Vera and Violet Emilia Sidney — Mrs Anderson, Mrs Greenwell and Thornes, the plumber. They, too, could all be dismissed. So could Lane, the gardener, and Lodge, the rat-catcher. The Duff children, John and Mary? He had dutifully investigated and could no longer seriously suspect them. Tom Sidney and Grace Duff? He had questioned them, gone over the ground minutely, assessing them for himself and viewing them through the eyes of their servants, past and present. And got precisely nowhere. Two months . . . and he was still completely baffled.

On the positive side, nothing.

What he needed was a break. One small positive factor pointing in a definite direction.

Arsenic had been found in Vera Sidney's body, but even that was inconclusive, for the doctors still could not be certain as to whether the amount was sufficient to justify a verdict that she had died of arsenical poisoning.

Since as long ago as March 23rd, he had been wondering about the two deceased children of Mrs Duff — Margaret Kathleen and Suzanne Violet Amy — lying immediately beneath their father in the same grave. He had heard that one of them died rather suddenly after a short illness, but he decided that it would be advisable, at any rate for the time being, not to delve too deeply into the matter. After all, he already had three unexplained deaths on his hands, and that was quite enough to be going on with.

What worried him infinitely more at the moment was the death of Edmund Duff. He could not see how it was going to be possible to narrow the enquiry down unless Duff's body was exhumed, and his remaining organs analysed.

He felt certain that the answer to all his problems lay buried six feet down in the earth of Queen's Road Cemetery.

V

The bombshell for whose explosion Hedges had been so
anxiously waiting turned out a disappointing dud. At the
inquest sitting of May 6th, Tom Sidney emphatically denied
that he had entered his mother's house about lunch-time on
March 5th, and, under fiercely pressing cross-examination by
Mr Fearnley-Whittingstall, Mrs Noakes wavered in her conviction, and eventually agreed that she could not be *sure* that
she had in fact seen Tom Sidney in the hall at Number 29 at
the time that she *thought* she had.

Tom Sidney's conduct was again called into question as a
result of a visit which Hedges and Morrish paid on May 15th to
Mrs Dorothy Winifred Robins (formerly Gent), of Vann
Cottages, Hambledon, near Godalming, Surrey.

Mrs Robins told them that she had been in the service of
Mr Thomas Sidney since June 1928, and it was at his house in
South Park Hill Road that they interviewed her.

She said that one day in the September or October of 1928,
Tom Sidney was in the scullery, trying unsuccessfully to remove
the lid from a small tin that looked like an ordinary boot
polish tin. Mrs Robins had offered to have a try, and she began
to knock it with a blacking brush. But he told her, 'Don't do
that. It's a powder and will all spill.' In the end he managed to
twist the lid off himself. In reply to Hedges' probings, Mrs
Robins said that she had no idea what Tom Sidney did with the
powder, though while opening it he had mumbled something
about rats and that he was going to try to get rid of them, and
later in the day she did see some pieces of bread near the dust-
bin.

Leaving Morrish behind with Mrs Robins, the Inspector went
off and collected the tin of Eureka weed-killer which he had
previously taken from Tom Sidney's house, and two tins of
Rodine rat-poison.

When he returned with them, he showed the contents of the
Eureka tin to Mrs Robins, who maintained that the powder
which it contained was exactly similar to the powder which she
had seen in the small tin in the scullery that day.

He then produced the two different-sized tins of Rodine.
Mrs Robins identified the smaller tin as being similar in size to
the tin seen in the scullery, but was quite firm that the dark-
brown paste which it contained was nothing like the contents of
the tin which Mr Sidney had shown her.

On hearing this, Hedges immediately went round to Number
29, where Tom Sidney was sorting out some of his mother's
belongings, to challenge him with Mrs Robins' statement.

Tom Sidney's reaction was unequivocal. 'Nonsense. She is

dreaming.' Then, according to Hedges, he seemed to work himself into a passion. 'You can't believe her, as I've already
proved her a liar over some brandy which she drank and then
denied that she'd had it.' He did not, however, offer any
explanation regarding the alleged tin, beyond saying that they
had some rats at Pauliva, and that he might have used paste,
though certainly not powder, to try to get rid of them.

On May 16th, as the result of an important letter which
Sir Trevor Bigham, the Assistant Commissioner (Crime) at
Scotland Yard, had written, at the instance of the Commissioner,
to Sir William Joynson-Hicks, the Secretary of State for Home
Affairs, Inspector Hedges was summoned to the Yard.

After discussing the developments in the case with Sir Trevor,
the Inspector paid a visit to the Home Office, where he had an
interview with Mr Arthur Locke, C.B.E., an Assistant Secretary
in charge of a division dealing with criminal justice administration and allied matters. And that same night, Hedges received
the Secretary of State's licence for the exhumation of the body
of Edmund Creighton Duff from Grave No. 35134 at the
Queen's Road Cemetery.

He promptly telephoned Sir Bernard Spilsbury, and they
made mutually convenient arrangements for the exhumation to
take place at 10 a.m. on May 18th.

And when, at the appointed time, Hedges, in the presence of
Sir Bernard Spilsbury, Drs Binning and Roche Lynch, Tom
Sidney, Sydney Gardiner, Superintendent Brown and Inspector
Morrish, watched Duff's coffin being raised from the grave with
the carved-stone angel guardian, he felt that now at last he
would have a fighting chance of bringing the case to a satisfactory conclusion. It was just a matter of waiting a few weeks
to see what results the experts would report from their forensic
examinations, and then, surely, the stalemate would be resolved.

But Inspector Hedges was not the man to sit back. While the
doctors studied slides, mounted their chemical tests and weighed
and measured their answers, he pounded stolidly on, seeking
out and interviewing witnesses, taking down their statements,
tirelessly pursuing red herrings and scribbling off those inter-
minable reports of his to his superiors at the Yard.

There was a moment when he half-believed that he had
stumbled upon something really important. On the evening of
May 18th, Tom Sidney telephoned and asked him if he would
come to see him in regard to a matter of the greatest importance. The Inspector, accompanied by Morrish, went along to
6 South Park Hill Road.

When they arrived, Tom told Hedges, 'I want to discuss this
case with you.'

Hedges replied that if he wanted to make a statement, he

and Morrish had come prepared to write it down.

But Tom said, 'I'm going to make no statement in writing, but I want to discuss this matter.'

The Inspector replied bluntly that he was not prepared to discuss it, but that if there was anything that he wanted investigated he would be quite ready to look into it. To discuss the case would, however, be a dangerous proceeding, and Tom had better seek the advice of his counsel before making any verbal statement.

But Tom insisted on having his say. Slowly and very deliberately he told the detectives, 'If any poison is found in Duff's body, Dr Elwell was the person who administered it.'

Flabbergasted, Hedges asked, 'Are you aware of the serious allegation that you are making? Only a few days ago you were openly expressing yourself in a similar way against Mrs Noakes in connection with the deaths of your mother and sister.'

'I look upon the death of Duff as an entirely separate matter,' said Tom. 'Do you know that Dr Elwell has not charged my sister any fees during the whole time he has been attending her, and that's about ten years? Do you know that there is something between them? He has visited my sister many times, and they have been out together.'

Tom added that he knew for a fact that on one occasion Elwell had been called in to settle a dispute between Grace and her husband.

The Inspector then asked, 'Do you really mean to tell me that you believe that Dr Elwell has been seducing your sister?'

'Oh, no, the friendship was only platonic, but he has taken her out.'

Shortly afterwards Hedges and Morrish left.

Frankly, Inspector Hedges did not believe a word of it, but in so serious a case as this it is a detective's job to check on *all* rumours, no matter how manifestly absurd he may secretly consider them. So he lost no time in contacting Dr Binning and telling him of this particular rumour. Binning said that his partner was away on holiday in Cornwall, but that he would get in touch with him at once.

A thoroughly alarmed Elwell returned to Croydon posthaste and, on May 22nd, was seen by Hedges and Morrish at his home in Addiscombe Road.

Dr Elwell admitted that since the inquest on her husband he had felt it his duty to assist Mrs Duff as much as possible. He had felt guilty because it was his refusal to issue a death certificate which had originally thrust so much anxiety upon her, and when it turned out that Duff had apparently died from natural causes, he had been eager to compensate in any way that he could. He vehemently denied, however, that there had been anything between them.

'Up to the time of Duff's death the family did not appear to be in very flourishing circumstances, and, on one occasion, he visited me, apologised for the fact that he had not paid my account, and asked if I minded waiting. I told him that it would be all right, but that I expected him to pay as soon as he could. I certainly did not regard the Duffs as intimate friends, but sometimes, if it happened to be around tea-time when I visited the house to attend one of the children, Mrs Duff would ask me to have a cup of tea, and I would accept. But it is ridiculous for anyone to suggest that I was fascinated by Mrs Duff. When, after her husband's death, she asked my advice on matters relating to her pension and other financial troubles, I did my best to help her. I have never visited London with Mrs Duff in my life. In fact the only time that I can recall when Mrs Duff has been out with me was once when I had to go to Limpsfield on business, and she said that she was going there to see an aunt.[1] I gave her a lift and I think I brought her back, too.'

Elwell denied that Mrs Duff had ever complained to him in any way about her husband. On one occasion, however, he had observed bruises on her shoulders. He had asked her what had caused them and, most reluctantly, she explained that it was her husband, who was very excitable in moments of sexual passion. The doctor had subsequently mentioned the bruising to Duff, who said that they were only the result of 'ruxing', which expression he understood to mean romping together. Elwell added that he had always thought of the Duffs as a devoted couple.

Having heard all this, Hedges was perfectly satisfied that there was absolutely nothing in the accusation against Dr Elwell. After all, it was he who had originally communicated with Dr Jackson asking for an inquest to be held. If he had had anything to hide, if he had poisoned Duff, it would surely have been the easiest thing in the world for him to have issued a death certificate.

Back to square one.

Hedges began again to turn his attention to the servants.

He and Morrish journeyed to 2 Cairo Place, West Croydon, on May 23rd. There they saw Mrs Barbara Smith, who had been employed as a daily help at Hurst View from November 1927 to January 1928. As she worked at Hurst View from 8.30 a.m. until 2.30 p.m., and Mr Duff did not usually get home from business until about 7.15 p.m., Mrs Smith, as a rule, only saw him on Saturdays. So far as her observations went, the Duffs had been a devoted couple. She had never heard them quarrel

[1] Eleanour Kathleen Stafford Sidney lived in Limpsfield. See: *The Voyage Home* by Richard Church (Heinemann, 1964).

and Mrs Duff always spoke well of her husband. Mrs Smith had left when Mrs Duff got a maid to stay in. After that she had worked for Mrs Thomas Sidney. She had only remained about four weeks in that situation, leaving because she had had an accident. The Duff family had the whole house to themselves. They used only four bedrooms upstairs, the ground-floor back drawing-room, the breakfast-room (ground-floor front), the kitchen and scullery. The other room on the ground-floor (front), where the old lady — Miss Kelvey — died, was empty.

Mrs Smith said that she never saw Dr Elwell, as Mrs Duff would always open the door to him, but she remembered his calling frequently.

'Sometimes Mrs Duff would say that the baby was ill, though I had not noticed anything the matter with him, and I used to look after him. Mrs Duff told me that Dr Elwell was Alastair's godfather, and that he had bought the child a cot. When the doctor came he used to go straight upstairs to Mrs Duff's bedroom to see Alastair in the cot. I remember he was there about twenty minutes when the baby had bad eyes.'

Mrs Jessie Bonfield, a widow, who was staying with her brother, Alfred Perry, at 16 St Peter's Road, Hammersmith, was seen on May 24th.

She had been employed as a daily maid at Hurst View between October 1926 and March 1927, working from 7.30 a.m. until 8.30 p.m. She, too, had found the Duffs a devoted couple, and had never heard them quarrel. She had seen Dr Elwell at the house frequently, but had never had reason to suppose anything other than a perfectly normal doctor and patient relationship between him and Mrs Duff.

Mrs Marian Hartley, seen a week later, on May 31st, at 63 Coldharbour Road, Waddon, where she lived with her husband, James Oswald Hartley, a labourer, told much the same story.

She said that in February or March 1927, when her husband was out of work, she had applied at the Noah's Ark Registry Office for daily work and secured a situation with Mrs Duff at Hurst View.

'At that time there was a girl named Phyllis also employed by Mrs Duff. Phyllis did not sleep in. I used to go to Hurst View from 8 a.m. until 12 noon and do the charring. After Phyllis left, I went for the whole day, including Sundays. I never heard any quarrels between Mr and Mrs Duff. He was of a jolly disposition and they were always joking. Mrs Duff was a hard worker and did a lot of needlework so as to save expense.'

Mrs Hartley said that she had remained at Hurst View until February 1928. She was with Mrs Duff when her last baby was

born. Dr Elwell was attending her, and he was at the christening.
She had never observed any unusual degree of familiarity
between Mrs Duff and the doctor.

Then Mrs Hartley said something that made Hedges prick up
his ears.

'Once Mrs Duff told me she thought she had a curse on her
children. I took one of my children there on one occasion,
and Mrs Duff told me, "Don't bring her here again. She is
like Suzanne." She cried and was upset about it. She told me
that it was a mystery how her daughter, Suzanne, died. She was
out walking with her nurse and had a fall. There was no mark,
and she did not know how she had hurt herself. The nurse was
an old nurse of the family. Mrs Duff said that Suzanne was
taken ill the same night and died, and their dog died at the
same time, from what was thought to be the same complaint.
They had several cats and rabbits die. I don't think they looked
after them well enough. These pets were buried at the bottom
of the garden.'

That evening Inspector Hedges made a brief entry in his notebook — 'Check histories of diseases and deaths of Duff children.'

The last witness tracked down in May 1929 was Colonel
Charles De Vertus Duff, Edmund's younger brother. The
Inspector went to his home, 184 Cromwell Road, Earls Court,
London, S.W.5, to have a talk with him.

Colonel Duff was not able to contribute much. He said that
he had last seen his brother in the garden at Hurst View two or
three months before he died. He seemed very fit then. Hedges
broached the subject of the deaths of Suzanne and Margaret
Duff.

'Suzanne died very suddenly, and my brother told me that it
was the result of an accident. I was led to believe that she had
a fall and knocked her chin. My brother was very cut up over
her death. He was also upset over the death of Margaret. She
died after a long illness, from rheumatoid arthritis.'

A fortnight had now gone by since the exhumation of Edmund
Duff, and a preliminary report had been received from Dr Roche
Lynch.

On May 30th, in company with Dr Jackson and Inspector
Morrish, Hedges attended at the office of the Director of Public
Prosecutions and, in the presence of Sir Trevor Bigham, had an
interview with Sir Archibald Bodkin. The matter under dis-
cussion was the advisability of re-opening the inquest on
Edmund Creighton Duff.

Dr Jackson was of the opinion that nothing definite ought to
be decided there and then. He would, he said, prefer it if they
were to wait until Dr Roche Lynch's examinations and analyses
were completed. He had in mind Mr Candy's negative findings

on the occasion of his first analysis in May 1928, and he would like Inspector Hedges to investigate the method of the despatch of Duff's organs to Mr Candy after Dr Brontë had removed them at the first post-mortem.

And, in the course of the next few days, he accordingly made the necessary enquiries. He found that on April 28th, 1928, John Henry Baker had received Duff's body at the Mayday Road Mortuary from the firm of Messrs J. B. Shakespeare, undertakers. The body was kept, untouched, at the mortuary until Dr Brontë arrived there on the morning of April 29th, and performed the post-mortem. He removed a representative selection of organs — portions of intestines, brain, liver, spleen, kidney, heart and stomach and contents. These were placed in: (1) a stone jar, which was labelled and sealed by Dr Brontë. (2) a glass jar, also labelled and sealed by Dr Brontë. Both jars were immediately put away in an otherwise empty cupboard, which was then locked by Baker. The only two people having access to this cupboard were Baker and his assistant, Donald Arthur Smith. There was only one other post-mortem carried out that day at the Mayday Road Mortuary. It, too, was conducted by Dr Brontë, and was on an old woman. None of her organs had been removed.[1]

On April 30th, Baker had handed the glass jar to a representative of the Croydon Medical Officer of Health, for conveyance to a bacteriologist.

The stone jar was left in the cupboard until 2 p.m. on May 3rd, when it was handed by Donald Arthur Smith to Samuel John Clarke, who conveyed it intact to the London Hospital Medical College, Mile End Road, and delivered it personally to Mr Candy at 4 p.m. the same day.

These facts were duly reported back to Dr Jackson. Hedges had done all that he could. Now it was out of his hands. Out of Dr Jackson's, too, for that matter. If there was to be a second inquest on Duff, the decision would have to be taken by the highest legal authorities in the land.

May 31st. Tomorrow it would be June. Hedges needed no calendar to remind him that his investigations had now been going on for three months. It had been a gruelling, abortive business. One after another every promising avenue had rapidly deteriorated into an improbable blind-alley, a cul-de-sac of impossibility. Twist and turn as he might, he could be sure of only three things — the deaths by arsenic of Edmund, Vera and Violet.

---

[1] Another conflict. Baker stated when seen by Inspector Morrish on June 4th, 1929, 'He (Brontë) did *not* remove her organs for analysis, and none were taken away. *He only removed them for his own examination.*'

Assiduously he had sought the source of that arsenic. No
good. Another blank wall. There had been routine work . . col-
lecting bottles, tins — full and empty — of weed-killer, samples
of rat-poison and foodstuffs. Tedious. Boring. But he had not
minded that. At least it had provided the illusion of fruitful
activity. It was getting something done.

Now, the whole thing was beginning to prey on his mind.
Long after his family had gone to bed, long after he should have
gone to bed, he sat up alone in the small back living-room in
Trafford Road, smoking his pipe and turning the case over and
over in his head. All his training told him that he should not
become emotionally involved, but these three murders on his
manor had begun to assume the proportions of a personal
challenge. The days, the weeks, the months now, had dragged
on. Somewhere at the back of his mind there was *something* —
if only he could get it into focus. He sighed, shrugged, got up
wearily, knocked the cold ashes out of his pipe into the dead
embers of the fire, and went moodily up to bed.

VI

The time had now come, Hedges decided, to try to clear up
something of the mystery which appeared to surround the sudden death of Suzanne Duff.

He started off, on June 1st, with a preliminary visit to
Dr Elwell, who had certified the cause of Suzanne's death as
tubercular meningitis.

Elwell was most co-operative. So far as he could recall after
so great a lapse of time, it was in the early part of February
1924 that he had been called in to see the child. She was
reported to have had a fall. She did not appear ill, but had a
slight bruise on the chin. Mrs Duff was very distressed about it,
fearing that some complication might arise, but he had not
thought that the child was badly hurt, and had said so. Shortly
afterwards, however, Suzanne became fretful and went off her
food. He then found that she was running a high temperature,
and concluded that she must be sickening for something. The
indisposition lasted for about ten days, and he called in to see
the patient every day. About the tenth day, he was summoned
urgently because Suzanne had had a convulsion. He put her in a
bath and applied restoratives, and the child came round. Mrs
Duff told him that although Suzanne was not persistently sick,
she could not keep any food down. There was no report of
diarrhoea, in fact constipation was the difficulty. Suzanne died
on March 16th, following a severe convulsion from which she
did not recover consciousness.

Elwell did not think that the fall was the cause of the trouble, as there were no signs of injury to the skull. In his opinion, death was due to meningitis of tuberculous origin.

'My examination of the child after the accident did not lead me to expect fatal results, and my diagnosis of tuberculous meningitis was based on symptoms shown in the course of the illness, and not on a pathological examination.'

Two days later, Hedges, accompanied this time by Inspector Morrish, went round to 59 Birdhurst Rise to see Mrs Duff. He told her that he proposed to take a statement from her, adding the warning that, since the matter into which he was enquiring was a serious one, he must caution her that what she said might be used in evidence. He then asked her if she had any objection to Inspector Morrish's writing her statement down in shorthand. She had. 'I wish to write my own statement, and if you will ask me questions I will write down my own answers.'

She began by outlining the course of her life from the time that she married in 1911. Her husband was nearly twenty years older than she was, and she used to tease him about growing old. He always had a dread of this, and would go so far as taking thyroid gland tablets and such things to retain his vitality. Coming to the matter of the death of Suzanne, Mrs Duff stated that in 1921, following the birth of Suzanne, her husband was not so well and seemed to be in rather a depressed state. After they moved to Hurst View, however, he was soon his normal, cheery self again. He was passionately fond of Suzanne, who met with an accident. She fell in the garden and knocked her head back. She was out with Mrs Duff's old nurse, Gertrude Russell, who had lived with Mrs Duff for twelve years or so.[1] Suzanne had had a brief illness lasting only a day and a night,[2] in the course of which she was seen by three doctors — Dr Elwell, Dr Purdom, and another whose name she could not recollect. The child had fits and convulsions and died of meningitis. Before her death her temperature was 106°F.

Margaret Kathleen, her eldest child, had died of rheumatoid arthritis in 1919. She had been treated by Dr Curtis and Dr Gayner, of Redhill, Surrey, and Sir Arbuthnot Lane had operated on her at a nursing home at 17 — or was it 19? — Manchester Square, London. She was brought home with a hospital nurse, who stayed with her to the end — two months after the operation.

[1] Gertrude Russell was actually engaged by Mrs Duff as a nurse in 1913, and remained in her service until May 1924. She continued on friendly terms with Mrs Duff thereafter, visiting her about every two months.

[2] This statement that Suzanne died within forty-eight hours conflicts with Dr Elwell's testimony, but it is likely that his memory was at fault.

The only other death that took place in her home was that of Miss Anna Maria Kelvey, who lodged with them at Hurst View. She had died of her third stroke, and Mrs Duff herself had attended her by day, while a nurse, brought in by Dr Elwell, attended her at night.

Mrs Duff had given Hedges Gertrude Russell's address — Long Ends Farm, Marden, Kent, — but it was at 23 Prestlands Park Road, Sidcup, where she was in a situation with a Mrs Shanks, that Hedges and Morrish interviewed her on June 5th.

Miss Russell told them that Mr and Mrs Duff had been a most devoted couple. Mrs Duff she described as 'very erratic in her manner. In her affections true.'

The child, Margaret, was about three when she developed rheumatoid arthritis. It started with a swelling of the wrists. Margaret had received treatment from many doctors and specialists and was eventually operated on at the Manchester Square nursing home. She had made progress at the nursing home after the operation, but when she came home she developed internal trouble. She was attended at home by Dr Gayner of Redhill, but died about six weeks after the operation. A nurse was sent from the nursing home. She lived in the house and Margaret was entirely under her charge. Mrs Duff was very worried over the child and had been greatly distressed when she died.

Suzanne was a very healthy child and had never had any fits or anything prior to her fatal illness. She was bonny and had a beautiful colour. She died within the space of about twenty-four hours.[1]

'This was a terrible tragedy to me, as I could not account for it. I was with Suzanne when, in a little passage at the bottom of the garden, she just had a little stumble. She fell on to her hands and rolled a little. It was quite an ordinary child's fall. I picked her up and found it had left no mark at all. I took her indoors to Mrs Duff, and told her of the fall. Mrs Duff pointed to a very minute scratch on her upper lip and asked me, "Do you think she got that scratch then?" I said, "She has a small scratch, but she didn't fall on her face." This happened at about 11 a.m. on March 14th.

'I used to give Suzanne her food, and I am quite certain that I gave her nothing that day to upset her. She ate her food as usual that day and was quite lively. I bathed her and she went to bed quite well. Suzanne slept with me, and when I went to bed at ten o'clock that night I thought she looked flushed. Thinking she might be too warm, I pulled the bedclothes back a bit. Up

---

[1] Yet another discrepancy. The likelihood is that Suzanne was taken fatally ill on the night of March 14th, 1924, and died some thirty-six hours later.

Appealing Grace. 'Those clear lake-blue eyes.'

Miss Anna Maria Kelvey. Paying Guest. Does her corpse still hide a secret?

Kate Noakes. The only one to emerge alive from that ill-starred house.

Dr Brontë and Dr Beecher Jackson.
Anxious Pathologist and ailing Coroner.

Mr Hugh Charles Herbert Candy. Chemist. Could
he have prevented two deaths?

Dr Binning. Family doctor who saw them
all die.

Dr Roche Lynch. Analyst. An expert with arsen:

to this time Suzanne had not been sick and was quite normal. About 2 a.m. she said, "I've got a pain in my tummy." I took her in my arms, and she was very unhappy and violently sick. She vomited twice, but did not have diarrhoea. I nursed her in my arms all night. At about 7.30 the next morning I saw Mr Duff and told him that Suzanne had been seedy all night. He went upstairs and told Mrs Duff. She came and looked at her and said that she looked very ill, and that a doctor must be sent for. So Mr Duff went and fetched Dr Elwell. He came at, I think, about 8.30 a.m.

'Dr Elwell examined Suzanne and said that she was suffering from a bad bilious attack. As he was leaving, he told us that he had to go away from Croydon on business at about twelve o'clock, but if Suzanne was ill in the meantime we were to let him know at once. After that the child became drowsy.

'Around half-past twelve Mr Duff decided that Suzanne ought to see the doctor again. Knowing that Dr Elwell would have left Croydon by then, he went off in search of another doctor, but returned later saying that he could not find one at home. While Mr Duff was away, Suzanne had a fit. That would have been at about one o'clock. I then went out and managed to get hold of Dr Purdom. He came at once, examined Suzanne and put her in a hot bath. He said that she had had a meningital fit of the worst type, and that there was no hope of her recovery. He gave her a brain sedative, and after that she seemed to me to look better in herself. But the doctor said that he could do no more, and she did not recover consciousness from then until the time she died.

'Dr Elwell came in at about eight o'clock that evening and was very shocked to find Suzanne so ill. He was also greatly puzzled as to the illness, and I have a faint recollection of Mrs Duff's telling me that he had used a stomach-pump on the child, as he thought that she might have swallowed something. I did not see any other doctor in the house that night, though I do have a recollection of a Dr Morris coming there. In the night Mrs Duff came to the nursery and told me that Suzanne was dying, and I went down to the drawing-room, where the cot had been moved. Mrs Duff and I were alone with her at 7 a.m. when she died.'

Gertrude Russell said that at the time of Suzanne's illness and death the only persons living in the house were the family and herself. During the day a domestic named Mrs Cooper came in to do the cleaning and cooking. The only visitor was Vera Sidney.

'I have always regarded the death of Suzanne as a great mystery. I am an experienced nurse and I have seen children fall endless times. I have had eighteen years' experience with

children, but I could not be convinced that a child could die
from such a slight accident.'

Puzzled, Hedges set off straight away to see Dr Thomas Eadie
Purdom, in practice at Ellerslie, 25 Park Hill Road, Croydon.

Dr Purdom had made no notes of the case, but remembered
being called in to see Suzanne Duff. As near as he could recollect, he had arrived at 16 Park Hill Road at about three
o'clock in the afternoon. He found the child unconscious, in a
fit of convulsions. He had recommended a hot bath and given
her very weak belladonna. He paid a second visit at 4 p.m. The
child was then in a bath, still unconscious, and running a very
high temperature. He did not recollect any history of the child's
having had a fall, and he did not see any bruises on the head
or face. He had diagnosed a meningital fit. The Inspector
noted the fact that Dr Purdom was very deaf, and wondered if
that might not account for his having missed the story of
Suzanne's fall.

When Hedges saw Sir Bernard Spilsbury the next day at the
coroner's court, he made a point of mentioning Suzanne Duff's
symptoms to him, and Spilsbury said that they appeared to
be consistent with tuberculous meningitis, which was common
among children.

He also reported the facts to Dr Jackson, who said that, in
his view, the circumstances were hardly sufficient to justify his
asking for an exhumation of the body.

But it is a detective's prerogative to suspect, and Hedges was
still far from satisfied. Elwell and Purdom might have been
convinced at the time that the child had died of meningitis, but
hadn't three medical men — one of them a specialist at that —
decided that Vera Sidney had died of gastro-enteritis? And
hadn't the medical men said that Edmund Duff died from heart
disease? He wondered. Wondered enough to seek out an independent medical man of considerable experience, who had dealt
with many cases of tuberculous meningitis. After turning up
various reference books on the condition, he told the Inspector
that in such cases invariably death does not occur until a period
of from ten days to three weeks has elapsed from the commencement of the illness.

Neglect no possibility.

Just to be sure, Hedges sent Morrish, on June 8th, to inter-
view Dr Francis Gayner, of Old Linkfield, Hatchlands Road,
Redhill, regarding the alleged history of Margaret Kathleen
Duff's illness and death.

The story that Dr Gayner told after looking up his record
books cross-matched satisfactorily.

'I attended Margaret Duff, aged about seven, in the year 1917,[1]

[1] She was actually five in 1917.

and found her suffering from rheumatoid arthritis. The record also shows attendances by my partner, Dr Frederick Curtis, and consultations with Sir Arbuthnot Lane and Dr Nathan Mutch. The child was operated on on July 17th, 1919, by Sir Arbuthnot Lane.[1] I personally was not in favour of the operation, which was for removal of the colon. On September 19th I visited the child with my partner, Dr Curtis, who concurred in my opinion that the child was suffering from intestinal obstruction. We decided that no further operation was desirable, or possible. The child died on September 21st, and at the time I myself and the other doctors were quite clear that the certificate given described correctly the causes leading to the child's death.'

Hedges subsequently discovered that medical men generally ridiculed Sir Arbuthnot Lane for performing such operations, and ascertained that it was indeed strictly against the advice of Dr Gayner that the operation was carried out on Margaret Duff.

On June 6th Inspector Hedges had been handed a copy of Dr Ryffel's report of his analysis of the organs taken from Vera Sidney's exhumed corpse. They contained arsenic, as Hedges had anticipated.

And, on June 17th, he received Sir Bernard Spilsbury's report on his post-mortem examination of the exhumed body of Edmund Duff. In it, Spilsbury wrote that it was impossible to state the cause of death from the post-mortem examination alone, and although the history of the last illness and the emptiness and internal reddening of the intestines pointed to some form of gastro-intestinal irritation, nothing could be known for certain until Dr Roche Lynch reported his analyses.

Hedges had not long to wait.

Four days later, on June 21st, a copy of Dr Roche Lynch's analysis of Duff's organs was delivered to him. The unfortunate man had apparently been stuffed to the gunnels with arsenic.

Finally, on June 22nd, a supplementary report from Sir Bernard Spilsbury on his post-mortem examination of Vera Sidney arrived on Hedges' desk. It confirmed that beyond any shadow of doubt she, too, had been liberally, and fatally, dosed with arsenic.

In view of the fact that he was virtually certain in his own mind that a second inquest would eventually be held on Edmund Duff, Inspector Hedges drove down to Fordingbridge

[1] Sir William Arbuthnot Lane (1856—1943). Lane had his own view on chronic intestinal stasis, for which he recommended a surgical method of short-circuiting the bowel — Lane's operation. He divided the ileum near the caecum, closed the portion attached to the caecum, and anastomosed the other end with the upper part of the rectum, or the lower part of the sigmoid, thus by-passing the colon.

on June 10th, to see Mr Harold Stanley Whitfield Edwardes. He was amazed, and not a little annoyed, when he arrived at Armsley to find a number of newspaper reporters from London already there, waiting for him. The news of his intended visit must, he supposed, have leaked out via the local police, through whom he had made an appointment with Mr Edwardes.

Mr Edwardes gave him a brief outline of how he had first come to know Duff when they were both serving in Nigeria.

'In 1911 I heard that Duff was married,' he continued, 'and later I received a letter from him asking me to be godfather to his first child, Margaret. I visited Mr and Mrs Duff at Redhill for a few days in 1917 and saw Margaret. The child was a pitiable object, suffering from rheumatoid arthritis. That was the first and only time that I met Mrs Duff. I heard of Duff's retirement in 1919, and some time afterwards I paid him a visit at the pensions office in London, where he had obtained employment. I heard of the death of Margaret, but know no particulars of it. Duff adored his wife and from my observation they appeared perfectly happy.'

Edwardes then went on to recount the story of Duff's fishing holiday with him, much as he had told it to Superintendent Jacobs thirteen months before and adding nothing to what Hedges already knew.

The Inspector also questioned Mr Edwardes' wife, Joane Margaret Edwardes. She, too, thought that Duff had seemed very devoted to his wife. 'He spoke to me a great deal about his wife and family, and appeared to be exceptionally fond of them all.' Her sole item of new information was that one morning before breakfast she saw Duff, dressed in his overcoat and slippers, hurrying from his room to the lavatory.

Neither could the Edwardes' cook, May Ford, nor their housemaid, Ellen Vincent, contribute anything of significance.

No one else in the household had been ill. In accordance with the Food and Drugs Act, the Medical Officer of Health had paid a visit to the house after Duff's death, and had taken away with him two pots of Patum Peperium for analysis. This proved negative.

Not much wiser, Hedges got back into his car and, carefully avoiding the clamorous 'gentlemen of the press,' was whisked home to Croydon.

Miss Amy Clarke, seen again on June 18th, made a statement giving details of an illness which Mrs Duff's youngest child, Alastair, developed about five weeks after his father's death.

'I was sleeping in the house at the time. First the child went off its food and then he was partly unconscious. One day he seemed to be quite stiff. During the early part of his illness he had diarrhoea and a high temperature. He was dangerously ill for about three days, and Mrs Duff was afraid that she was going to lose him. It was fully a fortnight before he really recovered.'

Also on June 18th, Inspector Hedges interviewed Miss Violet Wood, of 22 Kemerton Road, Croydon.

She told him: 'I am a single woman and live with my mother. I am now employed by Messrs Lyons, caterers, at their Streatham High Road branch. Three years ago, I worked for seven weeks as a daily maid at Mrs Duff's house. She was then living at 16 Park Hill Road. Mr and Mrs Duff appeared to be on very good terms with each other. Dr Elwell used to call to see Mrs Duff. I understood that she was suffering from haemorrhage. I did not notice any undue familiarity. He always called her Mrs Duff, and she called him Dr Elwell. There was an old lady named Miss Kelvey living with Mrs Duff. She seemed rather eccentric, but I did not have much to do with her. She was attended to by another maid, named Joan O'Regan. I was only engaged during the temporary illness of Mrs Duff and when she recovered I left.'

He succeeded, too, in tracing Miss Clara Caroline Collett, who had worked for Mrs Violet Emilia Sidney for a period of fifteen months immediately prior to Mrs Noakes. She had also worked for a time for Dr Elwell.

Interviewed on June 20th, Miss Collett, temporarily employed as a domestic at Sanderstead, and living at 31 Lebanon Road, Croydon, said that she was leaving her present situation in about a week's time, and planned to take a holiday before looking around for another temporary job.

One point in Miss Collett's statement particularly interested Hedges — 'On one occasion, Mrs Thomas Sidney entered 29 Birdhurst Rise by the side-gate and through the back-door. This happened because her child ran round to the back of the house and Mrs Sidney followed it. I can imagine Mr Thomas Sidney entering the same way if he had a child with him.'

Could it have been, he asked himself, that the child did the same thing when accompanying Tom Sidney on the day that Mrs Noakes had thought she had seen him with the child in the hall?

By June 24th, when Hedges attended yet another of those conferences with Sir Trevor Bigham at Scotland Yard, he was able to report that at least one minor mystery had been cleared up. He had managed to track down the source of Tom Sidney's tin of Eureka weed-killer. He had purchased it for three shillings from Boots, the chemists, of 83 Southend, Croydon, on September 26th, 1927, duly signing the poisons book with his correct name and address.

The mood of despair with which the month had opened had

passed. The Inspector was beginning to feel almost optimistic.
Any day now surely he would hear that the authorities had
decided to reopen the inquest on Edmund Duff. And then . . .

June ended with Hedges still hoping, Micawber-like, that
something would turn up.

VII

This time — for once — he was not to be disappointed.

The second inquest on Edmund Creighton Duff opened on
July 5th.

But all the time the inquests were passing through due process,
Inspector Hedges kept busily ferreting away at his run-of-the-
mill investigations.

On July 6th, Miss Amy Clarke was seen, by Inspector Henry
Moss, of the Lewes Division of the East Sussex Constabulary, at
the Dewdrop Inn, Peacehaven, where, since June 19th, she had
been working as a waitress for the summer season. Hedges had
wanted to know whether Dr Elwell had called at Hurst View
before she left to go home on the evening of April 26th, 1928.
She could not remember.

Still questing that 'something tangible', Hedges went along
to 20 Tanfield Road, Croydon, where, on July 11th he saw
a widow named Alice Mary Ann Matthews. In September 1928,
she had been sent by the Registry Office in Selsdon Road to see
Mrs Duff, who was requiring someone to look after Alastair.
Mrs Matthews had been given the job, and had remained with
Mrs Duff until January 1929.

But there was nothing tangible there. All that her evidence
amounted to was a repetition of that, by now, oft-told tale,
namely that Dr Elwell was a very frequent caller, and that
both he and Mrs Duff always comported themselves in a most
exemplary manner. And, with a touch of unexpected belli-
gerence, Mrs Matthews had added, 'If anyone says that I've
ever said anything about Dr Elwell and Mrs Duff, it's a downright lie.'

The Inspector had a long and interesting chat with Tom Sidney
on the evening of July 16th.

'Last May,' Sidney told him, 'acting on the advice of some
friends, I examined the interior of the tool-shed in my garden
in order to satisfy myself as to whether there were any finger-
prints which might assist the police. While I was doing this,
I moved a cardboard box which was used by me in 1927 to
contain a small bag of cement, as the cement was escaping
through a tear in the bag. When I bought the tin of Eureka in
1927, I removed the cement bag from the box and placed the

weed-killer tin inside the box, I used only a small quantity of this weed-killer powder in September 1927, and from that time I handled neither the cardboard box nor the weed-killer tin, and to the best of my belief no one else living in the house has touched them either. But when I lifted the box down off the shelf last May, after having previously handed the tin of weed-killer over to you, I observed that the interior of the bottom of the cardboard box was covered with a mixture of dust and white cement powder, and there were clear indications that the tin of weed-killer had been removed several times, and replaced in the cardboard box in different positions. I have examined these marks through a magnifying glass, and I have come to the conclusion that the tin has been left in one position for varying periods, probably ranging from a few weeks to a few months. As near as I can judge, the tin has been moved on four separate occasions.

'So far as I can recall, the only person that I have had in my garden from outside is an ex-railway porter from South Croydon Station. His name is William Monkton, and he was engaged by me for seven or eight consecutive weeks during the summer of 1928 to do a bit of gardening. He would not have any occasion to enter this shed, although the key was in the lock, and so far as I know he never went there. The shed which contains the gardening tools is at the bottom of the garden, and the shed in which the weed-killer was stored is looked upon more as a private shed of mine.

'At the time of Mr Duff's death I had in my employ a Mrs King. We got her from a registry in Purley, close to the terminus, a fancy shop where they sell stationery. She left before Mrs Gent (Robins) came. Mrs King worked for me for about twelve months. She had access to the shed, but I don't know that she would go there.

'You have previously questioned me about my nephew, John Duff, and my niece. I have always eliminated them, and I still do, but I think I had better tell you that whilst in bed at 10 Egerton Road, Bexhill,[1] with my wife and son, Cedric, aged six, yesterday morning, I was talking to my wife about the case, and John Duff's name came up. Then I asked Cedric if he had ever seen John go into the tool-shed. At first he said no, but afterwards he said, "I did once, but he wasn't in there very long." He said that it was during the summer of last year. This set me thinking, as some weeks ago my wife mentioned to me that on one occasion she was greatly surprised to find John on the landing as she came out of her bedroom. She asked him how he'd

[1] Tom Sidney had taken his family temporarily to Bexhill in order to get away from Croydon. He was, he said, alarmed in case anything should happen to them.

got into the house, and he replied, "I climbed over the gate and came in the back." My wife said that that happened last summer, too. So I asked Cedric whether he had ever seen John climb over the back-gate. He said, "Yes, he often comes that way." Now the side-gate is about seven feet high, but it can easily be climbed, as there are supports on which a boy could put his feet.'

Next day, Morrish was despatched to Bexhill to see Mrs Thomas Sidney, who confirmed all that her husband had said.

'John is an inquisitive boy,' she told him, 'and his hands are in everything, but he always appeared contented and had plenty of interests. At school he always went in for sport, was always busy. He is very fond of his mother, and she of him. He was given a great deal of responsibility in relation to money matters, and I think his mother would talk to him about financial affairs and difficulties. He is careful about saving his money and did little things for his mother.

'Mary is a quiet girl and would not be interested in money matters.

'I know that the children kept quite a number of animals at Hurst View. There were dogs and kittens in the house, and white mice, rabbits and chickens outside. I heard that two kittens had died. I think that was before Mr Duff died. It would probably have been about September 1927, after he bought the weed-killer, but I can't say for certain. I seem to remember that weed-killer was mentioned. I understood that Mr Duff had been using weed-killer in the garden, and the animals had got hold of it and were poisoned.'

The following day — July 18th — Hedges, together with Morrish and Tom Sidney, travelled to Monkton Combe School, near Bath, to see John Duff.

Tom Sidney knew the headmaster, to whom he introduced the detectives, and they were given permission to interview John in the headmaster's library.

To begin with, Hedges and Morrish saw the lad on their own. A statement was then taken from him in the presence of Tom Sidney and the headmaster.

John told them: 'I used to go two or three times a week to my Uncle Tom's, and if I got no answer at the front-door I used to shout through the letter-box to my cousin, Cedric, and if I got no reply then, I would go away. Once or twice, I'm positive not more than twice, I climbed over the side-gate. When I did that, I'd go into the house to find Cedric. I'd look in the kitchen first and see if the maid was there. Once, Auntie found me in the house and asked me how I'd got in. I said that I'd climbed over the side-gate, and she told me not to do it again.

'I used to play with Cedric in the garden with his fairy-cycle. I would get it out of the shed close to the house, where it was kept. The shed was unlocked and I didn't know there was any weed-killer in there. I've certainly never touched any. I don't know what it is like. I've never seen Uncle Tom use any. I didn't know he had any. My father used salt for his weeds, and black weed-killer in a tin. He always warned me not to touch it.

'I am not a cruel boy. I am fond of animals. I have killed mice by smashing them on the wall or ground. I think I drowned one kitten. My father killed some rabbits that had a disease, and Mother told me a long time ago about her chloroforming a cat that went mad. I think she said she bought the chloroform at Noble's, or some chemist or other.'

The whole interview lasted about three hours, and when it was over, Hedges, Morrish, Tom Sidney and the headmaster all felt that the boy had been telling the truth.

Hedges took Morrish with him to see Mary Duff on July 19th, and Mrs Duff insisted that her daughter's statement should be written down in longhand in her presence.

Mary said that she remembered seeing a tin of liquid weed-killer falling over in the yard, and some of its contents being spilt.

'You know that's wrong,' her mother interrupted sharply.

'Oh, Mother, what have I said?' the child asked. Then she started to cry. 'I've got a bad memory,' she sobbed, 'and I'm afraid I shall say something that's not right.'

She was obviously very nervous and the Inspector did his best to soothe her.

When Mary had calmed down she continued, 'I know a tin of weed-killer was put down in the cellar. As far as I can remember, I saw only one. I saw it in the cellar one day when I went down there to get a book. I don't think I saw Daddy use the weed-killer, as he used to do his gardening in the evening and I would go to bed. I was with Daddy when he ordered the weed-killer at Noble's. I thought that he ordered the two together. I think I remember going into Uncle Tom's shed once, but I am sure I didn't touch anything in the shed. I used to play in the garden sometimes. I love animals and I have never killed one. John killed a kitten by drowning it, but I hated the idea of it. John would never touch weed-killer. He is very kind and good.'

Tom Sidney had mentioned Mrs King and William Monkton as people who *could* have had access to his tool-shed had they so desired.

Neglect no possibility.

Both were interviewed that same day.

Mrs Evelyn King, of 110 Godstone Road, South Croydon, was

employed as a housekeeper at Oakleigh, Monahan Avenue,
Woodcote Valley Road, Coulsdon. She had been in the service
of Mr and Mrs Thomas Sidney from November 1926 — at
which time they were temporarily renting a house at 24 Godstone Road, South Croydon, as their own house was let — until
May 14th, 1928, and had lived-in with them at 6 South Park
Hill Road.

'I found Mr and Mrs Sidney a most devoted couple. During
the time I was with the family, Mrs Sidney's mother, Mrs
Elizabeth McConnell, came on a visit from America. She was a
very nice lady. She appeared to be in good circumstances.
During her visit she had a slight illness, through blood pressure
and indigestion, and was attended by Dr Binning. I heard
that she went back to America soon after I left the Sidneys.
During the time I was with Mr Thomas Sidney I went into the
tool-shed near the house several times to get nails and other
oddments. I went in there much more frequently than Mrs
Sidney, as I am fond of gardening. The shed was kept locked
and we kept the key out of the children's way on a shelf. I
knew they used weed-killer for the garden, but they used it
after the children had gone to bed. I saw Mr Sidney use it, and
he brushed it up in the morning. I saw the tin of weed-killer
high on the shelf in the shed, but I never saw anyone interfere
with it, and I never used it or moved it myself.'

On to number 2 Hurst Road, also in South Croydon, where
William Monkton lived.

'I'm an ex-foreman of the South Croydon railway station. I
remember doing some gardening for Mr Thomas Sidney at
South Park Hill Road. No, I never used the shed near the
house. Never even been in it. I used the shed at the bottom of
the garden. That's where the tools were kept. There wasn't any
weed-killer in there, and I never saw any at the house at all.
No, I definitely didn't use any.'

And all the time, that seemingly endless series of inquest
hearings dragged on . . . July 5th, 11th, 12th, 13th, 16th, 20th,
26th, 29th, 31st.

As he sat through session after tedious session, Hedges was
perpetually alert for some word, hint, look, gesture, that might
provide a clue. His concentration never wavered, but the
eagerly-hoped-for clue never came.

He began again at the beginning.

Back to Tom Sidney. Over the same ground yet once more.
Nothing.

Back to Grace Duff.
Nothing.

He knew all they had to say by heart. They said it. He
listened. Then moved grumpily off.

He and Morrish discussed the case *ad nauseam*. They always ended up precisely where they had started.

There was one more inquest sitting. One more week, to go.

VIII

August 6th, 1929. Just after four o'clock in the afternoon. And it was, at last, all over. The evidence had been presented, recorded, and weighed. The long procession of witnesses had come, said their pieces, and gone. The rest would be silence. And cloaked in that silence was a triple murderer — who would go scot-free. For the third and final inquest had ended, like the others, with a verdict of wilful murder by some person or persons unknown.

Unknown? Standing in the corridor outside the fast-emptying courtroom, Inspector Hedges emphatically did not agree. In these last days that missing piece which he had so long been seeking had clicked dramatically into place. It was as though he had been turning the wheel of a pair of binoculars and suddenly, quite by chance, the blurred horizon of doubt had hardened into a sharply-patterned focus of certainty. Of course it *was* still, in a sense, only a theory, and Hedges was no fool. He knew that half a hundred theories weighed less than a feather in the scales when one of the pans was loaded with the guilty burden of three mysterious deaths. Even so, it was good to feel that the punishing efforts of the last five months had not been entirely wasted.

And punishing indeed those last five months had been. He had left not a single stone, not even a pebble, unturned. Tirelessly, he had followed every tangential line, laboriously checked, re-checked, and then checked again, every infinitesimal possibility. Into his perpetually cocked ear had poured a stream of rumours, reports, canards and wild suggestions. He had not ignored one of them. Even the most improbable conjectures, formulated in a spate of anonymous letters, had been examined and investigated with time-consuming thoroughness. Not one, but a whole shoal of red herrings had been drawn across the harassed Inspector's track. Practically everybody — Tom Sidney, Grace Duff, Mrs Noakes, John Duff, Dr Elwell and even Violet Emilia Sidney — had been accused, in a series of constantly-changing attacks, that moved without rhyme, reason or discrimination from one person to another.

From month to month, the pendulum of suspicion had swung backwards and forwards in the mind of Inspector Hedges. Now he wondered about Tom Sidney. Exonerated him. Now about Grace Duff. Exonerated her. Now he wondered if there had been a conspiracy between brother and sister. Dismissed the notion.

All speculation, of course . . . the purest speculation. Still, theories are a detective's stock-in-trade.

But you couldn't make bricks to build a case without straw, and, cast about as he might, he could not discover a solitary wisp of graspable straw, either for brick-making or to indicate the quarter from which the hurricane of killing had sprung.

Sometimes Tom Sidney had put his back up. He had made what Hedges regarded as ridiculous statements. He seemed to have gone out of his way to cast reflections on the Inspector's handling of the investigations, forever popping up with 'clues' which, he implied, Hedges had carelessly overlooked. There was his demeanour at some of the inquest sittings, too. That had left a lot to be desired. How had the police solicitor, Mr Barker, put it? 'Tom Sidney's levity may be useful to him at entertainments, but it is not a happy feature at inquests.' Very neat that. Yes, Tom Sidney had sometimes behaved like a fool, but allowance must be made for his profession in life, which was that of an entertainer.

Was it Tom Sidney . . . or Grace Duff . . . or the two of them in collusion, who had murdered Edmund, Vera and Violet?

Or was it, (Hedges did not, could not, close his mind to the possibility,) some other person, who might have had good reason to nurture a savage enmity against the entire family?

He was to find the answer to that question — or at least the answer which satisfied him — by August.

And now, when the strong solution of suspicion which had ebbed and flowed in his brain, finally saturated it, and had been precipitated into crystal-clear conviction, it was all over. The juries thanked, dismissed and dispersed.

Now, he was anxious to make an arrest. But at the same time he was too old a hand to imagine that, without considerably stronger evidence than he was in a position to provide, he could hope to make out a case to answer. To have a conviction is one thing; to secure a conviction is something quite different. It was tantalising, infuriating — and insurmountable. He would have staked his pension that he could accurately name the killer — and there was not a thing that he could do about it.

Dogged to the end, Hedges went to see Sir Archibald Bodkin on September 21st. The Director of Public Prosecutions listened sympathetically to all that he had to say.

'Can you supply evidence of actual administration of arsenic?' he asked.

Sadly, Hedges admitted that he could not.

'Then,' said Sir Archibald, 'I'm afraid that I must decide to take no action in the case.'

The file was closed. Hedges was defeated.

IX

Frederick Hedges retired after thirty-five years unbroken service on February 28th, 1932. He took with him into his retirement a presentation clock and a host of memories. He had earned more than a hundred commendations from judges, magistrates and the Director of Public Prosecutions. He loved police work and hated having to give it up. For a time he compromised by undertaking some private enquiry jobs, but they did not really appeal to him. He would have liked to have taken over a country pub, but his wife was not keen on the idea. 'If you do, you do it without me,' she told him jokingly. As a matter of fact, there was, too, as a direct result of his work on the Sidney-Duff case, the offer of a position in the New York Police Department. But Hedges turned it down. He could not bring himself to leave England.

So he just settled quietly down on pension in the little house at 19 Trafford Road, Thornton Heath, where he, his wife, son and daughter had lived since 1919. Now, on dark winter's nights, sitting puffing at his pipe in his favourite chair beside the fire in the comfortable back-room, he could look quietly back on his cases. The mysterious disappearance of Eric Gordon Tombe, whose murdered corpse was found down a well at The Welcomes Stud Farm, at Kenley, Surrey; the case of the murdered night-watchman of Sanderstead, whose killers he had tracked down and arrested 176 miles away at Doncaster; and, above all, there would come constantly back to his mind the Sidney-Duff poisoning mystery.

Now, too, on long summer's evenings, he had at last time to do all the things that he had always planned to do in the garden. Time to prune and tend the roses that he loved with that special brand of rose-grower's enthusiasm.

Always a home-loving man, who seldom went out except when he had to, Hedges enjoyed the twenty-two years of his well-earned retirement. He pottered happily in the garden, growing bigger and better roses. He had boxed in his youth and liked now to go to the occasional boxing match. Never a great reader — he rarely picked up a book, and when he did it was strictly non-fiction — he was, however, very fond of light music, and got a great deal of pleasure from listening to the wireless.

Then there was always the family's annual seaside holiday, spent at places like Eastbourne and Worthing, to look forward to.

And so, with these small excitements, in final peace and contentment, the years of his life wound slowly down.

On January 31st, 1954, a day when his cherished garden was dark and locked with frost, and the rose-bushes looked as though they would never again carry blossoms on their bare, black twigs, surrounded by those he loved and who loved him, Fred Hedges died, in his seventy-ninth year.

Officially, the Croydon Poisoning Case must be regarded as one of Divisional Detective-Inspector Hedges' few failures.

Unofficially, privately, Hedges was convinced that he had solved it.

Suddenly, in a moment of illumination, an epiphany, he had seen clearly, and the vision remained with him to the end of his days.

9

A SECOND HEARING

I

By now the documentary spade-work was complete.

I had succeeded in tracing the outlines of the movements and events which shaped the lives of the Sidneys and the Duffs. I had examined the tragedies which befell them, and observed the impact of those tragedies upon those who, for one reason or another, found themselves drawn into the consequent vortex. In the process I had discovered a good deal about the principal actors, their antecedents, what they had done, and what had been done to them; but I still knew remarkably little about the wider reality behind the reported appearance. The protagonists remained scarcely more than puppets, jerked on the strings of circumstances external to themselves. I had plotted the directions of those jerkings; disentangled some of the strings.

Now I needed to uncover the animations from inside — the motivations born of their individual characters and personalities, which had tempered their actions, reactions and destinies. I was eager for any data which would help me to transform those wooden puppet figures into purposive, emotion-orientated flesh and blood. I wanted to learn something of their likes and dislikes, their attitudes and avowals, their responses to joy and sorrow, their conventions and vagaries, their inter-personal relationships with one another, their neighbours and their friends: to expose the basic pattern of trivia which made up their daily lives in the living.

The time had come to exchange the library for the field.

Edmund Duff and Vera and Violet Emilia Sidney were dead, but there must, I reasoned, be people alive who remembered them. Tom Sidney and Grace Duff would be in their seventies, but might well be living. If so, where were they? That was something that I should have to find out.

After the inquests had come to an end, the surviving members of the Sidney clan had left Croydon.

On September 5th, 1929, Tom Sidney, who had previously announced his decision to depart to America, put up for auction his South Park Hill Road home and a quantity of furniture which he did not want to take to the States with

him. The sale, which began at two o'clock, was held in the
garden. The house was offered first, but was withdrawn at
£1,550. The garden was crowded that hot, sunny September
afternoon, but sensation-seekers outnumbered bidders and good
furniture was knocked down for next to nothing. The auction
lasted for three hours, but realised only £165. Tom Sidney,
his wife and children left England for America in November
1929.

Grace Duff, who had at first declared that she had no intention of leaving Croydon, changed her mind when she found
crowds gathering round her house to get a glimpse of her.
Wherever she went fingers pointed and heads turned, and
before the end of 1929 she, too, had left her house in Birdhurst Rise for an unknown destination, where she hoped that
she and her three children could find the peace of anonymity. It
was rumoured that she had gone to start a new life in Australia.

For several months after the inquests the newspapers continued to print occasional references to the Croydon Arsenic
Mystery.

The *Daily Chronicle* of August 7th announced:

'Now that the last of the Croydon inquests has been concluded, the next move of the police will be watched with
considerable interest. Inquiries by detectives, which have
been secretly made during the many weeks the inquiries
lasted, will be continued with renewed energy. The possibility of a fourth exhumation, that of the body of Miss
Kelvey, an elderly spinster, is being considered, but no
decision has yet been reached.'

The *Daily News* of August 8th commented:

'Now that the protracted inquest proceedings . . . have
closed, the police are in a position to pursue a new line of
inquiry which they hope will yield some definite result.
Hitherto, to afford every assistance to the coroner, they have
been compelled to suspend their activities in several quarters.'

And on August 8th the *Daily Mail* asked:

'Was Mr Duff Afraid? — Had Mr Edmund Creighton Duff . . .
a presentiment that he was going to be murdered? The *Daily
Mail* is able today to reveal the fact that three weeks before
Mr Duff died he walked into the office of an old friend in
Fetter Lane, E.C., and deposited with him all the literary
work which he had done during and after his sojourn as a
Government official in Nigeria. As he handed these documents

over, he said, somewhat mysteriously, and with intense earnestness: "Guard these papers with your life, for they will be found to contain most important evidence." Then he walked out of the room, leaving the documents with his friend. They now appear to have no bearing on the tragedy of his death, but they show Mr Duff in a new light.

'Apparently he had for some years been anxious to make a name for himself as a literary man. During his stay in West Africa he paid special attention to the habits and customs of the natives, and wrote a number of interesting articles which were published in African and British periodicals under various names. He also wrote a 10,000-words story called "June's First Adventure", dealing with a Croydon typist who went to West Africa.

'The friend to whom these documents were handed said to a *Daily Mail* reporter yesterday: "A few days after Duff handed these papers to me I sailed to Brazil, and have only just returned. In the meantime there has been this inquiry into his death. Although I have looked at the papers he left me and have found nothing startling, I am certain from the way he spoke when he handed them to me that there is a peculiar significance in some of the passages in these manuscripts. " '

The next day, August 9th, under the heading, 'The Revenge Theory,' the *Daily News* asked:

'Were the three deaths in the Croydon poisoning mystery due to revenge? This theory has been placed before Scotland Yard by people who have lived in Nigeria where Mr Edmund Creighton Duff was for many years a Government official. A ship's surgeon who spent an hour at Scotland Yard yesterday, elaborating the theory, said to a *Daily News* reporter: "Immediately I saw that Mr Duff had been in Nigeria it occurred to me that the solution of the mystery might be found in that circumstance." This belief is based on the possibility that Mr Duff, in the course of his official duties, may have incurred the enmity of someone who swore vengeance against him and his kin. . . . The statement published yesterday in a newspaper, that Mr Duff, before his death, handed some papers to a friend, saying, "Guard these papers with your life . . ." is not taken seriously by Mr Duff's relatives. Mrs Charles D. Duff, wife of Colonel Duff, a brother of the dead man, said last night to a *Daily News* reporter: "I will never believe he said it, except in fun. Edmund was very fond of a joke." '

The *Sunday Express* of August 11th contained an: ' . . . amazing analysis of the case', written by Edgar Wallace, 'criminologist and master of mysteries, after a long and deep study of the Duff poison mystery . . . It is real life drama; one of the most absorbing mystery stories which even Edgar Wallace has ever written. His deductions, his conclusions and his predictions will be read throughout Great Britain with intense interest.'

It was, in fact, an assessment hinting at a great deal more than it actually said.

Wallace thought that it was possible to eliminate as a motive the desire of any person to benefit from the estate in the Sidney case. No person who had access to the three victims did benefit to any appreciable extent. It would be ludicrous to suppose that one of the servants or one of the relatives poisoned for pecuniary gain. He also ruled out the possibility that the poison was maliciously administered by one of the servants. The mentality of the murderer, he maintained, was that of Dr Neill Cream,[1] who poisoned at first for insignificant profit, and then from the sheer desire for destruction. It was the work of somebody who was mad, in the sense that all desperately wicked people are mad. Wallace did not believe that the killings were the work of an enemy of the family cold-bloodedly pursuing a vendetta. There was no historic precedent for murder by poison administered by a casual and totally disinterested outsider.

'Poisoners, even lunatic poisoners, choose only those with whom they are on terms of intimacy. In all the history of criminal jurisprudence I can find no instance of a man or woman who has administered poison to a total stranger[2].'

Wallace agrees with the juries who had dismissed the likelihood of accidental death.

'What strikes me as being extremely probable in this particular case is that the murderer had an accomplice. Whether that accomplice was innocent or guilty will perhaps one day be known. I am satisfied in my mind that there is a third person who, if he did not actively assist in the murders and was not actually privy to their committal, must in the case

---

[1] Dr Thomas Neill Cream, Victorian mass-poisoner. Executed November 15th, 1892, for the murder of a prostitute, Matilda Clover.

[2] Dr Neill Cream did just that.

of Mr Duff be well aware of the unknown motive. Unknown
if not unsuspected by the police, but for the moment entirely
unknown to the public.

'That mysterious third person is in as dreadful a position as
the murderer, for any moment he may find his secret
surprised and, because of his very silence, go to the scaffold
for the person who actually administered the poison. He may
have been entirely innocent. He may have been horrified
to discover the tragic turn that events had taken, and the terrible
solution which the murderer had found for some immediate
problem. Experience teaches us that men and women who
occupy what is known as respectable positions in society
will often risk the most ignominious of deaths to avoid any
scandal being attached to their name, and I have an idea
that something of the sort is happening here. It is a big price
to pay for the illusion of respectability.

'Were the three people killed by weed-killer at all? Were
they destroyed by a purer form of arsenic? And if so, how
was that arsenic procured? This may well be the point on
which the case will eventually turn. Was the third and unknown accessory, innocent or guilty, the agent from whom
the poison was obtained on some pretext or another?

'My own view is that the murderer will never be discovered. . . . I am not in the confidences of the police, but
I imagine that they are concentrating at the moment upon
only one of these deaths. That of Mr Edmund Duff. For
here may be discovered, and will be discovered sooner or
later, a significant motive. In this case two people are
directly and indirectly concerned, and when the crime is
brought home to its perpetrator it will be on the evidence
concerning the Duff murder. . . . What was the motive here?
To put out of the way a troublesome man? Mrs Duff testified to his being the best of husbands and the kindest of
fathers, and indignantly denied that he was a man of bad
temper or that he was jealous. No suggestion was made in
court as to the cause of his jealousy.

'It is because I believe that we shall find a definite motive
in this case — not a motive that would appeal to any sound
person but which may very easily bulk largely in the crazy
mind of the murderer — that I am satisfied that it will be
upon this crime that the police will erect the fabric of their
case, just as soon as the foundations can be laid. At present
there is no foundation.'

That week-end of August 10th–11th, in consequence of the
rumours of a further exhumation, crowds of people made
their way to Queen's Road Cemetery and clustered around the

graves of Violet and Vera Sidney, and Edmund Duff and his two little daughters, Margaret and Suzanne, There were also visitors to the grave of Miss Kelvey.

On the Monday, August 12th, the *Daily Express* came out with Thomas Sidney's own story of how the inquests had affected his life. Not to be outdone, the *Evening Standard* of August 17th published Mrs Thomas Sidney's own story. Neither account was particularly illuminating. Both praised the police and expressed relief that the long ordeal was over. They added little or nothing to the total picture.

According to the *Daily Telegraph* of August 28th, the authorities had now decided that they would take no further proceedings in connection with the Croydon arsenic mysteries, but that evening's *Star* printed an official statement from Scotland Yard:

> 'The matter is in the hands of the Director of Public Prosecutions, and the Commissioner of Police has received no intimation of any decision reached in regard to it.'

In the *Sunday Express* of September 1st, Ex-Chief Inspector Walter Dew, the man who caught Crippen, kept the pot boiling with an article on the Croydon case. He remarked on the tremendous difficulties involved in the solving of poison cases, expressed his sympathy for the officers concerned with the investigation of the Sidney-Duff killings, opined that one hand was responsible for all three deaths, and feared that it looked as if the police were faced with an unfathomable mystery.

Finally, on October 7th, the *Daily News* intimated:

> 'By the decision of the Law Officers of the Crown and the Director of Public Prosecutions not to proceed further in their inquiries, the Croydon arsenic poisoning mystery is added to the list of unsolved crimes.'

The following year, on June 26th, 1930, the *Evening Standard* printed a story that the Assistant Commissioner of the CID, Sir Trevor Bigham, had ordered the reopening of inquiries into the Croydon case. This was subsequently denied in the *Daily News* of July 17th.

Rumour flared up for the last time in September 1930. The *Daily Express* of September 6th understood that

> '. . . sensational developments in an entirely new direction, based on fresh evidence, are expected to take place in connection with the Croydon poison mysteries . . . Investigations which have never stopped are now leading in a startling

direction, and may ultimately furnish the solution of the mysteries.'

But nothing happened. The Croydon files continued to gather dust. The 'sensational developments' apparently failed to develop.

From time to time there were echoes of the case in the press. In books of strange stories and popular crime histories, the Croydon case took its place as a chapter in the sections dealing with unsolved mysteries. Occasionally it turned up in magazines. In one such article, Julian Symons suggested that fifty years must elapse before criminal historians could hope to offer an answer to the triple riddle. Accepting the implicit challenge, I resolved at least to have a try.

A new generation had grown up in Croydon and the five-months' wonder was long forgotten. Even so, Croydon seemed to me the only rational place in which to seek the answers to the questions which plagued me.

So I went to Croydon.

II

It is disconcerting to find how slight a trace the average person leaves behind, even when he or she has lived in one place for a decade. I came across a few people who remembered Violet Emilia Sidney and her daughter, Vera, but after more than thirty years their figures had grown dim.

Mrs Sidney? Yes. She was an aristocratic old lady of the old school. Very upright. Very correct. Rather religious. Somewhat severe. Kept herself to herself. You would see her out walking with her daughter sometimes.

Vera, the daughter? A good girl. Very devoted to her mother. Used to ride around on a bicycle when she was not driving her car. A keen golfer and bridge-player. Always very polite and pleasant.

Little snippets of information. All trivia like that. And those were the only ripples which their lives had left after ten years of living in even so tight-knit and inward-turning a little community as that of the Croydon of forty-odd years ago. Not much to go on, but surely the very paucity of the information was in itself a hint at the kind of people that the mother and daughter at 29 Birdhurst Rise were.

Then, after a great deal of searching, I managed to discover the whereabouts of Mrs Kathleen Noakes — the only person to emerge alive from that ill-starred house in Birdhurst Rise. Now, at last, I got a glimpse of life as it was lived behind the ugly red bricks of Number 29.

I found Kathleen Noakes, a slim, grey-haired woman of seventy-three, living alone in a small cottage in Surrey. Apart from a slight deafness and a tendency to anaemia, she seemed to be in good health, and her mind remained vivid and alert. She struck me as a respectful woman of the old servant class, who still retained a simple piety — 'Every night I always pray to God that before I die we shall know who did the murders.'

Born Kathleen Fleming, at 5 Queen Street, Croydon, on June 26th, 1889, before entering Mrs Sidney's service in August 1928 Mrs Noakes had spent three-and-a-half years as house-parlour-maid with a family in London Road, Thornton Heath. Leaving there in June 1912, she went as a nursing orderly to the Royal Earlswood Asylum in Surrey. Towards the end of the First World War she joined the Queen Mary's Army Auxiliary Corps, serving as a cook. From 1919 to 1921 she worked with the West Ham Union, first at a nursing home in Margate, and then at Forest Lane, East London. On October 7th, 1922, she married a Portsmouth seaman, Robert Henry Noakes, then serving in the Royal Navy, but the marriage was not a success and they separated five years later. It was in 1927 that she first met a 44-year-old man who had a small carting business in Croydon, and who was also unhappily married. A close friendship grew up between them. And that was the situation when, on August 31st, 1928, Mrs Noakes went to work for Mrs Sidney.

'I was waiting for my divorce to come through. My friend needed £9 to buy another horse for his pantechnicon, and I took a job to earn the money for the horse. From the start I only regarded the job as a temporary one. I intended to leave as soon as I'd saved up the nine pounds. When I was interviewed by Mrs Sidney I told her I was a widow. I didn't want her to know about my friend.'

The household in which Mrs Noakes now found herself was, in some respects, a curious one.

'Except for the family, we were so isolated that we might have been living on a desert island. At first I found the loneliness very trying. Although it was a lovely house with nice furniture, it was rather dark and gloomy, but Mrs and Miss Sidney actually tried to make me feel at home when I was there. The work was hard. I had to clean the whole house and was also expected to do all the cooking. The household was run regular as a barracks. I had to be up by seven o'clock, and after breakfast spent the morning cleaning. Then I cooked and served lunch, and between half-past two and three o'clock every afternoon I would be in my bedroom, putting on my black dress before serving tea. Supper, which I prepared, was at seven o'clock, and I generally went to bed at about ten o'clock.

'Mrs Sidney was a sweet old lady. She never interfered, but she was rather stern, and had very rigid ideas about what her servants should and should not do. She was not the sort of person to be approached by anyone in her service. Quite often she would chat with me, but she had to be the one to open the conversation, and it was she who always chose the subject. I don't mean to say that she was hard or mean with me. She was a good mistress and a fine type of woman, but she was not like Miss Vera.

'Miss Vera was the most normal, healthy-minded woman I have ever known, and I was much fonder of her than of anybody else at Birdhurst Rise. She was quite slim, not very tall, sort of medium height, and had rather a sallow complexion, with warm brown eyes that looked at you gratefully, and a sunny smile that made it a pleasure to work for her. I often wondered that Miss Vera had never married. She spoke of it once.

' "You're a widow, Kate," she said. "Are you very unhappy about it?"

'I was very embarrassed. I'd have liked to have told her the truth, because she always seemed to trust me, but I knew that she wouldn't want to keep anything from her mother, and I didn't think that Mrs Sidney would forgive a deception, however innocently intended. Anyway, I murmured something about having grown fond of somebody else. I was sewing at the time, and I pointed out that the curtains I was making were for the home of the man for whom I cared.

' "I can't quite make it out, Kate," said Miss Vera. "Do you really do all that work for love?"

'She saw that I didn't know how to answer, and so went on to tell me that marriage had never appealed to her. She liked her golf and her motoring, she said with a cheerful laugh, and added that about all she prized her freedom. Men didn't interest her particularly. She wasn't a man-hater or anything like that. She was far too normal. It was just that she liked being independent, fairly free of household responsibilities, and leading an out-door life. I know that some people suggested that Mr Duff cared for Miss Vera more than a brother-in-law should. Mr Duff was dead before I entered the service of the family, so I can't say anything about him, but I do know that Miss Vera was the most loyal, straightforward woman that ever lived, and that to give a thought beyond that which was sisterly to her sister's husband would have been contrary to everything that made up her character. Miss Vera played absolutely square with everybody, and I would stake my life on that.

'Had it not been for the fact that Miss Vera made a friend of me from the very first night that I arrived there, I should

have left Birdhurst Rise weeks and weeks before the tragedy
happened. Actually, Mrs Sidney offered me a rise before the six
months I'd agreed to stay for were up, but I told her that I
intended to leave. It was really to oblige Miss Vera that I
stayed on longer than I had planned.

'If I had been the strictly obedient servant that Mrs Sidney
thought me, I should never have been poisoned by the soup on
that Monday evening. The mistress had told me that she considered fish, potatoes and pudding ample as supper for a servant,
and had forbidden me to take soup or cake in the evenings.
Sometimes I used to buy little cakes for myself from the
baker's, but I had never taken any soup until that Monday
night. I only took it then because I had such a bad cold that
I was afraid it might turn into the 'flu if I didn't have something to warm me up. And so I "stole" the cupful of soup. I
only had a little of it, and was violently sick. I was not sick
before drinking the soup, as Mrs Duff suggested in court. Bingo,
the cat, was a dear creature, a beautiful cat. But cats are
cunning and he took only one mouthful of the soup. Even so
he was awfully sick.

'I didn't know until the last minute that Mrs Greenwell was
coming on the Wednesday. Mrs Sidney told me on the Tuesday
evening that there would be a visitor to lunch next day.

'When Miss Vera died the mistress was dreadfully distressed.
"I never want to see anybody like that again," she said to me.

'I shall never believe that Mrs Sidney committed suicide. If
you'd known her, you'd know that she just wasn't the sort of
person who would.'

I asked Mrs Noakes who she thought it was that had murdered
Vera and Violet Sidney.

'Well, I always suspected Mr Tom,' she said. 'I never really
liked him. But I don't think it can have been him, though. To
be absolutely honest, I simply can't imagine who could have
done it.'

I took up with her the point that she gave in evidence,
about having seen Tom Sidney in the hall at Number 29 shortly
before one o'clock on the day of Mrs Sidney's death.[1]

'I definitely did see him in the hall,' she told me, 'but I
suppose I may have made a mistake in the day perhaps.'

Finally, I asked what sort of a person Grace Duff was. She
paused for a moment or two. Then said, 'She was a shifty person.
She never seemed to be able to look you in the face. I didn't
like her.'

And what of the fifth member of the family, Grace's husband,
Edmund?

[1] See page 62.

Mrs Noakes had never known him. I would need to look elsewhere.

Perhaps if I were to seek out Dr Elwell . . .

III

Dr Robert Graham Elwell was not hard to find. Although eighty-five years of age, he was still in practice at Eastmead, 14 Addiscombe Road, East Croydon.

A short, slightly built man, with fair hair, a pale face and shrewd blue eyes, he looked considerably less than his years. His manner was professionally wary and cautious.

'I have made it a rule never to discuss the case,' he told me, and it took a great deal of persuasion before I succeeded in inducing him to change his mind. Even then it was only on the strict understanding that I promised to reveal nothing of what passed between us 'within the four walls of the arcanum of this consulting room' until after his death.

On December 26th, 1961, three months after our meeting, he died peacefully at Eastmead, and I was at liberty to disclose his guarded confidences.

It was from Dr Elwell that I received the first hint of the real man behind the public image of Major Edmund Creighton Duff.

'Duff was a tough sort of a man,' he said. 'Not quite a gentleman. He was very different from the Sidneys. They were a very nice refined family, and Duff was the odd man out. Mrs Sidney did not care for him at all, and, in my view, anybody less complacent and adaptable than Mrs Grace Duff would soon have found the marriage a wreck.'

That uncomplimentary opinion of Duff was to be amply confirmed from other sources. Dr Binning was to describe him quite categorically as 'A brute who behaved like a beast, and deserved to die.' Neighbours recalled him as rather a crude, coarse personality; an obvious misfit in that very refined family circle. And 95-year-old Mr Douglas Cator, whom I ran to earth at Hertford, and who had served with Duff forty-five years before in Nigeria, remembered him as a 'disagreeable, overbearing and quarrelsome little man'.

Here, then, were the first indications that Duff was far from being the amiable, forbearing, good-humoured fellow portrayed at the inquests.

And there was more to come.

Apparently, too, the marriage of Grace and Edmund was not the idyllic union that the witnesses at the inquest would have had the court believe. In some respects at least, things were not, I had by now discovered, quite what they had seemed.

In fact, it turned out that Dr Elwell himself was not quite what he seemed, either.

The old man that I met struck me as the perfect embodiment of the old-style family doctor, Rather quiet, serious, professionally reticent and very correct. I met many, many people who spoke of him with great affection and in terms of the highest praise, but I never met one who denied that he was a great ladies' man. Women adored him and, by all accounts, he was far removed from indifference to them. He never married, but there is little doubt that he was a busy man of affairs.

Among those who succumbed to Dr Elwell's ubiquitous charms was Grace Duff.

I was first told of this by neighbours who, after her husband's death, had observed Elwell's car standing outside Grace Duff's house night after night. 'It was constantly there,' one of them had said. I was, initially, inclined to dismiss this as mere gossip. When, however, several professional colleagues of Elwell's confirmed that he was a well-known Lothario, I had second thoughts. And when, finally, Thomas Sidney admitted that he had no doubt at all that his sister, Grace, had an affair with Elwell, I accepted it as a fact. 'The family knew that they were lovers,' said Sidney, 'and I know that my mother hoped that they would eventually marry.'

Normally, when the family doctor makes his appearance in a murder case of this kind he takes his place in the witness-box as a sort of lay-figure, his involvement is only professionally incidental. As my investigations proceeded, however, it soon became evident that Dr Robert Graham Elwell was hardly to be described as an incidental figure in the Croydon case.

In these circumstances, it is not perhaps surprising that he should have summed Grace Duff up to me as 'A happy, carefree, gay person. Very nice. Very charming.'

Naturally, I asked him who he thought had been responsible for the murders.

'I was, and still am, completely baffled by the mystery,' he admitted. 'But whoever it was, I'm sure it can't have been Mrs Duff. I observed her demeanour throughout the period of her troubles. She was either innocent, or a consummate actress. And I have always believed that she was innocent.'

IV

Gradually, as the tally of months lengthened, I went on building up my dossier. I could still find no trace of Tom Sidney or Grace Duff, and I had to rely, for the moment, upon such impressions as I could gather at second hand.

Information about Tom Sidney was almost as sparse as that about his mother and sister, Vera. Seen through the eyes of those who had known him, he emerged as a quiet, pleasant, rather reserved man, but with an unexpectedly sharp sense of humour. No one who had been personally acquainted with him — except Mrs Noakes — considered it even remotely possible that he could have killed his mother and his sister, let alone his brother-in-law. 'He just wasn't the sort of man who'd commit a murder,' I was told again and again. 'Whoever did it, you can be sure *he* didn't.'

Of all the Sidneys, it was Grace Duff who seemed to have left the most vividly-etched impression behind in the minds of those who had known her. She was clearly a stronger character than her brother, Tom, and, as is the case with all strong characters, the reactions which she evoked were extremely varied. I met several people who spoke of her with considerable affection, said how kind and generous she was, and what an exemplary mother she had been. Others were less enthusiastic.

The words 'wild', 'erratic', 'odd', more politely 'artistic', and less politely 'unstable', consistently cropped up in the personality sketches that those who remembered her gave to me. So did the words 'stoical' and 'unfeeling.'

One woman neighbour described her as 'An erratic, rather artistic, but unstable kind of a person.' Another told me unequivocally, 'That woman was a liar.' Said a third, 'Mrs Duff struck me as a pseudo-intellectual. She used to dress herself up in sort of loose robes and went in for coloured veils. She was always rather interested in the gentlemen. There was a wild, artistic streak about her.'

But the clearest portrait of Grace Duff was painted for me by a man who had lived a few doors away from her in Birdhurst Rise. 'She was the queerest female I ever met in the whole of my life. A frightfully excitable person. Amiable and pleasant enough on the surface, but with an underlying queerness. Yes, an exceedingly peculiar woman, I'd say — so self-possessed, so able to accept those frightful tragedies. She showed no feelings whatsoever about the suspicions that were going around concerning her and her brother's possible guilt. I won't deny it, I found Mrs Duff sinister. I was afraid of her. Mainly because I felt that she was a man-eater. I thought to myself, "Show any interest, put a foot out of proper step there, and she'll develop a hysterical attachment to you and make a lot of trouble for you. She's that kind of person." She would look at you in an appealing little-girl-lost way, making you feel that you were the big, strong man, on whose understanding and aid she was relying.'

According to this same gentleman, Grace Duff's demeanour in the public limelight of the inquest court was very different from that which she displayed in the privacy of her own home.

'She didn't give the impression of being at all upset by the deaths of her mother and sister. Actually, she seemed excited rather than sorrowful. I remember meeting her coming down the road on the evening of the night that Vera died, and she said, "My sister's dreadfully ill. Terribly ill. Her face has altered so much I can hardly recognise her. I've been with her all evening." But all this was said with breathless excitement. Not a trace of sorrow, such as you might naturally expect.

'What's more, Mrs Duff hadn't the least reticence about the tragedies. Not the least. I remember her shouting out of her window to me on one occasion, "They think I murdered my husband." The whole street could hear her. She was very cool and collected all along, and would go into the local shops and tell the shopkeepers, "Imagine it. They think I murdered Mr Duff." She seemed to me to enjoy the notoriety, and I used to see her laughing with the newspaper reporters and posing for the press photographers with her children in the garden.'

So much for what may be termed the evidence of parochial gossip. I turned my attention next to the collection of the opinions of the official side.

First of all there was Inspector Hedges. Unfortunately he had died in 1954, so I was not able to question him. But I met his widow, his daughter and his son, and they told me that he had, in his own mind, come to a very definite conclusion.

No one now can be absolutely sure when it was that the moment of *éclaircissement* came for Hedges. All that we can certainly know is that it *did* come, and from the various notes that he left it is possible, piecing together the fragments, to trace the genesis of suspicion, and plot the course of its hardening into irrefragable conviction.

It was somewhere about the middle of May 1929, that Hedges began to have his first serious misgivings concerning the innocence of the tearful widow of Birdhurst Rise. Tentatively, one can almost *see* him hesitating as he scribbled the words in his notebook, 'Mrs Duff is an erratic, irresponsible woman. She is also a very clever actress. I think that she is typical of a woman who would be likely to carry out a system of secret poisoning, though her subsequent conduct has been such as would cast aside all suspicion, unless one is specially trained in the investigation of crime.'

In fact, this was a return to an earlier position, for Hedges had begun by suspecting Grace Duff at the very start of his investigation. A week after Violet Emilia Sidney's death he had written, 'Mrs Duff is an exceptionally difficult woman to assess.

She is obviously very clever, and there is some evidence that she is also very extravagant. She would, of course, benefit considerably by the death of her sister, and even more by the death of her mother. There seems, too, to be a strong motive for her doing away with her husband.'

But it was not long before the curious conduct of Tom Sidney caused Hedges to have second thoughts.

In his notebook Hedges wrote: 'Throughout this enquiry Tom Sidney has been the most disturbed person. Perhaps this is because he takes a more serious view of the matter than Grace Duff? He has also been a most unsatisfactory witness, trying to throw dust in the eyes of the juries, and to discredit me by producing various objects which he says he has found in his mother's house *after* my search. Perhaps this is his way of trying to draw their attention away from the tin of weed-killer which I found in his possession? I was previously more favourably impressed by him than I am now.'

For months Hedges found himself riding a kind of see-saw of suspicion between the pair of them. Gradually, however, the weight of suspicion piled up, factor by tiny factor, on the side of Grace's guilt, and by the end of June the balance, so far as Hedges was concerned, had irrevocably tipped against Grace Duff. Tom Sidney had been annoying, awkward, provocative and prevaricatory, a thorn in Hedges' side. But it was Grace, with her ready tears, and equally ready wheedling smile, who finally impressed him as being the more likely poisoner.

'There is no doubt in my mind that she was secretly in love with Dr Elwell. I believe that she poisoned her husband, perhaps hoping that Elwell would marry her. I am sure, too, that she put the arsenic in the soup *before* she knew that her aunt, Mrs Greenwell, was coming to lunch (a fact which she only found out when Vera, who was unwell, asked her to meet their Aunt Gwen at the station) — and then it was too late to do anything about it. I think that she killed Vera because she thought that she would stand a better chance of catching Elwell if she had more money of her own. And she murdered her mother in order to acquire still more money. There is something cold and sinister about that woman. She is a born actress, and her sorrow for the loss of her relatives is obviously all on the surface.'

It was all speculation, of course, but from that time onwards, Hedges bent his every endeavour to drawing the net securely about her.

In July, an incident occurred which strengthened Hedges' belief that Grace was the culprit.

On July 23rd, he, together with Morrish, went to see Tom Sidney with regard to an anonymous letter which the coroner had received, containing a scurrilous reference to Mrs Margaret

Sidney, and suggesting that she was responsible for Edmund Duff's death. Tom Sidney most vehemently denied the allegations in the letter, and it was then that he told Hedges, 'Prior to my knowledge of the anonymous communication, my sister, Grace, had made veiled suggestions as to why Margaret, my wife, had not been called upon to give evidence at the inquests. My sister intimated that my wife could easily have committed all three murders. My sister further mentioned the strange illness of my mother-in-law whilst in this country[1] . Grace said, "You know you said once that Margaret had an aunt who was not quite right." The aunt in question had suffered from mental strain, due to a love affair. I said to Grace, "There has never been any insanity in Margaret's family."

'My wife has always been on good terms with all the members of the family. She has had no occasion to be otherwise. Naturally I was annoyed at my sister's suggestion, and I told her that if the coroner called my wife he would eliminate her in two minutes.

'I said no more until after I was shown the anonymous letter received by Dr Jackson. After I was shown it at the inquest sitting of July 20th, I had a telephone message from Grace the next morning, asking me to go and see her. On my arrival, she brought up the subject of our previous conversation relating to my wife. Grace said, "I want to say that I don't really believe in that business about Margaret." I then told her about the anonymous letter received by Dr Jackson, making allegations similar to those which she had made to me personally.

'She said, "I have received a similar letter, and the writer told me they were sending a copy to the police." I asked to see the letter. She said, "I can't find it now." I persisted, and she then said that it had been destroyed. I asked her about the envelope and paper. Grace said it was a yellow envelope. She described it exactly as I had seen it. She did not mention the paper. I don't want to say anything damning about my sister, but I think the anonymous letter was inspired by her. I have carefully examined the letter, and am of the opinion that the signature, "M. King", is written by a different hand from the other part.'

It was on July 23rd, too, that Tom Sidney introduced Hedges to the Reverend Mr Deane, at St Peter's Vicarage, South Park Hill Road.

And Mr Deane had some very curious things to say.

'I can only give you my opinion about the case,' he began.

---

[1] Tom Sidney's mother-in-law came to England on a visit from America, and had a slight illness from blood pressure. The illness occurred in the absence of the Sidneys' servant, Mrs King, and only immediate members of the family knew of it.

'I have met Mrs Duff when I conducted the funerals of the family. Mrs Duff showed me her daughter, Suzanne, lying dead in her coffin, which was covered with flowers. Mrs Duff was remarkable to me on that occasion. She appeared quite unmoved, callous, and not a bit like a mother. She appeared to be merely interested in the sight of the child in the coffin. I have never in all my experience met such a woman. When Mr Duff died, I formed the conclusion that he did not die a natural death, and when Miss Vera died I felt convinced that she had been put out of the way, and told my wife so. Mrs Duff was at the grave, and I felt throughout the service at the grave that there was antagonism to everything I was saying on the part of Mrs Duff. I can't explain it. Whilst in the carriage at the time of Mrs Sidney's funeral, Mrs Duff again seemed extraordinary. She said, "Tom wants an inquest. He wants to disturb her ashes. Her ashes are sacred. The goodness in her ashes would cry out." '

By August, Hedges was pressing for permission to arrest Grace Duff. 'I asked my superiors, begged them, to allow me to arrest her,' he wrote in his diary. 'The coroner's summing-up in all three cases showed extreme weakness, and he seemed to go out of his way to be kind and protective to Mrs Duff. I feel sure that I could place sufficient weight of circumstantial evidence to convict her before an impartial jury.'

But it was no use. The powers that were just could not see a prosecution succeeding. The great stumbling-block was, as Hedges had to acknowledge, the utter impossibility of *proving* administration of arsenic. They were sorry. They were sure Hedges was right. They regretted. But they were adamant. The meshes of Hedges' carefully-spun net were, in their considered judgment, too wide. And that was that. Hedges had ended up not so much baffled as frustrated.

When, some time later, I met a former colleague of Hedges', ex-Chief Detective-Inspector Herbert Iredale, he told me: 'I often used to have a chat with old Fred Hedges, and many's the time he'd say that in his opinion Grace Duff was definitely guilty.

"I reckon she's one of the luckiest women alive," he'd say. "Yes, one of the luckiest women alive." '

I learned that Hedges' assistant, Detective-Inspector Reginald Morrish, was living on his pension in retirement in Surrey. I went to see him, but he steadfastly refused to discuss the case.

A request to Scotland Yard for assistance met, perhaps understandably, with a similar stone-wall response. It was, after all, hardly one of their most successful investigations.

So I switched my enquiries to the more exalted reaches of the law, the legal personalities who had been involved in the inquest proceedings.

Mr H.D. Roome, counsel representing the interests of the Commissioner of Police at the second inquest on Edmund Duff, had died in a motor accident in 1930, but Sir William Bentley Purchase, who had been his pupil and who had acted as his junior in the Croydon case, was very much alive.

'My chief, Roome, was quite certain that Grace Duff was guilty,' Purchase told me. 'So was the police solicitor, Barker. And so was I. I didn't like Mrs Duff at all. She seemed a very hard sort of woman.'

I asked Purchase what he thought the motives for the killings could have been.

'Well to begin with, when Duff gave her another child it was something she didn't want,' he told me. 'Duff was very vital and sexually demanding. Probably took monkey glands or something of the sort. Anyway, the fellow got on his wife's nerves. They weren't very well off, you know, either. Couldn't afford to go on having children. As regards Vera, Grace was having an affair with Elwell. Vera was a bit of a conventional type, disapproved, and told her, "If you're going to set your cap at the doctor, I think you're acting wrongly. I don't like it, and I shan't go on helping with John's school fees unless you stop." A fortnight after that rash remark Vera was dead. Grace probably killed her mother because the old woman was sick, a bloody nuisance and holding up the money. She may also have suspected that Grace had done for Duff and Vera.'

Purchase certainly seemed to have it all cut and dried, at least to his own satisfaction.

He went on, 'Barker summed it up very neatly in a bit of doggerel he composed. It went like this:

> Who killed poor Edmund Duff?
> I, said his wife,
> Because of his life,
> I'd had quite enough.

> And who killed poor Vera?
> I also, said Grace,
> As 't'would appear a crime hard to trace,
> To kill yet another,
> I, too, murdered Mother.

> From one I got peace,
> From the other two cash,
> And though it seems rash
> To murder all three,
> Since keen the law's edge is,
> I've quite baffled Hedges.

Sir Bernard Spilsbury. Medical Witness. 'His was a divine afflatus only one celestial notch below that of the Almighty.'

Dr Henry Ryffel. Toxicologist. A preoccupation with Metatone and Eureka.

Inspectors Hedges and Morrish with Mr Thomas Sidney. Seekers after truth.

William Arthur Fearnley-Whittingstall. Barrister for the Defence. 'The one outstanding forensic figure in court, the most formidable cross-examiner.'

Grace and her Counsel wind-swept through the Workhouse Gardens. But the gale did not blow away the mist. . .

'I don't mind telling you, Spilsbury was perfectly sure that Grace was the murderess, too. Jackson, the coroner, made a botch of things. Bodkin, the Director of Public Prosecutions, had told him at a conference at his office that it would be best from every point of view to hold the three inquests together. But the damn fool misunderstood him, and took them separately. The result was that protracted series of useless inquests, and the loss of vital evidence of opportunity to administer poison that might have made all the difference.

'But Mrs Duff was a cool customer. I remember one week-end my wife and I went down to Bath for a breather. We were staying at the Empire Hotel there. At breakfast I noticed a well-dressed, good-looking woman sitting at the next table. There was something vaguely familiar about her. I looked again. Bath and Croydon are more than a hundred miles apart, and there are scores of hotels in Bath. I leant across to my wife and said, "Don't ever talk to me about coincidences. It may surprise you, but the woman at the next table is Mrs Duff of Croydon." I'm quite sure that she recognised me, too, but the said Mrs Duff completely ignored me!'

Since Purchase, Roome and Barker all represented the police at the inquests, it was only to be expected that they might hold hostile views concerning Grace Duff, but I must admit that I was considerably surprised to discover that her own counsel, Mr William Arthur Fearnley-Whittingstall, shared their convictions regarding his client's guilt.

Fearnley-Whittingstall was dead, but his widow, Mrs Margaret Nancy Fearnley-Whittingstall, left me in no doubt as to what her husband's views had been.

She had herself attended several of the inquest hearings, and saw Grace Duff 'act the part of the meek, pathetically bewildered and defenceless woman, the innocent, blue-eyed and fluttering little widow, who was casting herself upon the protection of the big, chivalrous, capable barrister.'

'But,' said Mrs Fearnley-Whittingstall, 'on one occasion my husband saw the mask slip. I remember he came home one evening and told me, "I've seen the most extraordinary thing today. A completely different Mrs Duff." Apparently, they were standing talking together outside the court, when some small incident occurred which angered Mrs Duff. In an instant, the sweet, tragic look vanished from her face, which was transformed by an expression so vicious and venomous that Bill was utterly taken aback. "She looked like a devil," he told me. "I would have believed her capable of anything." It was from that moment that he felt certain that she was the murderess. And when the inquests were over, he said that he thought he'd been exceedingly lucky to get her off without a charge of murder.'

Fearnley-Whittingstall's views as to the probable motives for the killings are interesting. They display the controlled imagination of a great advocate.

Grace Duff, he said, absolutely adored little children. They were the be-all and end-all of her life. In fact, he thought that the deaths of her two young daughters, Margaret and Suzanne, had temporarily unbalanced her mind. Edmund Duff retired from the Colonial Service on a very small pension, and was not much use as a wage-earner. To make matters worse, not only was he inclined to be extravagant, but he lost £5,000 of his wife's own personal money for her by bad investments. That upset her, because it menaced the security of the children whom she adored, and she began to see him as a liability, a danger to her children's well-being.

She also knew that her mother disliked Edmund, regarding him as not quite a gentleman, not good enough to be a member of the Sidney clan, and wasteful and improvident. Grace feared that, with Edmund alive, her mother would leave more money to Vera and Tom — both of whom she seems to have preferred to Grace in any case — because Mrs Sidney thought that whatever she left in her will to Grace would only be appropriated, and wasted, by Edmund.

Grace saw that if her husband were to die, not only would she miss his earning power very little, but she would be restored to her mother's financial good graces, and her children would no longer be endangered in their security, because she herself would have sole control of all monies.

There was another consideration, too. Edmund continued very sexually demanding. He had recently given her a fifth child, and might quite easily give her several more. This she did not want, because she felt that in their precarious financial circumstances it was as much as they could do to provide properly for the three surviving children whom they already had. Any additional mouth could be fed, any additional body clothed, only at the expense of the existing children.

And so she determined to be rid of Edmund.

Having got away with that killing, she then decided to murder Vera. The motive here was either that she saw the chance of improving her financial circumstances — more money for the children — as a result of Vera's death, or it was because Vera had threatened to discontinue her contribution towards John's school fees. That would be to menace the future of Grace's elder son.

Mrs Sidney was killed, perhaps for her money — again with the children's security in mind — perhaps because she had begun to suspect the way in which Edmund and Vera had met their deaths.

A week or two after my visit to Mrs Fearnley-Whittingstall,
I travelled down to Devon to see 73-year-old Mrs Hilda Jackson,
the coroner's widow, who was living in a private nursing home
at Torquay.

Mrs Jackson told me that, at first, Dr Jackson had suspected
that Tom Sidney would prove to be the murderer.

'I remember that when I attended the hearings my husband
told me to watch Mr Sidney's feet. Beecher thought that if he
was guilty he would shuffle them about. I watched, but he kept
them quite still. My husband didn't like Tom Sidney. He thought
him very impertinent.'

Subsequently, however, Dr Jackson changed his mind regarding Sidney's guilt — to the extent of privately suspecting
collusion in the murders between him and Grace Duff.

It was from Mrs Jackson that I learned, incidentally, that
Mrs Greenwell, Grace's aunt who was poisoned by the soup at
that Wednesday lunch at Birdhurst Rise, had very definite
views as to the identity of the poisoner.

'At one of the hearings I was sitting next to Mrs Greenwell.
Of course she didn't know who I was. Suddenly she turned to
me and said, "She did it, you know. My niece. She did it." I
moved away and called Mr Clarke, the coroner's officer, over,
and asked him to tell Mrs Greenwell that I was the coroner's
wife, and that she mustn't say things like that to me.'

But Mrs Greenwell was an irrepressible chatterbox, and later
in the proceedings Mrs Jackson heard her telling somebody else
in the court, 'Vera and her mother suspected Grace. That's
why she poisoned them. *She* did it, you know.'

Mrs Jackson also provided me with independent confirmation
of several facts which had emerged from my previous investigations.

'Edmund Duff was pretty beastly, you know,' she said. 'My
husband heard afterwards from a barrister friend who had
known Duff abroad that he was not at all a nice type of man.'

She also told me: 'Dr Elwell was a very attractive man. He
used to wear a straw-hat with elastic under his chin, and he
would wave to all the nurses. I remember he even tried waving
to me.' As she spoke, I saw a momentary flash of long-dead
coquetry come back into the old lady's eyes. Then, primly, she
continued, 'Of course I ignored it. It wouldn't have done for the
coroner's wife . . . But he had an affair with Mrs Duff. I know
that for certain, because when he reported Duff's death to my
husband he told him, "I'm afraid I've been indiscreet with Mrs
Duff."'

Revealing, as well as amusing, was the anecdote that Mrs
Jackson recounted of Dr Brontë's discomfiture in the course of
a visit which he paid to Mrs Duff's house in order to question

her on one or two points.

'She was all over him and sat on the rug up against his legs.
Poor Dr Brontë was frightfully embarrassed. He told my husband
afterwards, "Beecher, I don't want to go and see that woman
alone again." '

After leaving Mrs Jackson, I crossed the border into Cornwall,
where Dr Binning was living in a picturesquely situated bungalow
near Liskeard.

A tall, stringy Scot, alert and vigorous in his bucolic retirement, Dr Binning obviously knew considerably more about the
affair than he seemed prepared to say. He was, after all, a very
important — a key — figure in the case. He was the man who
knew all the Sidneys and the Duffs intimately. He was the man
who watched the progress of their various illnesses. He was the
man who witnessed the moments of each of their deaths. I felt
as soon as I met him that, if he wanted to, he could provide
me with a unique eye-witness account of a trained observer
whose judgments would be unclouded by prejudice of any kind.

But *did* he want to?

Dr Binning was hesitant.

When, four hours later, I took my departure, he was still un-
decided. But he had promised to think the matter over very
carefully. 'I'll write and let you know what I decide,' were his
last words to me.

V

In the course of our conversation, Dr Binning had told me
that Tom Sidney was now living in New Orleans, where he had a
flourishing antique business. Binning, who still kept up a
friendly correspondence with him, had recently heard from
Sidney that he would be coming to London in the following
Spring. I made up my mind that when he arrived I would pay him
a call.

It was in May 1962, that I first met Tom Sidney. I recognised
him easily, although the only photographs of him which I had
seen had been taken more than a quarter of a century before.
He was balding now and rather plumper, but with his bronzed
complexion, clear blue eyes, that regarded one quizzically and
humorously from beneath dark, luxuriant eyebrows, he looked
a remarkably spry seventy-three.

It turned out that Dr Binning had already written to him and
told him that I was engaged upon a study of the case, and Mr
Sidney generously agreed to do his best to answer any questions
that I cared to put to him. We met several times during his
stay in England and spent many hours together going over the

whole affair in the most minute detail. I found him a charming companion, patient, good humoured and astonishingly frank, and we have since become, and remained for more than a decade now, very close friends.

'Of course I was originally suspected by both Hedges and Morrish,' he admitted, 'though I was never actually accused. Not in so many words. But I know that Jackson, the coroner, thought that I was guilty. I heard afterwards that he had said as much at a dinner-party.

'I never cared for Duff, and he didn't like me, either. I saw as little of him as possible. He wasn't an attractive personality and none of the family could ever understand what Grace saw in him, or why she married him. She'd had quite a few offers of marriage, all from fine-looking men with plenty of money, and turned them down. I couldn't help feeling there was a touch of masochism in her choice of Duff. He could be pleasant enough when he wanted to, but he was unpopular with his colleagues. His clothes were always soiled and crumpled, and his hat was frightfully disreputable. I once offered him one of several old hats of mine, all of which I may say were in considerably better shape than the one he was wearing. I suppose it was a bit tactless of me, but I only meant it kindly. Duff was very, very angry indeed with me over it. He was an extremely proud sort of an individual.

'I'm pretty sure that he knew about the attention that Elwell was paying to Grace. That would have infuriated him. Grace had a temper, too, and I know for a fact that she and Edmund quarrelled. He was a rough kind of chap, and very intemperate sexually. I remember Elwell saying to me, "That man's not fit to be your sister's husband."

'Mother didn't like him either. Very shortly before he died, I heard that he was saying that he was going to sell something or other. I'm not sure what it was, but it may have been his life insurance policies, which he had settled on Grace when they were married. I can see my mother now, standing beside the fireplace with her head in her hands, telling me, "That *dreadful* little man is going to sell them." If he had done, that would have left Grace with no security of her own if anything had happened to him, and she would have been completely dependent on Mother. It seems a strange coincidence that Duff's death should have come at just this particular convenient and crucial moment.

'When his body was being taken away, Grace lay on a sofa shrieking and kicking her legs about hysterically in the air, and Mother told her to control herself. She was always a bit of an actress, and somehow I didn't feel that she really cared about the loss of Duff. Vera said to me shortly afterwards, "I don't understand Grace at all; she has got over Edmund's death so quickly."

'Later on, when they found the arsenic in Duff's body, I thought that Elwell had done it. It seemed to me that he had a very strong motive. We all knew that he and Grace were lovers, and my mother hoped that they would eventually marry. But Elwell wasn't the marrying sort. He was very promiscuous. My Uncle Willie[1] thought that the poison must have come from Elwell, and I actually accused him of being involved. The police went down to Cornwall and fetched him back from holiday, and took him to Scotland Yard, where they had him in tears.

'At first I was absolutely flummoxed. I couldn't imagine who had done the killings. But the more I studied the evidence, the clearer it became that it *must* have been either me or my sister. Well, I knew it wasn't me . . . so it *had* to be Grace.

'I know that Mr Ðeane, the Vicar of St Peter's, who lived opposite, thought that it was her, too. He told me, "I've known all along. I didn't like to mention it before, but when I buried Mr Duff I thought to myself, "This man has been put away." It was an odd thing to say, but Mr Deane never liked Grace. As a matter of fact, he didn't like Elwell either. I once saw him in a towering rage because a girl had confessed to him that Elwell had seduced her.

'Looking back now, I realise that Grace had not been herself for some time before Duff's death. When her daughter Suzanne died in 1924, she made the dead child's face up, dressed her in baby clothes, and propped her up in bed like a grotesque little doll. The nurse who had been called in to look after Suzanne during her illness told me, "I think your sister was mad."

'Grace behaved very oddly, too, shortly after Alastair was born. She upset the whole family by threatening that she would kill the baby unless she got some money. She said she needed £100. It was Vera who, in the end, gave it to her on "extended loan".

'I recall another remark that Grace made to me not long after Duff's death. She said, "I can kill people without leaving a trace." I forget what the conversation was about, but I didn't think much of it at the time. She was always inclined to be a romancer, and she'd often talk wildly and say the weirdest things. I thought she just did it for effect, and I used to take them with a pinch of salt. But, thinking it all over now, I'm convinced that Grace killed Duff.'

I asked Tom Sidney if he thought that she had also murdered her sister, Vera.

[1] William Stafford Sidney.

'Well, Vera and Grace always seemed quite friendly, and my mother was absolutely devoted to Vera. She was a very nice girl, rather religious. Much more so actually than my mother. Mother was a good woman, warm and kindly, and I was deeply attached to her, but she was a very strange person in some ways. She was rather intense, full of suppressed emotions and had a depth of character and a certain secretiveness which, from one point of view, might make her seem a much more likely poisoner than Grace, who was rather superficial. On the other hand, Grace had a curious, almost mesmeric influence over Mother. I sometimes wonder if she knew that Grace had poisoned Duff, perhaps even helped her to do so. Grace could have had some sort of hold over her. I just don't know.

'But one thing I *do* know is that Mother would never have harmed Vera. Yes, I think it must have been Grace who killed her.

'The morning Grace came to tell my wife and me that Vera had died, she seemed so happy about it that I said to Margaret, "There's something wrong with that girl."

'One reason why Grace might have killed Vera was because she thought that Vera was leading a useless life. I know that she held very strong views about people who were living lives that were, in her opinion, of no use to the community. It was almost a mania with her. And if a person who was leading a useless life could by their death provide Grace with money, she would probably have seen nothing wrong in their dying.

'I'm sure now, too, that Grace murdered Mother. *She* was leading a "useless" life. *Her* death meant money for Grace and her children. Grace and Mother were never particularly close, and judging by the way I saw Grace look at her sometimes, it almost seemed as if she hated her.

'I know the jury thought it possible that Mother might have poisoned Vera, and then committed suicide, but I think they were influenced by the fact that the mother of one of the jurors had tried to poison her entire family. I can imagine Mother killing herself in some circumstances, but not painfully. She had seen the agony in which Vera died, and nothing will ever convince me that she would knowingly have inflicted the same agony on herself.

'Again, Grace behaved extremely oddly after Mother's death. She made her face up heavily, and wandered around in a pair of silk pyjamas. I know it all sounds completely crazy, but that was the way it was.

'Uncle Willie was the first to accuse Grace to her face. He said to her in front of Fearnley-Whittingstall and Mr Smythe, the solicitor instructing him, "You must have poisoned them." Grace never batted an eyelid. She just got up and walked out of the room.

'At that time, I myself thought that it was Mrs Noakes who had poisoned Mother and Vera. She was a very strange witness, you know, saying that she'd seen me in the hall at Birdhurst Rise the morning of the day that Mother died, which was utterly untrue. It occurred to me that she might not be all there. Anyway, I decided to telephone Aunt Gwen[1] in Newcastle, to see if she could give me any evidence, but a newspaper friend of mine, Robert Kelly, told me that my telephone was being tapped. So instead, I travelled up to Newcastle by a circuitous route, and called on my aunt. I told her that I thought it was Mrs Noakes, but she said, "I'm sure it's your sister." And, later on, Aunt Gwen actually faced Grace with the accusation.

'I know that Hedges thought Grace was guilty. He told me so. So did Morrish. "I've been through the whole thing again and again," he said, "and I always come back to Mrs Duff."

'And that pretty well expresses how I feel about it today. It simply *had* to be Grace. It couldn't be anybody else. I admit that I shielded her at the inquests, but you see I just couldn't bring myself to believe that she would have killed Vera and Mother. I thought she was odd, but I didn't think that she was wicked.

'I went down with the police to John Duff's school, Monkton Combe, at Bath, to ask him some questions. Grace, who was fanatically devoted to her children, especially John, was absolutely furious. I tried to explain to her that I'd only done it to try to clear the matter up for her sake, but she turned on me in a frightful temper and said, "I'd rather die a hundred times than have a child of mine involved." And all through the inquests she was acting like an enemy to me.

'Then you must realise that at that time I wasn't a hundred per cent. certain in my own mind that Mother hadn't been somehow involved — at least in the death of Duff. About a year before he died I was using weed-killer in my garden and Mother said she wanted some for her gravel-path. I gave her a large quantity mixed with water in a watering-can, but I never saw her use it. I also considered it possible that she might have moved the Eureka tin, because I saw her coming out of my shed one day. It could have been that she got the arsenic for Grace to use on Duff.'

I asked Tom Sidney what were his views on the matter of motive.

'I think that Grace poisoned Duff because she had grown to hate him. I think that she killed Vera and Mother for their money. She was always careless about money. We all thought

---

[1] Mrs Gwendoline Greenwell.

her an awful fool the way she spent it when she had it. She once said that she was being blackmailed. When she came into her legacies from Vera and Mother's wills, I said to Hedges, "She should be all right for life now." Hedges was a wily old bird, a bit rough, but knowledgeable about people, quite a psychologist in his own way. "That'll all be gone in three years," he said.

'He was a year out. Within two years she had the brokers in. Her Aunt Amy[1] had to come to her aid. She paid off a hundred pounds for Grace, to get the bailiffs out of the house. Aunt Amy asked Grace what she had done with all the money that had been left to her, and she made the rather strange reply, "I had to get rid of it; it was blood-money."

'My mother's sister, Aunt Claire[2], seeing the ease with which Grace had got through the money, asked me, "Do you think she's being blackmailed?" I've often wondered.

'I remember that while the inquests were going on Elwell, who by the way got himself worked up into a terrible state when Mother died, told me, "Keep out of it. And steer clear of Grace. I know you know nothing about it, but keep clear." And Dr Binning, whom Grace had always disliked, said all along that he was certain that she was the murderess. Incidentally, while the case was on I saw a clairvoyant, and she told me, "Your sister is the killer."

'When the inquests were coming to an end, Superintendent Brown, of Scotland Yard, warned me to get away from Grace. He said he thought that she might try to poison me, and to tell you the truth I was afraid that she might. That's why I went to America. To get out of her way.'

Tom Sidney last saw his sister on the day after the third inquest ended — August 7th, 1929. She wrote to him once, but he did not answer her letter.

'By then I felt sure that she had murdered my mother and my sister,' he told me, 'and I never wanted to set eyes on her again.'

And, indeed, to the day of her death, he never did.

VI

Finally, I set to work to find Grace Duff.

Tom Sidney had told me that he hadn't the faintest idea where she was, and for weeks it looked as if I would never

---

[1] Gertrude Amy Stafford Sidney, who lived at St Leonards-on-Sea.

[2] Violet Emilia Sidney had two sisters, Alice, who died in childbirth, and Claire. She also had two brothers, Charles and Edward Lendy.

succeed in tracking her down.

Then I got a clue. Somebody knew somebody, who knew somebody, who thought that he had heard that she was living somewhere on the south coast. It was not much to go on, but at least that was better than Australia. I checked the voters' lists of every town in the area. It was a long, tedious business, but in the end I found her.

Within twenty-four hours, I was face to face with her.

It was at a quarter past three on a Sunday afternoon that I knocked at the door of a pebble-dashed house in a quiet seaside road. Grace Duff herself opened the door — a plump, slack woman, with a muddy complexion, a bush of wiry white hair, and bold, startling blue eyes, their whites stained a disconcertingly bright yellow. We shook hands, and while I told her who I was she stood warily at the door. She did not invite me into the house and was continually on the point of closing the door. I had the impression of a forceful, not very pleasant personality. Hostile, suspicious, she struck me as a hard, unyielding woman. Age, which so often softens people, had done nothing to make her gentle. It had withered her into harshness. She seemed like a bulky grey erratic, scored by the ice of an old guilt.

I explained that I was writing a monograph on the case, apologised for reopening an old wound, but said that I would be grateful if she would help me by answering a few questions.

'I don't know how you found me,' she said, 'but I have nothing to say to you.'

I was watching her closely all the time. Her lips said, 'It was all very painful and tragic for me,' but her eyes remained untouched by the slightest glimmer of recollected emotion.

Then, suddenly, her voice rose angrily.

'I will tell you nothing — NOTHING!'

And with a flash of the old decisiveness, she slammed the door in my face.

But her attitude had in fact told me a great deal. There was a curious quality of malevolence about her such as I had never encountered in anyone before. This, I felt, was a woman fully capable of murder.

Her ethos extended even to the house in which she lived. It was shabby and cracked, its paintwork flaking, and the shiny blue American cloth sun-blinds were all pulled down, as though in mourning for some half-remembered tragedy. There was a pall of seediness over everything. As I talked with Mrs Duff, I was aware of people moving stealthily, furtively, inside the house. The whole place seemed alerted and uneasy. I caught a glimpse of an old white-haired man creeping quietly through the hall and, later, as I walked down the road, I saw a younger man peeping out at me from behind the twitching curtains of an upper window.

I was to meet Grace Duff again some months later. This time the encounter was stormy. By then I had a great deal of evidence in my hands which I had lacked on the occasion of our previous meeting. This time, too, I was not alone. Dr Binning accompanied me.

It was the first time that he and Grace had seen each other since 1929.

Again, Mrs Duff did not invite us into the house, but she and Binning chatted quite amiably in the porch. The moment, however, the talk turned to the subject of the murders, her whole attitude changed, and when Binning mentioned the fact that some people had suggested that he had been implicated in the deaths she said with a strange laugh, 'That's absurd. You had nothing to do with them. But that's all I will say. I will not discuss anything of the past at all.'

The barriers were up. Mrs Duff was on the defensive.

I remained behind for a few minutes after Binning's departure, and it was then that a conversation took place between Grace Duff and myself which must, I think, be unique in the circumstances of a literary murder investigation.

R.W.E.: 'I know who committed the murders.'

Grace Duff: 'Many people think they know.'

R.W.E.: 'I have been into this case minutely, and I know who did them. You and I know that *you* did them. But don't worry, I shall publish nothing until . . .'

Grace Duff: (interrupting) 'Until I'm dead. Don't be too sure that you won't die first!' (She began to close the door.)

R.W.E.: 'Just one question. Where did you get the arsenic? From Tom's shed?'

Grace Duff: 'What arsenic?'

R.W.E.: 'The arsenic that killed your husband.'

Grace Duff: 'I wouldn't have killed my husband. He was a very nice man.'

R.W.E.: 'He was a very disagreeable man. He knocked you about, and was sexually intemperate.'

Grace Duff: 'He did not. There was no sex about him.'

R.W.E.: 'I have a large body of evidence to the contrary.'

Mrs Duff did not reply.

For a second or two she looked at me with an expression of undisguised hatred.

Then, for the second and last time, she slammed the door in my face.

VII

So now I had met them all — Grace Duff, Tom Sidney, Dr Elwell, Dr Binning, Mrs Noakes, Bentley Purchase and Inspector Morrish.

Through Purchase, I knew the views of Roome, Barker and Spilsbury. Through Hedges' family, I knew the views of Inspector Hedges. Through their respective widows, I knew the views of Fearnley-Whittingstall and Dr Jackson. I even knew what Mrs Greenwell and William Stafford Sidney had thought.

Only Morrish's views remained unexpressed. Only Dr Elwell remained half-convinced of Grace Duff's entire innocence — and he could scarcely be counted an unprejudiced witness.

Then, in March 1962, I received a communication from Dr Binning. He had, he said, thought the matter over, and had reached a decision. He was prepared to break the silence of thirty years.

What he had to tell was so important that it must have a chapter to itself.

10

DR BINNING REPORTS

I

'At about 8.20 a.m. on the morning of April 23rd, 1928, I had just finished breakfast when there was a ring at my front-door bell, which I answered personally, and there was Mr Edmund Duff. He apologised for calling unexpectedly but, as he was going off for a day or two's fishing, he hoped that I would be able to give him relief for some abdominal pain accompanied by diarrhoea. I took him into my consulting room and, after further questioning, took his pulse, which was normal; nor had he any temperature, and a clean tongue. I got him to undress sufficiently for me to examine his abdomen, which I did, but could find no definite signs of any condition, excepting some slight tenderness around the appendix area. I prescribed a bismuth mixture for him, and told him to go fishing as he had arranged.

Duff, fifty-eight years old, was of medium height with a tendency to obesity. He never looked a clean type of man, sallow yet swarthy complexion — perhaps tanned by Nigerian suns. He was not a lovable man, even in his habits. For instance, on the morning in question he produced live fish bait from his jacket pocket with no wrapping around it. Then he was always very nervous as to his health and I was often consulted by him for very flimsy reasons. I thought that this occasion was on a par with some of his previous visits.

I did not see Duff again until the morning of April 27th, when he told me that he had been fishing in Hampshire after leaving my house, and had been fairly comfortable. He had eaten something at Salisbury — sandwiches, I think, with beer — and then, when he got home, he had a light supper, accompanied by two bottles of beer. His night had been very disturbed owing to severe diarrhoea with gastric pain and cramp in his legs, all of which were increasing.

He was also seen by Dr R.G. Elwell, whose partner I was. Seen later by me, his condition had deteriorated considerably; pulse rapid, temperature subnormal, abdomen generally tender. He was walking about in his agony, doubled up with pain, and had extreme tenesmus.

I should like to make a note here concerning tenesmus. This

is a spasm or continual straining of the rectum and anal canal
to empty the bowel, without any evacuation of faeces, and so
extremely painful — as it was in this case — that the patient
holds his hand to his anus to try by his own manual pressure to
relieve the spasm and pain. I shall be referring to this condition
again later.

The man's agony — cold beads of sweat were on his brow and
there was some retching — compelled me to give him two injections of morphia. In about an hour he gained some relief but,
at about 11 p.m., in the presence of his wife, who watched the
closing scene standing at the end of the bed, he died.

Mrs Duff was most helpful, and apparently very solicitous as
to his condition, but I had cause to know something of her life
with Duff. About a year before his death she had given birth to
a child, and some *twelve days* after her confinement I had
occasion to examine her. I found her body, especially the arms
and legs, covered with bruises. She told me that her husband had
forced her, much against her will, into sexual intercourse. I felt
very sorry for her and a loathing contempt for Duff.

As to the cause of Duff's death I knew not, and asked that a
post-mortem be made. It was performed by Dr Brontë. The
result — a finding of death from natural causes. This I always
felt had been quite wrong, and in conversation with Dr Beecher
Jackson I made it quite clear that I did not agree with the
verdict.

I now come to February 14th, 1929, when I was called to
29 Birdhurst Rise to see Miss Vera Sidney. The patient gave a
history of gastric pain with diarrhoea in the course of the
previous forty-eight hours, but had so far recovered that the day
before she had got up and gone out. On returning home, and
after eating lunch, the diarrhoea and vomiting had returned.
She was put on a milky diet and a bismuth and opium mixture
prescribed. She was told to remain in bed. Examination gave
no definite physical signs. There was a slight temperature,
pulse slightly increased, and she complained of general body
pains. When I saw her, between 4 and 5 p.m. on February 14th,
she said that she had had a very disturbed night on account of
continued diarrhoea with some retching. Increased doses of her
mixture had been ordered, with milk and chicken broth as diet.
A visiting nurse was now in attendance.

At about 8 p.m. I was hurriedly called, and arrived to find
her condition much worse — temperature under 100°F., but
pulse now rapid, and diarrhoea with tenesmus present.

As the patient had become very dehydrated, I gave her an
intravenous saline up to one pint, and there was an improve-
ment in the pulse and general condition, but this was not
maintained and I attempted to give a further intravenous saline,

but was unsuccessful because of the collapse of the veins. I then substituted for this a subcutaneous saline in the sub-mammary area.

The visiting nurse had left, and I was helped thereafter by Mrs Duff, until Elwell, who had gone off to get a night nurse, returned. I found Mrs Duff's single attendance somewhat em-barrassing, especially as I had failed to give a second intravenous saline, when I was giving the subcutaneous injection. I felt that I would be better by myself and asked Mrs Duff to leave me, and here I really did get a shock for, happening to glance at the lady, I saw that she was looking at me with what I can only describe as a look of intense hatred. However I persisted, and she did go, while I did my best for the patient, who was now obviously dying.

Some five minutes later, there was a gentle knock at the door, and Mrs Duff reappeared with a cup of tea in her hand. She said she felt I ought to have it as I looked very tired. I could only say thank you, and asked her to place it near me on the bedside table, adding that I would drink it presently. I was then fully engaged in giving the saline. She was very charming — such a change from her previous look — and left me.

At this point I must make a digression to relate a scene being enacted in a house not a quarter of a mile away. About the time Mrs Duff brought me that cup of tea, a patient of mine who had a very ailing baby and who felt very dependent on my daily visits, suddenly awoke and, declaring that "Dr Binning was in great danger," implored her husband to ring my house, or get in touch with me at once.

This lady was, in her own words, "psychic". For instance, when her husband was blown up and buried by a shell burst while fighting on the Somme, his wife was at that very moment conscious that he was in great danger.

When, at about eleven o'clock that night of February 14th, she insisted upon her husband's communicating with me, he apparently remonstrated with her, but as she got into an almost hysterical state, he got up, put on his dressing-gown, and was going downstairs to telephone, when suddenly she said that there was no need to do anything now as the danger was past.

All this I was told next morning by the lady herself, and it was then that I realised that at the precise moment when she had this "psychic storm" I was being presented with that cup of tea by Mrs Duff. I may say that the lady in question could not have known that I was tending a death-bed the previous night.

To return to the sickroom.

I continued the saline until Elwell returned with a nurse, but my efforts were useless and, at 12.20 a.m. on February 15th, Vera Sidney died. I watched Mrs Duff standing at the end of the bed. She showed no emotion whatsoever. Just those clear blue eyes of hers concentrated on the death-bed scene.

I, for one, felt very upset over the whole illness, and was glad to get out of the room for a few minutes to visit the toilet. On returning, I found that that special cup of tea prepared for me by Mrs Duff had gone, taken away by Mrs Duff, who was going to make tea again for us all. We drank it with no untoward effects.

As to the death certificate, I believe Elwell gave one. I know I did not, for here again I was at a loss to account for death.

We proceed now to March 5th, 1929.

Mrs Duff called at my house at about 2 p.m. on that day, and asked me if I would come to her mother at 29 Birdhurst Rise, who seemed to be very ill — and that within the last hour. I went at once, only giving Mrs Duff time to get well ahead of me. But what was my surprise to see her walking slowly and almost nonchalantly up the road in front of me, so much so that I had to slow down my pace considerably, as I did not want to join her.

Arrived at the house, I found her mother, Mrs Violet Emilia Sidney, sitting in a chair in the dining-room. Then she got up and started to walk about, retching and in great gastric pain. This had all commenced shortly after her lunch. She had taken a dose of her tonic. She showed me the bottle, in which there was a small amount of medicine left. It should have been a perfectly clear red liquid, but in it I saw a fair deposit of what looked like sago grains. I at once took charge of the bottle, and later handed it to the coroner's officer.

Mrs Sidney kept on saying that she had been poisoned. I so well remember being left for a moment or two alone in the room with Mrs Sidney and asking her, "Who gave you this?"

And her answer was, "Please, Oh! please, Dr Binning, don't ask me that."

A minute or so later, a sudden illumination of her case came to me. When walking about in a semi-stooping attitude she began holding her anus — tenesmus having commenced — just as Duff had done some eleven months before. It was then that I thought to myself, "My God! This is the Duff case all over again."

We got her to bed, and when she was being undressed by Mrs Duff and her cook I noticed how soiled her undergarments were with faeces, diarrhoeic in character.

I left a message for Elwell to come, and tried to get Sir William Willcox, a well-known forensic expert, but he was unavailable. So, instead, I got hold of Dr F.J. Poynton, a first-class clinician on the staff of my old hospital (University College) who, when I was a student there, lectured us on forensic medicine.

I met him at the station about an hour later and gave him what information I could on the case. I also told him that I felt that there was a definite relationship in the three cases — Duff's, Vera Sidney's and now Mrs Sidney's.

Poynton made an examination — as much as was possible under the circumstances — but no diagnosis was made. That her condition was critical, was apparent — the increasing gastric pain, tenesmus, cramp and distress, subnormal temperature and rapidly increasing pulse. One or two injections of heroin were given to relieve the extreme agony suffered by the patient, and all was done to make her comfortable during the last hours of her life. In the early hours of the evening her heart failed her and she died. Again, Mrs Duff was a spectator from the end of the bed.

It has been reported that I "fell back on the theory of *food* poisoning." On poisoning . . . yes. But not specifically food. As to Mrs Sidney's having taken her own life, that was completely incompatible with her character and life. She was a gentlewoman, deeply religious, and in spite of her recent bereavement in Vera's death accepted the latter in a truly Christian way, and remained calm in her mind. This I know from one or two visits I had paid her after her bereavement. No, she did not take her own life.

I immediately informed the coroner of this death, and a post-mortem was subsequently performed by Sir Bernard Spilsbury, with what result we all now well know — "Death due to arsenical poisoning."

Previous to this case, Sir Bernard had made several post-mortem examinations for me on private cases. Never throughout my career did I sign a medical certificate unless I was quite certain of the cause of death, and as I had doubts on two or three occasions I got Spilsbury's help, so that I could give a valid certificate. I came in this way to know him quite well, and on hearing the result of his autopsy on Mrs Sidney I met him and told him that I was certain Duff died in the same way, going over his symptoms and comparing them with those of Mrs Sidney. As a result of our conversations, Sir Bernard got permission to exhume Vera Sidney's body, and later, Duff's.

I cannot say how many times I was interviewed by Inspector Hedges and his assistant Mr Reginald Morrish of our local CID. Every bit of knowledge on the case I had, I gave freely. Every channel of investigation was explored, but mistakes were made, as will be seen later, which precluded any chance of conviction.

At least once or twice a week I was interviewed, and always in the late evening. About the only amusing incident for me in all these meetings happened one night around nine o'clock when dusk was falling. I went to put my car away in a garage a little distance from my house, and was met on the doorstep by Hedges, Morrish and Superintendent Brown, one of the "Big

Five" from Scotland Yard. I asked them to come in and wait while I put my car away, but they said not to mind about it as they would not detain me very long.

An hour or so later there was a ring at my front-door, and I went to find a policeman. He apologised for disturbing me, but said that he required my name etc., for leaving a car unattended without lights, which was then a punishable offence in the metropolitan area. I said he might as well come in and get his information and I showed him into my consulting room, where were the CID officers. As in one voice they asked what he wanted, and I explained that he wanted particulars regarding my car offence. Poor chap, he made a very hurried exit, following a somewhat peremptory and unprintable order from the CID. I was sorry for him, but his introduction among that triumvirate saved my being prosecuted!

I was present at the mortuary at Mayday Hospital on the morning of May 18th when Spilsbury performed his post-mortem on the exhumed body of Edmund Duff. The coffin was placed on a couple of trestles beside a slab. The under-takers undid the screws securing the lid, and Baker, the P.M. room assistant, carefully laid out the operating tools. Spilsbury then turned to me and asked that I give my nose a thorough "blow", as he was doing. This done, he secured a strong screw-driver and prised open the lid of the coffin, on the side nearest us, to about an inch and, looking at me, said, "Give a sniff." This we did simultaneously and, standing up, Spilsbury said one word, "Arsenic." There was no delay, no hesitation, in saying the incriminating word.

The lid was removed, also the covering shroud, and with Baker's help ties were carefully put round the body to enable us to lift it out of the coffin. With Baker squatting on the slab, and we two on the other side, the body was gently raised and got on to the slab, and there divested of funeral garments. Not a very pleasant sight to me, unaccustomed to exhumed bodies, but poor Baker was as nauseated as I was. I remember saying to him, "Are you feeling sick?" And his reply, "No, but I'm ———— near it." The skin was very discoloured and on many parts of it a greenish-grey fungus was growing.

The post-mortem was proceeding quietly with that meticulous care bestowed on all work done by Spilsbury, when there was a peremptory knock on the door. Baker unlocked the door and Dr Brontë came in smoking his pipe. Spilsbury stopped what he was doing and fixing his gaze on Brontë said, "Good-morning. I have no objections to your being present but you must stop smoking, and I wish to have no remarks from you." There was a complete silence. Brontë stopped smoking and remained a quiet member of the party throughout the proceedings. Spilsbury addressed any remarks he made to me or Baker.

We had just opened the first p.m. wound, and what was most noticeable at once was the well-preserved condition of the tissues generally. As Spilsbury said to me, "Quite as good as any dissecting-room body." This preservation was due to the arsenic in the body. Shortly after this, Brontë, who had maintained the silence imposed on him, left us abruptly. The results of the investigations were later given at the inquest. The coroner's verdict — "Death from arsenical poisoning."

It is obvious that a great mistake had occurred at Brontë's previous examination. It is known that another post-mortem had been conducted at the same time, I believe a female body, and by the greatest misfortune the specimens of gut and so forth which had been sent for analysis were sent from that other body. What a tragedy, for had the true cause of death been found then, two other people, Vera Sidney and her mother, might have been saved the same fate.

The inquests on the three cases lasted over a period of almost five months and, as they proceeded to a close, tension increased among those concerned. One experience which I can never forget was this. A session had been held in the morning and we had gathered for the afternoon one. It was a beautiful and warm day and we waited outside until it was time to begin. I was walking on the grass lawn outside the entrance of the Queen's Road Homes, when I was joined by Mrs Duff. I had avoided the family as much as possible so far, however we walked about slowly, and talk was on the past sessions and of the evidence given.

Suddenly, Mrs Duff stopped, looked straight at me, and said, "Dr Binning, you think you're going to put a rope round my neck, but you're not clever enough."

I was speechless, and with a hurried adieu went to a room reserved for doctors and any counsel or solicitors concerned. There I met Fearnley-Whittingstall, to whom I related the episode. He was very upset over it and he walked about in a very agitated state, and suddenly lay down on the cold concrete floor, stretched right out on his back with his arms raised to support his head. After a few minutes he was fully himself again, and shortly we entered court.

As well as the inquests I had, as I have said, the CID to contend with. They were most keen to get a conviction in the case, and I think there would have been one had Dr Ryffel, who analysed the contents of the medicine-bottle containing Mrs Sidney's tonic plus a sago-like sediment, used only half the contents of that bottle for his examination, and left half of the original contents. The CID gave me a sample of the weed-killer thought to have been used by the poisoner, and I produced for them, from this weed-killer and a quantity of the tonic prescribed for Mrs Sidney, a mixture of exactly the same appearance as that which was in the original bottle that had been analysed.

I was very worried as the CID said my evidence was vital, and that they would go ahead for a conviction. Fortunately, I had a very great friend in the late J.G. Hurst, K.C., who wisely advised me not to accede to this request in view of the fact that it was only my word that could be given. As the latter said, I should be "torn from limb to limb under cross-examination." The standard of comparison had gone.

Then again, the CID had, rightly I thought, been investigating the very sudden death of Miss Anna Maria Kelvey, who had died on January 12th, 1927, while a paying guest at Mrs Duff's. My partner, Elwell, had been the doctor in attendance and he certified death as due to cerebral haemorrhage. I know that he was asked for, and gave, a report on the case, and maintained his diagnosis. But so often do I feel there should have been an autopsy on her body, and even as I write, over thirty years later, this could yet be done. For arsenic remains in a body for years, *and were it found it would give absolute proof of the guilty party* — and vindication of Dr Elwell if the findings were negative.

In all murder cases a motive is sought, and in these cases it is difficult to find. So far as Duff's case went, I feel that he deserved punishment for his behaviour towards his wife. But was there something more? Here was a very handsome woman, a brunette with good looks, a pleasing personality and beautiful eyes. I saw those eyes at their brightest when observing death was coming to the three victims. They were never lovelier than when she hovered over the three death-beds. There was a gloating in the look, combined with a transport. Very often have I wondered if there was not present a diseased psychological condition. Perhaps psychologists could have given a clue. When from time to time in later years I met Spilsbury, he would say, "And how are the clear lake-blue eyes going?"

I had heard rumours connecting Elwell's name with that of Mrs Duff, but, being a very charming man, his name was often talked of where other women were concerned. Of this I took no notice, and so far as Elwell is concerned I leave any judgment of him to others. I cannot, however, see his being implicated in the Duff case. He was, in my opinion, too clever a man ever to allow himself to be a party or a shield to anything criminal. He was the "Prince Charming" to many of his — especially lady — patients; but on the other hand, he was scurrilously referred to by others of the same sex.

Not long after the inquests had terminated, I was called on by Mrs Duff to attend her youngest child late one evening. I had seen her several times in the interim. The child was very ill, high temperature, rapid pulse and very infected throat. It looked suspiciously like diphtheria, and I secured anti-diphtheric serum, injected it, and saw the baby comfortable. As I was about to leave, Mrs Duff took me into her living-room. She was wearing a very loose and charming negligee and offered me a whisky, adding with a smile, "And I promise not to put any arsenic in it!" I felt home was the best place for me, and there I went without my whisky.

Watching a television play a short time ago — to be exact, "The Evil Flower" — I saw the villainess in the play looking at a man dying. With a gloating, sadistic expression on her face, she exclaimed, "Death is like wine to me." Could there, I wondered, be any resemblance between that scene and Mrs Duff's presence at the three death-beds?

Again, perhaps the psychologists could explain.

I had it on good authority that this charming lady, in the course of a discussion on social problems, said that she felt that individuals who were of no social value to the community were of no further use in the world!

From the deaths of all the deceased Mrs Duff did get some financial gain, as did Tom Sidney, I believe, in the cases of his mother and sister. I was also informed that Mrs Duff's children, John and Mary, each received legacies under Miss Kelvey's will.

Of course there were many who suspected Tom Sidney. Even, I think, at one time the coroner himself, whose brother told my wife at a dinner at which they were both guests that Dr Jackson said that he had seen the same look on Tom Sidney's face during a hearing that he had once seen on a murderer's face. It was on this that he had apparently based his suspicion! My wife was very indignant but, maintaining the ethics proper to a doctor's wife, said nothing.

Tom Sidney, when his mother died, insisted that the very strictest investigation be made at once into all these deaths. Would a guilty man adopt that attitude? Solid weed-killer was found in his garden, but Mrs Duff had access both to his house and to the garden. Many discussions I had with him, many and searching questions put, but all were answered without evasion or hesitation. It is difficult for me to incriminate him.

My summation of Grace Duff — a psychopathic personality; and it is my opinion that she was the poisoner in all three cases.

Experts in criminology may come to a definite conclusion one day as to who the poisoner was. Assumption has been rife ever since the crimes were committed, but there has always been insufficient evidence against the culprit.

These notes, absolutely factual and unembellished, have been written with the hope that they may lead to a more intimate

understanding of these tragedies, and perhaps lead to further
investigations being carried out. The exhumation and examination of Miss Kelvey's body for instance.

For my part, I felt it was all a very sorry business. Here was
I, a generally well-experienced medical man, and had been
unable to diagnose acute arsenical poisoning. My only consola-
tion in this was the fact that Dr Poynton failed to do so in Mrs
Sidney's case. It is with a wry smile that I think of medical
students on examination in forensic medicine being "ploughed"
if they fail to give a clear exposition on arsenical poisoning.
Had I been asked at any time previous to the inquests if I had
suspected arsenic in these cases, I should have given an emphatic
"No" in reply. Never among such gentlefolk could such an idea
have been entertained.

I end these notes with one definite conclusion — namely that
any poisoner found guilty of such a crime, absolutely pre-
meditated, should receive capital punishment. The cruelty inflicted on the victims is indescribable. The excruciating agony
undergone calls for the most condign punishment.

Nearly eighteen months have elapsed since the foregoing notes
were compiled, and in this time certain events have occurred
on which I think I ought to remark.

Dr Elwell died in December 1961, aged eighty-six.

In June 1962, I visited Mrs Duff at her home on the south
coast in company with Richard Whittington-Egan.

I found Grace Duff looking very fit and well, and although
now her hair was quite grey, she was still a very good-looking
woman, and still had those clear lake-blue eyes as of old.

Personally, I was well received, though we never got beyond
the front-door. I think I would have been invited in had I been
by myself. We chatted about the past — the death of her son,
John; the death of our daughter, Elizabeth; her daughter, Mary;
her son, Alastair.

When she realised who was with me, her whole attitude
changed from what had been friendliness to one of defensive-
ness, especially when Whittington-Egan began asking questions.
She tried to close the door on us.

A day or two previous to this visit, I had a meal with Whittington-Egan, who informed me that on a visit to Elwell in 1961
they discussed those who might have murdered the three victims, Whittington-Egan even mentioning my name. Elwell's
reply was (and I quote his words here), "Yes, I think Binning
was quite capable of it." Had I known when he was alive that
he had made such a statement, I should have taken very strong
action.

When I visited Mrs Duff I told her what had been said about

me. Her comment, without the slightest hesitation, was, "That's absurd. You had nothing to do with them (the tragedies)."

When further I referred to Elwell's death in the previous December, she said, "Yes — and left £80,000. He told me he was going to leave his money to his three godchildren. Alastair was one. But he never left him anything." It was obvious she felt very hurt in this matter.

Candy, the analyst who has been spoken of in this book, and I had an interesting conversation. He was an old, sick man. We were talking about the fact that he had failed to find any arsenic in Duff's body after the first post-mortem. He told me that he had tested for it, but must have missed it, or words to that effect. Then he added, "It really doesn't concern me much. I am more concerned with the next world now."

I have been asked at this time to express my opinion of Elwell. The ethics of my profession preclude me from being candid. All that I will say is that I was most thankful when our partnership ended and, as I have said previously, I leave others to assess his character.

I should like to conclude these notes with an interesting episode in the life of Vera Sidney a year or so before she died. She went with some golfing friends to the Mitcham Fair, and each went in to see a clairvoyant. Vera, asked by her friends what the clairvoyant had told her, said the fortune-teller refused any information on seeing her hands, as the reading of them was too bad for anyone to know. This I have on unimpeachable authority — a friend of the deceased's.'

John Archibald Binning

11

BY WHOSE HAND?

I

By whose hand then did Edmund Duff, Vera Sidney, and Violet Emilia Sidney meet their deaths?

Leaving aside the opinions — and no matter how well-informed the sources, or vehemently expressed the suspicions, they are only opinions — of those who gave their testimony to me at a second hearing, is it possible to formulate a convincing answer to that question on the basis of logical argument and legitimate inference?

Let us look more analytically into this matter of culpability.

As the coroner pointed out, the three crimes were clearly the work of one hand. Unconsciously, every criminal hall-marks his crimes with the stamp of his individualistic procedure. The *modus operandi* is what the police grandiloquently call it. In the Croydon affair a simple analysis shows that each of the killings presented three common factors:

1. The victim was always despatched at a time when he or she was vaguely unwell of demonstrably natural causes. Edmund Duff was off-colour. Vera Sidney was suspected to be suffering from gastric influenza. Violet Emilia Sidney was shocked and below par.

2. The victim was always given the poison in a vehicle to which, normally, only he or she might be expected to have access. Only Edmund Duff drank beer. Only Vera Sidney took soup. Only Violet Emilia Sidney was taking Metatone.

3. In each case it was always the same poison — arsenic — which was employed, and it was always administered in liquid.

As to the identity of the poisoner, there are only two alternatives. Either the criminal was an outsider, or he or she was a member of the family — that to include servants who were employed in the respective households.

Taking stock of the first two of the three factors which the crimes present in common, it becomes apparent that the poisoner must have been intimately acquainted with the conditions and habits of the victims. Must have known the day-to-day states of their health. Must have been familiar with their individual tastes and idiosyncrasies in matters of food and drink.

It follows that the outsider, maniacally roaming Croydon and, within eleven months, by incredible coincidence, picking first on the Duff household and then on the Sidney household, to sate a motiveless, meaningless blood lust, vanishes into the mist of fancy, from which no reasoning mind could ever have conjured him. The side-doors of the houses in South Park Hill Road and Birdhurst Rise may have remained habitually unlocked in the daytime. So, no doubt, did the side-doors of scores of other houses in the South Croydon area. That circumstance is not in dispute. But the mere fact of its being so does not justify the assumption that they provided ingress to some hypothetical killer, concerning whose possible identity, or even existence, there was at no time the barest hint of evidence.

We are left then with a handful of rational suspects — the members of, and visitors to, the households where the deaths took place.

Such visitors as there were at the material times — two doctors, Mrs Sidney's sister-in-law, a clergyman's wife, several tradespeople — are hardly serious candidates for suspicion.

The servants surely can be dismissed. None of them, except the near-blind, deaf and aged jobbing gardner, Arthur Henry Lane, had access to both households. What is more, neither he, nor any of the others for that matter, can be demonstrated to have had either the mentality, or any conceivable motive, for murder.

There remain only two feasible suspects — Tom Sidney and Grace Duff.

But it is possible even further to narrow the field by selecting the case in which the conditions surrounding the commission of the crime were most restricted. That case is the murder of Edmund Duff. In my submission, answer the question 'Who killed Edmund Duff?' and you can name the triple poisoner.

II

Accepting the premise that these crimes were — and it seems logically inescapable that they undoubtedly were — the work of one hand, let us apply the three classic criteria customarily employed to establish guilt of homicide — means, opportunity and motive — to the two prime suspects.

In the case of Edmund Duff opportunity is the crucial factor.

Duff returns from Fordingbridge to Hurst View on the evening of April 26th, 1928, off-colour, sorry for himself, but, according

to the medical evidence, by no means a man at death's door.
In that house there is a maid, Miss Amy Clarke, there are
three young children and there is his wife, Grace. The only
visitors who see Duff in the twenty-eight hours that elapse
before he dies of arsenical poisoning are Dr Elwell and Dr
Binning.

It is, I suppose, within the bounds of possibility, I will put
it no higher, that Tom Sidney, or Vera Sidney, or Violet Emilia
Sidney, could, at some time previous to the early evening of
April 26th have stolen into the larder at Hurst View, either to
doctor, or more probably to replace with an already-doctored
bottle, one of the half-dozen or so bottles of beer that were
habitually stored there. But even if one or other of them had
done so, how could that person have known that Edmund Duff
would return from Fordingbridge indisposed? And, as we have
seen, the prior natural indisposition of the victim appears to
have been a constant and essential prelude to the commission
of these crimes. How, moreover, could he or she have been sure
that Duff would have selected the one arsenic-laced bottle on
that appropriate evening?

There is the possibility that he had deliberately taken poison
home Duff met somebody who gave him something to eat or
drink that was poisoned. But if so, he would surely have said
something of that meeting.

There is the possibility that he had deliberately poisoned
himself. But if so, is it likely that he would have displayed the
bewildered alarm which he did display during his terminal illness?

Weighing all the relevant factors, the one person who would
seem to have had sufficient reason, together with adequate
opportunity, to administer arsenic to him was Grace Duff.

Take now the case of Vera Sidney. It is rather more compli-
cated. There are two distinct occasions on which arsenic is
administered to her. Firstly in the soup which she had on the
evening of Monday, February 11th, 1929, and secondly in the
soup served to her at lunch-time on Wednesday, February 13th,
1929.

According to Mrs Noakes, the soup consumed at supper on
February 11th had been prepared by her on Sunday, February
10th. She made the soup for Wednesday's lunch on the morning
of Tuesday, February 12th. In both cases the soup was kept in
the pantry. This pantry was situated in the cellar of 29 Birdhurst Rise, and was approached by a flight of stairs which
descended from a passage leading from the side-door of the
house. The entrance to the cellar stairs was only a few feet
from the side-door. That same side-door which was so frequently
left unlocked. Who was it who, on two separate occasions,
crept stealthily down those dim backstairs to the cellar pantry,

on either February 10th or February 11th, and again on either February 12th or February 13th, and secretly slipped a quantity of arsenic into those two distinct pans of soup which stood upon the shelf?

Was it Violet Emilia Sidney? She could have done so. But where was the motive? For what possible reason should she have wished to destroy the daughter upon whom all her life she had doted? There is ample testimony that she was not insane. There is ample testimony that her grief at Vera's death was not simulated. One must apply the yardstick of common-sense in these cases, and it recoils from the suggestion that this devoted mother should, wickedly, feloniously and of malice afore-thought, have twice set a dish of arsenic before her ewe-lamb.

Was it Mrs Noakes, the cook-general? Again common-sense emphatically rejects her. Moreover, Miss Vera was the apple of her eye.

Was it Mrs Greenwell, Vera's aunt and Mrs Sidney's sister-in-law? One cannot think so. Besides, she had not been near the house when Vera, Mrs Noakes, and the cat were poisoned on February 11th.

Was it Tom Sidney? There is not a shred of evidence that he visited the house on February 10th, 11th, 12th or 13th. And you may be sure that the police looked long and hard for any such evidence.

Who *was* in the house on Birdhurst Rise on February 10th, 12th, 13th and 14th? Grace Duff. And she admitted that she might have been there on the morning of February 11th also.

Finally, we come to March 5th, 1929, and the death by arsenic of Violet Emilia Sidney.

Here a new problem is involved. Was this murder or suicide? Astoundingly in my submission, the jury could not decide. With two clear-cut cases of murder staring them in the face they theorised about suicide. Of course they must not be too severely blamed, for it was not within the legal province of their terms of reference to take cognisance of the other two cases. 'You must find your verdict entirely on the evidence you have heard, and you must disregard any rumours you may have heard,' the coroner warned them. The fault there lay squarely with Dr Jackson, who had misunderstood certain advice given to him by Sir Archibald Bodkin, the Director of Public Prosecutions, to hold all three inquests together. In fact, he opened them sep-arately. In consequence, the jury said, in effect, that this bereaved and bewildered old lady might have murdered Vera, and then poisoned herself. But would she, having witnessed the terrible agony of Vera's last hours, deliberately have selected for herself this same excruciating end? Would she have repeated, as she did over and over again, her suspicion that she had been

252 *Pursuance of One*

poisoned, if she had knowingly swallowed a self-administered
lethal dose of arsenic? It won't do. It simply is not consistent
with our knowledge of human psychology. She was a fairly
religious woman. A strong-minded, morally upright woman. She
had actually stated her view that suicide was an abominable sin.
I am sure that the suicide theory can be utterly discounted.

Who then struck her down?

Mrs Noakes? She was leaving Mrs Sidney's service, anyway.
There was not a whisper of evidence that she bore her mistress
any grudge. On the contrary, she appeared to have been quite
fond of her.

Tom Sidney? He was at his mother's house on March 4th,
though he denied having been there on the morning of March 5th.
Mrs Noakes was, at first, adamant that she had seen him in the
hall of Number 29 shortly before lunch-time on that day. Under
cross-examination, however, she subsequently agreed that she
could have been mistaken, as indeed she proved to have been
mistaken in her recollection of the dates of certain other
events. And even if Sidney *had* been at the house that lunch-
time, he could not have entered the dining-room, where his
mother was then sitting, and interfered with her bottle of
Metatone without her having seen him do so.

What of Grace Duff? She, too, was in the house on the afternoon of March 4th, and again on the morning of March 5th.
Furthermore, there is evidence that she was left alone in the
dining-room — where the bottle of Metatone was very likely
kept — while her mother went upstairs to fetch something. Less
than three hours later, Violet Emilia Sidney was to pour her last,
fatal dose from that same bottle. And six hours after that she
would be dead.

So much for opportunity. Let us turn now to the question of
means.

Here we come up against a very serious obstacle. Ironically,
it is not absence, but abundance of arsenic that is the embarrassment.

There was so much confusing courtroom talk of tins and drums
of weed-killer that it may be well at this point to enumerate
clearly and succinctly the sources of arsenic that were shown
to be in existence.

1   A tin of Eureka (solid) weed-killer.
    This was voluntarily produced by Tom Sidney from his
    shed in the garden at Pauliva, 6 South Park Hill Road.

2   A gallon tin drum of Noble's liquid weed-killer.
    This had been purchased by Edmund Duff on October
    16th, 1927. It was in the possession of Grace Duff until

September 1928, when she gave it to her jobbing gardener, Arthur Henry Lane.

3   An old, rusty Eureka (solid) weed-killer tin.
This was recovered from Mrs Sidney's garden shed at 29 Birdhurst Rise. It contained only a few specks of arsenical weed-killer.

The balance of the evidence indicates that this last tin was of no importance. We are left, therefore, with Tom Sidney's tin of Eureka (solid) weed-killer, and Grace Duff's drum of Noble's liquid weed-killer.

It is now necessary to introduce one or two technical considerations.

Eureka weed-killer was a solid powder, consisting of a mixture of 291 grains of arsenic, in the form of arsenious oxide, to every ounce of powder. The substance mixed with the arsenic was caustic soda.

Noble's liquid weed-killer was a very much weaker solution of arsenic, containing only 140 grains of arsenic, in the form of arsenious oxide, to every fluid ounce of the mixture. According to Mr Henry Atkinson Noble, the son of Samuel Noble, the South Croydon chemist who supplied it, water was the base in which the mixture of arsenic and caustic soda was suspended.

In Dr Ryffel's view, the arsenic in suspension in Noble's liquid weed-killer was not present in sufficient quantity to produce the observed strength in the fluid analysed from Mrs Sidney's medicine-bottle.

It was also stated by both Dr Binning and Dr Elwell that, of the mixtures of Metatone and weed-killer experimentally produced by Dr Ryffel, the one which was obtained by mixing the solid Eureka weed-killer with Metatone bore the closest resemblance in appearance to the fluid which they had originally observed in Mrs Sidney's medicine-bottle.

Moreover, Dr Ryffel himself gave it as his expert opinion that Eureka solid weed-killer was more likely than Noble's liquid weed-killer to have been the source of the lethal doses or arsenic.

Bear in mind Mrs Sidney's complaints of the bitterness and grittiness of her last dose of medicine.

I have myself recently tasted a sample of pure arsenic. It is quite flavourless. But caustic soda has a bitter, burning flavour and a gritty consistency. It might well have been the caustic soda content of Eureka weed-killer added to her Metatone that made Mrs Sidney's tonic bitter and gritty.

That is not to say, however, that it necessarily *was* Eureka, or any other weed-killer for that matter, which was the source of the arsenic used to murder Duff and the two Sidney women. Arsenic is available in many forms other than weed-killer. Dr Ryffel's experiments did not prove that the arsenic added to the Metatone was in the form of Eureka weed-killer, although they did suggest that it was very unlikely to have been derived from Noble's liquid weed-killer.

With regard to Tom Sidney's tin of Eureka, he purchased it perfectly openly from a chemist's shop in Croydon, signing the poison register for it with his correct name and address, and he subsequently produced it quite voluntarily for the police. Nevertheless, the fact remains that once he had acquired that tin of weed-killer he had in his possession the means of poisoning his brother-in-law, his sister and his mother, had he wished to do so.

If we accept Dr Ryffel's contention that Noble's liquid weedkiller lacked the essential observed potency, and I think that we must, then Grace Duff was not shown to be in possession of the arsenic, in the form of weed-killer at any rate, with which to poison her mother's Metatone.

But where is the evidence that it was *arsenic derived from weed-killer* that was used?

All that the evidence amounts to is that remains of fatal concentrations of arsenic were found in Edmund Duff's body, in Vera Sidney's body, in Violet Emilia Sidney's body and in the dregs of her tonic. It is perfectly possible, though not perhaps likely, that all this talk of weed-killer may have been a gigantic red herring. How do we know that the poisoner did not acquire the arsenic from some entirely different source which was never traced?

We will suppose, however, that it *was* Eureka weed-killer that was employed, and it is my own view that that was indeed the case. Does this exculpate Grace Duff? I say that it does not. I will go further than that. I believe that my investigations have revealed a source from which she could have obtained the necessary quantity of Eureka weed-killer, had she been so disposed.

Tom Sidney, as we have seen, purchased a tin of Eureka solid weed-killer on September 26th, 1927 — *but that was not the first tin which he had bought*. He had made a previous purchase early in 1926. In the spring of that year he went away to America for a period of about six months. The tin of Eureka was left behind in an unlocked garden shed, and during his absence in the United States he let his South Park Hill Road house to some Japanese tenants, a Mr and Mrs Sasaki.

I suggest that during those six months while her brother and his family were away it would have been a simple matter for Grace Duff to have obtained access to that garden shed, either surreptitiously or on some plausible pretext or other, and to have helped herself to a sufficient quantity of the arsenical weed-killer.

Again, Sidney stated in his evidence that shortly after his purchase of the second tin of Eureka in September 1927, he began a series of provincial tours which kept him away from home for a regular two days a week until April 1928. He further admitted that it was not until January 1929, when he saw his young son trying to get into the garden shed, that he started to keep it locked. Prior to that, anyone who wanted to could have had unimpeded access to the tin of Eureka which he kept there.

We must remember also that it was only in the case of Mrs Sidney's medicine that the evidence indicates the probability that it was Eureka and not Noble's liquid weed-killer that was used. There being no residual material available for analysis in the cases of Edmund Duff and Vera Sidney, there is no evidence that it was not Noble's liquid weed-killer that was employed to despatch them.

I think that we may be reasonably certain that no weed-killer from the drum which Grace Duff handed over to the gardener Arthur Henry Lane was used for purposes of homicide.

But that was not the only drum of weed-killer at Hurst View.

There is evidence that on September 24th, 1927, Edmund Duff had purchased a previous drum of Noble's liquid weed-killer. It is also a fact that a cat was found dead of poison in the Duffs' garden shortly after the purchase of that drum of weed-killer. Was that, perhaps, the poisoner's trial run? How do we know that Grace Duff did not acquire a secret supply of Noble's liquid weed-killer from that first drum and, having satisfied herself as to its lethal efficacy on the cat, carefully conserved the remainder towards the day, seven months later, when the conditions were favourable for her to embark upon a more ambitious adventure in venenation?

What it amounts to is this:

Tom Sidney certainly had the means to poison all three of the murdered persons, but against this must be balanced the fact that all the resources of the police, directed as they were by powerful suspicion, failed to establish that he had indisputable opportunity of doctoring his brother-in-law's beer, his sister's soup, or his mother's medicine.

Grace Duff had ample opportunity of poisoning all three, and I suggest that, with the exercise of a minimum of ingenuity, she could easily have obtained the means to do so — Noble's liquid weed-killer from her own garden, and Eureka weed-killer from Tom Sidney's shed.

Lastly there is the problem of motive.

Generally speaking, six categories of motives for murder have been loosely recognised — murder for gain, murder for revenge, murder for elimination, murder for jealousy, murder for lust of killing and murder from conviction. This does not mean that a murder is necessarily committed for one of these motives exclusively. It may be the result of an amalgam of several.

In the case of Edmund Duff, Tom Sidney would appear to have had no motive of any kind. True, he did not really like Duff, but their association was not so intimate that dislike would develop into murderous hatred.

There is absolutely no evidence on the score of motive to implicate Vera, and precious little to implicate Violet Emilia Sidney.

Grace Duff, on the other hand, had several grievances which could have amounted, certainly cumulatively, to motive. First of all, there is Dr Binning's objective testimony that she was ill-used by her husband — testimony confirmed to me in the course of conversations with Dr Elwell and Tom Sidney. Secondly, there is the fact that Duff was inclined to be a spendthrift, and is known to have lost the better part of £5,000 of his wife's money by irresponsible investment, and to have been, shortly before his death, on the verge of some new gamble. Thirdly, there is the strong probability that Grace Duff hoped that, with her husband out of the way, Dr Elwell might marry her. Fourthly, and most significant of all, there is the consideration that Duff, by his financial indiscretions and sexual excesses, constituted a menace to the welfare of her surviving children, to whom, whatever her other faults, Grace Duff appears to have been an exemplary and fanatically devoted mother.

It may be argued that Grace Duff would not willingly have destroyed her only certain means of support. And indeed it was this argument that veered public belief in her innocence.

But how adversely did the death of her husband affect her financially?

At the time of his death Duff was in receipt of a Colonial Office pension of £360 per annum, and was also receiving £182 per annum from his employment at Spicer Brothers. A total regular income of £542. When he died, Grace Duff received insurance policy payments totalling £1,500, which, after the deduction of charges amounting to between £300 and £400 in respect of repayment of a sum of money borrowed by Duff in 1921, left her with a net capital gain of between £1,100 and £1,200.

As stated in evidence, after Duff's demise her relatives made her a voluntary allowance of £300 a year, and she obtained the National Health Insurance widow's pension of £54.12s. per annum, together with a Colonial Office widow's and children's allowance of £52 per annum. This meant that following her husband's death she was in receipt of some £406 a year, plus sundry gifts of money which she admitted receiving from members of the family. Taking everything into account, she herself estimated her income as £460 per annum — that is some £82 a year less than the Duff family income during her husband's lifetime.

Allowing for the fact that the premiums on Duff's life insurance policies ceased to be payable, that her husband had no longer to be fed, clothed and provided with spending money, and that her purchase out of capital, for £650 leasehold, of 59 Birdhurst Rise, meant that she was no longer obliged to find the annual £105 rent which she had previously been paying for Hurst View, Grace Duff was, as it turned out, no worse off financially in consequence of her husband's death. Indeed, she probably found herself minimally better off.

In other respects she was certainly better off. What money she had, was hers to administer. A man who was by all accounts feckless, extravagant and, at times, downright brutal, was removed. Marriage with Dr Elwell loomed on the horizon of possibility. Her children's security was no longer menaced by their father's monetary ineptitude, and that overweening sexuality which might easily have resulted in the arrival of more children, to topple an already precariously balanced economy.

Take now the death of Vera Sidney.

Her brother, Tom, her sister, Grace, and her mother, all derived financial benefit from it. Vera's estate amounted to £5,530. Of this sum, Tom Sidney received a legacy of £1,000, Mrs Violet Emilia Sidney £2,000, and Grace Duff £2,000, plus a further £100 to her son, John.[1]

Of the three principal legatees, only Grace Duff stood in any real need of the money.

Tom Sidney's financial position had actually improved during the months immediately preceding Vera's death. He had securities to the value of approximately £5,000, his professional earnings were shown to have been steadily increasing throughout the last two or three years, and he owned his freehold house, on which there was no mortgage or charge of any kind. Neither had he any outstanding debts.

Mrs Violet Emilia Sidney's financial situation was also perfectly satisfactory. Not only had she ample means to supply her own modest needs, but she had, as we have seen, a sufficient surplus to be able to help her daughter, Grace. Indeed, when, the following month, she died, she left effects to the value of

[1] In his summing-up the coroner stated that John Duff had received £200 from his aunt's will. The additional £100 may have resulted from Vera Sidney's direction that after payment of specific legacies 'the residue of my estate (is) to be equally divided between my nieces and nephews.'

£11,439.

Grace Duff was overdrawn at the bank, albeit only to the extent of something under ten pounds, and was slightly in debt, although she was not, she said, being pressed by creditors. In dire emergency she could, of course, quite easily have raised several hundreds of pounds on her house. Nevertheless, it is an indisputable fact that, of the three of them, she was the one to whom a windfall of £2,000 would have proved the most useful, so that, in that respect at least, she was the one who would have had the strongest motive for killing Vera. Neither can one ignore the point made by Sir Bentley Purchase that, following the disagreement between the two sisters over Grace's continued cap-setting at Dr Elwell, Vera had threatened to withdraw her offer of help towards meeting the fees for John Duff's first two terms as a boarder at Monkton Combe school.

If financial gain was the motive behind the poisoning of Violet Emilia Sidney, and it is difficult to conceive of any other, then once again it is Grace Duff who is revealed as the person upon whom Mrs Sidney's death conferred the most timely benefit, and the person who, in consequence, might be thought to have had the strongest motive for encompassing it.

Certainly Tom Sidney was the richer by some £5,500 for his mother's demise, but his financial standing in March 1929 was such that the sum of his inheritance must have meant considerably less to him than did the £5,500 which Mrs Sidney's death brought into Grace Duff's bank account.

It is true that Mrs Sidney — like Vera — was already contributing substantially to Grace's income, but the money which she gave her was in the nature of a purely voluntary donation. When Vera and Violet Sidney died, the money which they bequeathed to Grace became hers by right. The element of reliance upon continued goodwill and charity was removed. Obviously a much more satisfactory state of affairs from the recipient's point of view.

There is also the possibility, and one is not entitled to dismiss it, that both Vera and Violet Sidney had guessed that Grace had poisoned Duff. Vera may, in turn, have been poisoned because she knew too much; and Mrs Sidney may have been despatched because, after Vera's death, she knew even more about her surviving daughter's fatal freeness with arsenic. In this connection one may recall Tom Sidney's statement to me, ' . . . judging by the way I saw Grace look at her [Mrs Sidney] sometimes, it almost seemed as if she hated her.'

Remember, too, that both Vera and Violet Sidney were leading what Grace Duff would undoubtedly have regarded as 'useless' lives.

Love, hate, greed — these are the most usual emotional drives to murder, but I do not think that any one of these on its own was enough to account for all three deaths. It is likely that a mixture of these emotions was present. I would hazard that, if it was Grace Duff who was guilty, it was primarily hatred, allied to love and fear for the well-being of the children, that accounted for the murder of Edmund Duff; and that it was primarily greed that lay behind the killings of Vera and Violet Emilia Sidney.

III

Aside from means, opportunity and motive, there is another factor to be taken into the reckoning. It is the respective characters of the two prime suspects.

Let us examine first their courtroom demeanour.

In the course of the twenty-six inquest sittings in 1929, Tom Sidney made twelve, and his sister, Grace, eight, appearances in the witness-chair. From the start, he was careless, truculent and obstreperous, where she was carefully circumspect and conciliatory. He didn't give a damn: she didn't miss a trick. Tom was tactless: Grace was tearful.

On March 22nd, 1929, when the inquest on Vera Sidney began, the coroner had barely opened his mouth to inform the jury that the deceased had died in the early hours of February 15th, when Tom Sidney corrected him from the back of the room — 'Late at night, sir.' (On February 14th). It was the first of many interruptions, many brushes between them.

Tom Sidney was not a good witness. His memory was erratic, his temper uncertain. He contradicted himself and antagonised the coroner by being undisguisedly belligerent on a number of occasions. A far more impetuous character than Grace, he was emotional with an actor's emotion.

In one outburst — at the seventh sitting of the inquest on Vera Sidney — he practically invited an accusation of murder — 'I should not mind being charged with the murder of my mother and sister. I should sleep quite soundly at nights because I should know quite well what would be the result.' One might think that that was the protest of a man angry with the outright anger of outraged innocence. He was always tripping up where Grace side-stepped, and even his most trivial and human little evasions and petty dishonesties consistently failed to deceive anyone, while his frankness sometimes militated against him.

At the eighth sitting of the inquest on Vera, for instance, he said that he did not know that Mrs Greenwell was lunching at Birdhurst Rise until half an hour before she arrived. That could have been a damning admission had he been guilty, for Mrs Greenwell was obviously poisoned by accident, and the inference might reasonably have been drawn that the poisoner was someone who did not know in advance that she, as well as Vera, would be having the soup. Grace Duff, on the other hand, said that either her mother or Vera (both conveniently dead and unable to corroborate her statement) had told her of the visit several days before it took place.

Again, at the sixth sitting of the inquest on Violet Emilia Sidney, Tom Sidney went out of his way to make it clear that he did not subscribe to the theory that an outsider might have tampered with Mrs Sidney's Metatone. 'My mother's house was very dark and a stranger would have difficulty in finding his or her way about inside if the doors were shut,' he said, thus effectively bolstering the case against himself and his sister.

And when, subsequently, he had the perfect opportunity to switch the focus of suspicion from himself to Grace, he was emphatic that he did not at any time inform her that he had weed-killer in his possession, and affirmed with equal positiveness his belief that she did not in fact know that there was a tin of Eureka easily accessible in his garden shed. It was a convincingly poor show of self-defence, completely consistent you may think with the bewildered candour of an innocent man. The sole pejorative judgment that one can make of his demeanour is that it made him his own worst enemy.

The image contrived by Grace Duff was infinitely more subtle. She chose for herself the natural role of the tragic widow, the bereaved sister, the sorrowing daughter, and filled her part with consummate skill. Discreetly dressed in appropriate crow-black mourning, soft-voiced, frequently trembling on the brink of tears, she made gentle play for the hearts of the juries. It was a superb performance, nicely punctuated with moments of head-hanging pathos and sympathy-winning touches of brave yet wistful humour. Her large blue eyes swam with tears, and, to a man, the hearts of the jury beat stoutly for her.

But analysis would seem to disclose a number of deft stratagems by which, using insinuation rather than any blatant denial, she endeavoured to blur the sharper edges of the evidence, especially when it tended to tell against her. Even her weeping has the savour of calculation — aptly-timed, reasoned and expected behaviour.

Thus, at the second sitting of the inquest on Vera Sidney, she said that Vera had told her that Mrs Noakes had been sick *before* she had the soup on the evening of February 11th, and poured scorn on the idea that the cat had had soup at all.

She made much of the fact that Vera had constantly complained of feeling 'tired and seedy' for some time before her death.

She also stated that Vera had left a little slip of paper with her will on which was written, 'Please burn my diaries unread at my death.' Grace maintained that both she and her brother were present when that slip of paper was discovered, but Tom Sidney said that he did not remember seeing it. The first that he knew of Vera's having expressed such a wish was when Grace told him of it.

Grace also asked the coroner if, when reading out extracts from Vera's diary in public, he would delete names of the family and matters which had nothing to do with the case. Was she, perhaps, anxious that the jury should not hear any reference which Vera might have made therein to her threat to withhold payment of John Duff's school fees, and to the affair with Dr Elwell?

Grace admitted knowing that her mother never touched soup, and also that she had heard about the time of Vera's illness that there was a good deal of gastric influenza about. In other words, she knew of a natural cause which might be accepted to account for Vera's sickness and death.

But she categorically denied any knowledge of Mrs Noakes' habit of leaving the side-door of Number 29 ajar.

She had to agree that she had visited the house on February 10th, 12th, 13th and 14th, but regarding February 11th — the one day concerning which there was no irrefutable evidence that she had called at her sister's home — she said that she 'did not think' that she saw Vera.

Grace Duff's evidence at the inquest on her mother was delivered with all the tears and emotion that could possibly be required of the most dutiful and heartbroken of daughters.

She agreed that, unlike Tom, she knew that her mother had been visited professionally by Dr Elwell, and that he had prescribed medicine for her.

On the day that she died, Mrs Sidney had told her that she had not taken a dose of her medicine that morning. Had Grace then been asking her mother about her tonic? Perhaps urging her to take it?

In reply to the coroner's question as to where she thought it likely that Mrs Sidney would keep the medicine-bottle, Grace suggested that it might have been kept upstairs in her mother's chest of drawers. Her 'little boy' (John was actually fifteen at the time to which this emotionally-weighted description refers) had, she explained, seen a bottle rather like that upstairs on his grandmother's chest of drawers. In any event, she did not see it in the dining-room.

In her evidence at the fourth sitting of the inquest on Violet Emilia Sidney, Mrs Noakes had testified that on the morning of

March 5th Grace Duff had called and stayed for a short time with Mrs Sidney in the dining-room. Mrs Noakes said that while they were together there she had gone upstairs. Presently, Mrs Sidney had come up, gone into her bedroom and opened her chest of drawers for the purpose, Mrs Noakes thought, of getting her purse or handbag. This suggests that Mrs Sidney was fetching some money to give to Grace, who was going to do some shopping for her, and that while her mother was upstairs in her bedroom getting the money, Grace was left alone in the dining-room.

Grace, who had heard this previous evidence of Mrs Noakes', was asked if, on the morning of the day of her death, her mother had in fact given her any money to make the purchases for her before she went off to the shops. 'No,' replied Grace, 'she settled up when I came back,' thus neatly scotching the implication that she had been left alone in the dining-room. One searches the inquest reports in vain for the question which should have been put directly to Grace Duff — 'Did your mother at any time in the course of that morning leave you alone in the dining-room?'

It was at the inquest on her husband that Grace gave her finest performance. Always the dark clothes, the tragic expression, the faltering, well-modulated voice, the innocent blue eyes mirroring her anguish.

She painted an idyllic picture of their marriage. He was a good husband, very fond of her, and she of him. Here she hung her head, and those limpid eyes filled with tears. Jealous? Yes. But she had never given him cause to be really jealous. They had never had a serious quarrel. Regarding the quarrel between them of which Tom Sidney had spoken, she had no recollection of it. He was a very good-tempered, cheerful man, without, so far as she knew, an enemy in the world.

She implied her disbelief in the suggestion that his beer had been poisoned, because, she said, her husband was very careful and fastidious and would probably have noticed if the seal over the stopper was not intact. Even so, she made much of the fact that the larder where the beer was kept was situated close to the side-door of the house, and that the side-door was always kept unlocked during the day. She successfully conveyed the impression that access from the road to Hurst View was pretty easy, so encouraging the idea that an outsider could have doctored the beer without too much difficulty, and drove her point home by remarking, 'Somebody once christened our house "the house with the ever-open door." '

Asked if she could explain how it was that the maid, Amy Clarke, had said that she took only one bottle of beer in for Duff's supper, whereas Dr Binning had said that Duff had told him that he had drunk two, she replied that he had probably snaffled it. It was an adroit piece of side-stepping. 'Snaffle', with its slightly humorous connotation, was exactly the right word to use, and it was said with a look that seemed to take the jury into her 'you-know-what-you-men-are' confidence, and turned the whole incident aside as something of a joke.

Clever, too, was her presentation of Amy Clarke as 'Very smart and intelligent in some ways and . . . rather observant.' As much as to say, she was a person who would certainly have noticed if anything odd had been going on.

And when Mr Roome suggested that it was a curious thing that if Duff had returned home ill Grace should not have told Amy Clarke that he was unwell, she was quick to make capital of the fact that Amy Clarke was deaf, saying that she must have heard only half the remark which she addressed to her — 'He looks well, *but doesn't feel as well as he looks.'*

Grace 'seemed to remember' her husband's telling her that he had vomited at Fordingbridge. Considering the capriciousness of her memory in respect of so many other circumstances, this was an exceedingly fortunate piece of selective recollection, for it tended to establish the likelihood that Edmund Duff was already a sick man before he ever set foot back in his home.

Indeed, Grace was even more forthright in this connection, stating it as her positive conviction that 'Whatever poison might have been had, he took it away with him, and had a little while he was away, and some more when he came home. That is, if he died from arsenic . . . I don't mean purposely. I mean he took it without knowing he was taking poison.' Referring to a small flask of whisky which, she said, she saw him tucking away in his bag before he went off on holiday, she said that she thought at the time that he had bought it himself, but afterwards she wondered if someone had given it to him already poisoned. Who that someone could possibly have been, she had not the faintest idea. Was this a deliberate attempt to sow a useful seed of doubt in the minds of the jury?

Certainly, she left them in no doubt of the accuracy of Tom Sidney's statement that she had not known that he had weed-killer in his possession.

So much for the publicly projected personae of Tom Sidney and Grace Duff. What of their informal personalities, their behaviour beyond the limelight of the witness-chair?

As we have seen, those who knew Tom Sidney have described him in such terms as 'amiable', 'genial', 'disingenuous' and 'thoroughly decent'. He emerges from all accounts as a pleasant, kindly and generally well-adjusted man. Binning liked him. Fearnley-Whittingstall liked him. Morrish liked him. The worst that Hedges could think of him was that he was deliberately shielding his sister. I myself have met him many times and can only concur in all these judgments.

It is Grace Duff who displays the widest disparity between her public image and her private face.

'Though perhaps emotional, a frank and truthful witness,' said the coroner of her. This description hardly accords with the expressed opinions of many who knew her in other contexts. Such epithets as 'callous', 'fanatical', 'intense' and eccentric', were frequently applied to her. Allowing for all exaggerations and promptings of hindsight, the picture that comes into focus is that of a woman of decidedly peculiar character. A woman of violent emotions, yet sufficiently strong and determined, when it suited her, to hold those emotions in iron control. A woman whose studiedly meek exterior sheathed formidable claws. An English rose — with thorns.

Her conduct in regard to Miss Anna Maria Kelvey, for example, conveys a very different impression from that which the weeping widow at the inquests sought to project upon the court.

I discovered an old lady in Nottingham who had been very friendly with Miss Kelvey during the last year or so of her life. This is what she told me.

'I first met Miss Kelvey in 1924. At that time I was living in South Croydon and she was lodging in Addiscombe Road, East Croydon. It was funny the way we met. That year I'd had an enormous number of sweet-peas in my garden, and I asked Dr Elwell, who was a dear friend of ours as well as our doctor, if he knew of anybody who would like to have some of them. He told me that a Miss Kelvey, an elderly lady who was a patient of his, would very much appreciate such a gift. So I went along one afternoon and took her a big bunch. She was a lonely old lady who seemed to have very few friends, but such a sweet and charming person. She was delighted with the flowers and as I was leaving she said, "Oh, do come and see me again."

'Shortly after that first visit of mine Miss Kelvey moved, I think it was at Dr Elwell's suggestion, and became a paying guest at the Duffs' house — The Limes, at number 16 Park Hill Road. It was a huge, rambling place and, so far as I can recall, Mr and Mrs Duff and their children lived on the first floor. I used to call there to see Miss Kelvey about once a fortnight. I didn't take to Mrs Duff at all.

'I'm sure that Miss Kelvey was afraid of her, and I think that Mrs Duff bullied the old lady. One day I found Miss Kelvey in a terrible state of upset. She showed me a gas bill and, almost in tears, told me, "Mrs Duff has given me this." It was for something over seven pounds — for a quarter — yet Miss Kelvey had only a tiny gas-fire in her little room. Miss Kelvey didn't have much money, just a few hundred pounds which she'd managed to save from her salary as governess to a county family in Northumberland. I'm sure that Mrs Duff was gradually draining the old lady's life-savings away by tricks like the one that she played over the gas bill, and by cashing cheques for her and giving her short change. The fact that Miss Kelvey's eyesight was failing would make it easier for Mrs Duff to deceive her.

'I had the impression that life in the Duff household was not happy. On one occasion while I was waiting for Miss Kelvey, who was getting ready to come out with me, I was chatting with Mrs Duff, and she told me that she didn't care how little she saw of her husband. I loved mine, and I thought it very nasty of her to disparage hers like that. I gathered that she hadn't much use for him. I remember, too, thinking that Mrs Duff was rather a slovenly housekeeper, because her home always seemed very untidy, very dirty and ramshackle as to the furniture. In fact it wasn't what I'd call properly furnished at all.

'When the Duffs moved from The Limes to Hurst View, Miss Kelvey went with them. I definitely know that she wasn't happy there. For one thing, she was desperately lonely. It was pathetic. She had her meals brought to her in her room, and spent practically all her time alone there. Sometimes, the Duff children would go in and talk to her, but mostly she was left by herself. The family didn't bother with her much. As I got to know Miss Kelvey better, I used to invite her every so often to come and spend the day at our home. The last time that I ever saw her was on one of those visits. She was very distressed and distraught that day. I can see her now, crying as she told me, "I'm very unhappy with Mrs Duff. I don't want to go back to that house." Soon after that she died.

'I knew that Miss Kelvey suffered with headaches, quite severe ones sometimes, but apart from that her health always seemed fairly good, and when she died so quickly I couldn't help feeling there was something queer about it. Afterwards, I felt sure that Mrs Duff had done away with her. I went to the funeral. Mrs Duff had hired a car, and when it took us back to the house afterwards she opened her purse to pay the driver, and I noticed that it was absolutely crammed with banknotes. Now I happened to know that not long before she died Miss Kelvey had cashed a largish cheque, but the money was never found among her effects. I was pretty certain, knowing all I did, that Mrs Duff had appropriated it. I am certain, too, that it was under pressure from Mrs Duff that Miss Kelvey left legacies to the Duff children. She seemed to think that she had more money to leave than she in fact had — after Mrs Duff had been at it.'

Significant independent confirmation of my informant's suspicions is provided by Tom Sidney, who told me, 'I believe that when she was dying Miss Kelvey turned to my sister and

said, "Mrs Duff, you are a wicked woman." Grace herself told
me this, and laughed about it.'

This heartlessness of hers, this curious lack of affect, has been
remarked by others who knew Grace Duff at the time of the
tragedies.

What woman with normal emotional responses would have
viewed with such meagre reaction the deaths of her husband,
her sister and her mother?

What normal woman would gloat, as Dr Binning has said that
Grace Duff gloated, over the painful death-beds of those who
were her nearest, and should have been her dearest?

What normal woman would dress-up and paint the face of a
dead child, as Grace Duff is said to have dressed-up and painted
the corpse of her daughter, Suzanne?

And what are we to make of those extraordinary outbursts of
passion which so amazed and alarmed Mr Fearnley-Whittingstall
and Dr Binning? Are they the sort of conduct that one would
expect of a person of normally adjusted emotions? All this
would certainly seem to amount, at very least, to a highly
irregular behaviour pattern.

When, thirty-three years after the last of the deaths, I met
Grace Duff, and had an opportunity to assess her demeanour,
I, too, found it odd.

I had envisaged four possible reactions to my sudden and unexpected appearance. She could have shut the door in my face,
because, guilty, she was afraid of the whole business being re-
suscitated. Or, perhaps, innocent, she would see no point in
going over it all again and reopening an old wound in her heart.
She could, if guilty, have discussed the case with me, gloating
over the skill with which she had accomplished her ends and
baffled contemporary investigators and subsequent speculators.
Or, if innocent, might she not think that here was a chance,
however slender, to reinvestigate the murders, and perhaps even
track down the unknown person who had killed her loved ones?

The attitude that I in fact encountered, was the one attitude
that I had not anticipated — a blank negativeness, which swung
with disconcerting speed into palpable hostility.

IV

If, then, the case against Grace Duff emerges so strongly, why
was she not committed for trial?

It is difficult to supply any single answer to that question.
The official reply would, of course, be that there was insuf-
ficient firm evidence upon which to frame an indictment.
Opportunity and motive could conceivably have been formu-

lated against her, but the most zealous police work had utterly failed to establish means. No arsenic could be conclusively traced to her.

But, over and above everything else, there was one cardinal factor that operated to the unknown poisoner's enormous advantage. It can be summed up in a single word — luck. Luck, allied to a series of unbelievable and totally unpredictable coincidences.

To begin with, there was the great post-mortem blunder.

At the first autopsy on Edmund Duff either the wrong organs were sent for analysis, or the analysis was bungled. At this distance of time it is impossible to do more than speculate as to how the error arose.

On Sunday, April 29th, 1928, Dr Brontë found two bodies awaiting examination at the Mayday Road Mortuary. One was that of Edmund Duff. The other, that of 84-year-old Rose Ellen Walker, the widow of a London dentist, Gilbert Walker[1]. She had died suddenly, on April 28th, at Miss M. G. Coulson's rest-home, at number 1 Birdhurst Rise, Croydon.

According to Dr Brontë, he conducted his examination of the female body first, and recorded a finding of death due to chronic myocarditis and chronic interstitial nephritis. The examination, he said, took place on a different table from that on which he examined Duff, and he kept the two cases absolutely separate.

According to the mortuary attendant, John Henry Baker, however, it was the examination of Duff's body that took place first. He said in evidence that Duff's organs were removed, placed in jars, and the jars sealed *before* the woman's body was opened.

It is at first sight a curious discrepancy, and to this day Baker maintains that the organs were removed from Duff's body first. And so they probably were — by Baker. It is a common practice on the part of some pathologists to allow the mortuary attendant to open up the bodies, dissect out the viscera *en bloc*, and lay them ready for inspection. Baker informed me that he had in fact prepared both cadavers in this way for Brontë before his arrival at the mortuary. Possibly, then, Brontë *did* examine the woman's organs — or what he *thought* were the woman's organs — first.

Assuming that the wrong organs were sent to Candy for analysis, I suggest that the mistake could have come about in this way.

It is not my view, however, that the organs received by Candy were those of Rose Ellen Walker. It will be remembered that Candy reported finding quinine and mercury in the organs

[1] Gilbert Walker, L.D.S. (1837-1922).

submitted to him for analysis[1] . We know that prior to his death
Duff had been dosing himself with quinine and calomel. Now
calomel is a mercurous compound (mercurous chloride), and the
discovery of 'medicinal quantities' of quinine and mercury in
the tissues would seem to indicate that the organs were indeed those of Duff, and that somehow Candy missed the arsenic.
In this instance, at least, I think it may well be that the unfortunate Dr Brontë was more sinned against than sinning.

Certainly the jury took that view, for at the conclusion of
the second inquest on Edmund Duff, as the coroner was beginning to thank them for the patience and attention which they
had shown, the foreman interrupted him saying that they wished
to add a rider to their verdict — 'We consider that the chemical
analysis of the organs carried out after the first post-mortem
examination was not conducted with sufficient care.'

Dr Jackson was taken aback. 'I am not, of course, in any way
responsible for that rider. You are entitled to express your
opinion, but if I may suggest, after a little more consideration,
it should not go on the inquisition. I think in fairness I should
say, after that rider, that in my own mind I am not satisfied
what is the real reason of arsenic not being found at the first
examination. You have had one suggestion of what might be a
possible explanation. I take it from your rider you have accepted
it.'

But the foreman of the jury was not to be persuaded. 'Had
arsenic been found on that first examination there might have
been a possibility of saving two other deaths,' he rejoined
stolidly.

'I agree it was a very unfortunate error at the first examination. What I will say is that there was conflicting evidence as
to what happened at the post-mortem and which body was
examined first. I think you are going rather far in coming to
that definite opinion that the mistake was in the chemical analysis,' protested the coroner.

Mr Candy, with Dr Jackson's permission, then addressed the
jury.

'As my conduct of the chemical analysis has been directly
challenged and as an English audience as a rule is willing to give
fair play, I might be allowed to say a few words in my own
defence after such a grave indictment. I had certain organs submitted to me for chemical analysis. I conducted a careful chemical analysis of those organs. I came to a certain conclusion and I
reported it to the coroner. I grant you that a year afterwards
on certainly justifiable grounds the body was exhumed again.
A further chemical analysis was made and positive evidence of

[1] See page 25.

arsenic was found. Whether or not positive evidence of arsenic would have been found in the organs that I examined by the same analysis I don't know, and I really don't think you do. I can only say I did not find it, and it would have been of no service, my not having found it, to say that I had. I am willing to say, if you are looking for an explanation, that in a human operation error is not impossible, and I should not say that if I conducted that operation myself it would not lead to an error. But that is as far as I can go. Had I, twelve months later, in the light of events, attacked those organs with the conviction that arsenic must be there, then possibly I might have found it. But further than that I cannot go, and I do think it is a very grave thing for twelve gentlemen to charge me, after thirty years or more reputation for care and skill in similar analyses, with criminal carelessness, for that is what it amounts to.'

At the conclusion of this speech, the coroner told the jury, 'I think you are going rather outside your province in putting that on as a rider. I am doubtful how far I can accept it.'

And the Foreman replied, 'It is definitely proved that in the first place no arsenic was found, and also definitely proved that at a later date arsenic was found, and therefore it must have been there in the first place.'

'It may have been in the body in the first place,' said Dr Jackson, 'but you have to distinguish between the different stages at which it was found, and the evidence is very conflicting as to what occurred in the post-mortem room. How are you going to say exactly at what stage this error occurred? You have witnesses speaking of events which took place fifteen months ago, events of everyday occurrence, and how should they remember exactly what occurred?'

The coroner paused briefly, then, in a manner that brooked no further argument: 'I shall not accept that rider. You have expressed your opinion, and I have expressed mine. I think that possibly later on you may be rather glad I have taken this course.'

Both Sir Archibald Bodkin and Bentley Purchase held that Dr Jackson had acted quite properly in refusing to accept the jury's rider, and in permitting Mr Candy to make a personal statement to the court. They were convinced that the responsibility for the mistake was Brontë's.

Sir Bernard Spilsbury also blamed Brontë. That he should have done so is not really surprising, for there was a strong mutual antipathy between the two men. Spilsbury despised Brontë, regarding him as slipshod in his methods and unsound in his conclusions. He would refer to him contemptuously as 'that person', and had been heard to remark that whenever Brontë had done the post-mortem there were never any stomach contents.

Brontë disliked Spilsbury because he felt that he was held in altogether too godlike an awe in the courts. It was enough that Sir Bernard said that a thing was so for it to be accepted henceforth as a fact.

The two most eminent pathologists of their time had first clashed in 1924, when they gave conflicting expert evidence in the Norman Thorne case. They crossed scalpels again during the Robinson Trunk Murder case in 1927, and were to have a classically violent disagreement at the trial of Sidney Fox for matricide in 1930.

As a pathologist, Spilsbury was meticulous, where Brontë was inclined to be slap-dash. As a witness, Spilsbury was cautious, lucid, and given to understatement and the use of the minimum number of necessary words, where Brontë was cocksure, circumlocutory, and combatively verbose.

But it was not only a question of professional rivalry — or jealousy. They were fundamentally different in their natures. Brontë was very much an Irishman — sharp-witted, pushing, boastful, sociable and quite unworried about personal dignity. Spilsbury was the typical reserved Englishman — austere, aloof, restrained, retiring and dignified. His one great weakness lay in his invincible conviction of his own invariable rightness. As his fellow-pathologist, Professor Sir Sydney Smith, has said of him, 'He was unique . . . in that he never admitted a mistake. Once he had committed himself to an opinion he would never change it.'

Where the fallibility of others was concerned, Sir Bernard was notably less rigid, and, recalling how in his first post-mortem on Duff Brontë had not only missed the organic indications of arsenical poisoning, but had also left the major portion of the intestines intact and unexamined, he was quick to see in these circumstances evidence of carelessness. A carelessness which led him to the not entirely unpleasing conclusion that, by an extension of that same carelessness, Brontë had despatched the wrong set of organs for analysis.

After all these years, the argument as to whether the blunder was really Brontë's or Candy's is of no more than academic interest. The tragedy is that it was made, and that, because of it, two further deaths occurred which might otherwise have been avoided.

The second stroke of luck — from the poisoner's point of view — was Dr Elwell's shamefacedness over approaching the coroner after the death of Vera Sidney.

'I had reported Duff's death to Dr Jackson,' he told me, 'and the post-mortem and analysis had revealed no grounds to suppose that it was the result of anything other than natural causes.

When a G.P. gets a coroner's report back that all was in order, he feels a fool. When, later, Miss Sidney died in much the same way as Duff, I remembered the result of the Duff post-mortem and determined not to make a fool of myself a second time.'

Had Elwell been a shade less sensitive, had he overcome his, in the circumstances, natural reluctance to demand another post-mortem, there would still have been a chance of averting a third death.

Even when the fact that murder had been committed was out, the killer's luck held good.

There was Dr Jackson's misunderstanding of Bodkin's directive that the most satisfactory procedure would be to hold the three inquests jointly. The Director of Public Prosecutions had obviously wanted them taken together, recalling how in two other murder cases, *R.* v. *George Joseph Smith* (1915), and *R.* v. *Herbert Rowse Armstrong* (1922), reference to other associated deaths had proved vital evidence of system and intent.

During the consequent separate and protracted proceedings, Jackson, a man in poor health, displayed a certain inadequacy. His ill-concealed prejudice against Tom Sidney, his unsympathetic, almost brutal, handling of Lane, the old jobbing gardener, his occasional prickliness — these were superficial expressions of a much more deeply-rooted trouble, exacerbated by stress and strain. Indeed, at one stage in the proceedings Jackson was taken ill in court and had to receive medical attention from Sir Bernard Spilsbury.

The coroner seems, on the other hand, to have gone out of his way to predispose the juries in Mrs Duff's favour at all the inquests. She was at no time subjected to any hostile battery of skilled cross-examination. Jackson asked one or two pointed questions in an oblique sort of way. Roome was consistently restrained and unfailingly courteous. The one outstanding forensic figure in court, the most formidable cross-examiner, was Fearnley-Whittingstall — and he appeared for her. Had she had to face an advocate of his dialectic ability, instead of being jollied along by the accommodating Dr Jackson, it might have been a very different story.

Then there were the lamentable performances of two of the principal medical witnesses.

As Dr Binning has pointed out, Dr Ryffel made the cardinal mistake of using the entire contents of the medicine-bottle containing the residue of Mrs Sidney's Metatone for his analysis, instead of leaving half of it to supply a standard of comparison. This meant that his subsequent experiments in producing mixtures of Eureka-and-Metatone and of Noble's-liquid-weed-killer-and-Metatone were completely useless evidentially. With the original fatal mixture dissipated, there was nothing with which to compare the relative appearances of the experimentally-produced samples.

Neither did Ryffel cut a particularly brilliant figure under cross-examination by Fearnley-Whittingstall at the eighth sitting of the inquest on Violet Emilia Sidney. He could not tell the jury how much arsenic he had found in Mrs Sidney's medicine glass. He did not know how much liquid was there. He was unable to say what was the proportion between the arsenic and the liquid.

Dr Brontë acquitted himself scarcely more creditably. At the seventh sitting of the inquest on Violet Emilia Sidney, all he did was to fog the issue — and, no doubt, the jury — with a meaningless rigmarole about arsenic in the finger-nails and hair of the deceased. He then turned round and said that its presence probably had nothing to do with the poisoning! He next proceeded to complicate the evidence concerning the arsenic in Mrs Sidney's medicine-bottle, embarking upon a tedious and tangential disquisition regarding solubility and elementary physics. Finally, at the fourth sitting of the second inquest on Edmund Duff, he made himself ridiculous by fatuously claiming that a pencilled 'A.S.' which he had written on his carbon copy of his report of his findings at his first post-mortem examination of Duff's body, indicated that he had had the possibility of arsenical poisoning in his mind all the time. And that, despite his initial categorical declaration that death was unequivocally resultant upon natural causes.

That such a concatenation of idiocies on all sides can be ascribed to anything other than a formidable run of sheer good luck for the guilty person, is undeniable. In any case, the secret poisoner certainly profited from the cumulative effect of this constellation of coincidences, this massive combination of blind chances and official ineptitudes.

All the long months of investigation, the expended energies of the seemingly endless inquests, came to nothing.

The dossiers were closed, the inquest papers stowed away to moulder in a municipal basement.

The crimes could never be brought home to anyone with the slightest hope of providing that secure proof which the law of England requires before it will abandon the assumption of innocence which it accords to everyone until he is shown to be guilty beyond all reasonable doubt.

In the Croydon Poisoning Case, the criminal found sanctuary within an impenetrable shadow of doubt. There is a vast, neck-saving difference between the convictions of moral certainty and the requirements of legal proof, but I put it to you that the mystery as to the identity of the person who was responsible for these three deaths is morally, as opposed to legally, solved.

Epilogue

THE FOURTH DEATH

JUNE 24th 1973

The *Sturm und Drang* was over.

Of a family of five, only two remained to live out a tranquil coda.

Grace Duff had left Croydon at the end of 1929, and moved a few score miles down the railway line to a quiet, old-fashioned town on the south coast. There, she ran a seaside guest-house, and found the anonymity that she sought.

In 1933, when her son John was eighteen, she articled him to a solicitor, and her daughter, now seventeen, took a temporary job to help out. Alastair, aged six, had just started his schooling, and was a heavy expense.

Towards the middle of the following year, the pound-a-week Colonial Office widow and children's pension ceased. Grace was surprised and shocked. She had miscalculated, thinking that it had been awarded for fifteen years, instead of only five. She missed the money. Things were not going too well financially. Its sudden withdrawal made life even more of a struggle, and it was not always easy to make ends meet. But, somehow, she managed — even though at one stage she had to go out and take a situation as a cook.

In September 1939 the war came, and a fortnight later John Duff enlisted in the Artists' Rifles. In May 1940 he was commissioned a second-lieutenant in the Royal Sussex Regiment, and posted overseas. He died in the British Military Hospital at Moascar Camp, on the outskirts of Ismailia, on September 28th, 1940, aged twenty-six. Grace mourned him — the third of her children to die.

The windows of her home faced France. Like everyone else in Britain, Grace Duff looked anxiously across the Channel for the invasion that never came.

The war ended.

Life trudged on.

Grace Duff, now in her sixties, went shopping, cooked meals, served them, did the washing, cleaned the house. She read the papers, listened to the wireless and watched television. Perhaps she saw the programme about the Croydon Poisoning Mystery. Books and magazines appeared with accounts of the case in them. Perhaps she read them. But if she did, she gave no sign, never broke cover. She continued to exist in the inviolable vacuum of her quiet routine.

Somewhat of a mystery surrounds the next dozen or so years.

In 1948 Grace sold her guest-house and took a flat in another south coast resort.

Five years later, a well-to-do old gentleman in his seventies moved into the flat as a paying guest, and in 1955 he and Grace went to live at another flat, not far away.

Then, in 1958, he bought a house in the town where Grace had first lived after leaving Croydon, and she accompanied him back there.

Her brother, Tom, was living four thousand miles away in New Orleans, where, after a false start as an entertainer, he had rebuilt his fragmented life, eventually becoming the proprietor of a vigorous antique business. But, materially successful, he was never really spiritually happy out of England, and he knew moreover that he could never hope to erase the scarring distress of those calamitous eleven months, which were to change for him the entire shape of the future. Grace had blighted his life, poisoned it as surely as if she had dealt him a measure of arsenic.

As the years wore on, Tom Sidney heard — muffled echoes from the past across the wide, grey waters of the Atlantic — reports of the successive deaths of Roome, Brontë, Barker, Candy, Dr Jackson, Spilsbury, Hedges, Roche Lynch, Ryffel, Fearnley-Whittingstall, Purchase, Elwell and Binning.

Time passed. Unhappy memories receded even further, grew dim, until at length Croydon and all those far-away events came to seem unreal.

But for the two who remained there were disquieting moments. Moments when an old man in the deepening twilight of a New Orleans evening, and an old woman in the curtained cosiness of her living-room within sound of the English Channel, were both — though differently — plagued by their memories.

The 1970s came.

Grace Duff had suffered a stroke. She seemed to make a fair recovery for a woman of her age, but it dented even her tungsten constitution. Her doctor watched over her carefully. She could no longer manage the stairs. Her bed was made up in a downstairs room.

On August 7th, 1970, the old gentleman whose home she shared died. Cerebral haemorrhage, states the death certificate. He left to Mrs Duff and her children his house, most of his furniture and personal effects, together with the sum of £13,000. The will was dated February 25th, 1969. It was her last and finest windfall. Grace Duff was still, forty years on, vitally concerned with other people's wills. *Plus ça change . . .*

In fact, familiar things *were* now changing, disintegrating with alarming momentum.

In 1972 came another fundamental change. Grace sold the house which had been her home for the past fourteen years, and moved into a bungalow — away from the sea, uphill, nearer the cemetery.

And there, paralysed, and speechless for the last two days of her life, on Midsummer Day, Sunday, June 24th, 1973, in her eighty-seventh year, she died.

At half-past two on the golden heat-wave afternoon of Friday, June 29th, a thin straggle of mourners followed her coffin from the rough-flint Church of England chapel in the town's cemetery to the waiting grave.

The small breeze ruffled the clergyman's white surplice . . . a stray scatter of seagulls moved through the clear, broad arc of sky over the cypress-trees . . . the age-old comfort of the ancient words of the burial service sounded on the still, humid air.

The little black knot about the open grave untied itself. Parson and mourners, one by one they moved slowly off, heading towards the last ritual of funeral high tea.

The sexton began to shovel in the earth.

It was the end of the story.

Dusk crept quietly over the tombstones. The sky fell to meet the sea. Grace Duff lay alone on this her first night in the silent darkness of her eternal earthen bed.

My business in that old-fashioned sea-side town was done.

An end — and a beginning . . .

For thirteen years I had watched and waited — for the incredible story of the Widow of Birdhurst Rise could not be told until after the fourth death. While Grace Duff lived, I felt myself privy to a terrible secret. We were united in an uneasy compact of silence. Now the pact was broken.

Standing beside the new-dug grave, one of the first to disturb the soil of the consecrated square of cornfield annexed as extension to the old cemetery, I wondered about those last forty-four years. Had they really been as untroubled as they seemed? Had Grace Duff been the innocent victim of coincidence? Or secretly tormented by guilt? Or eased by self-delusion? Had some strange mechanism of her mind wiped the slate of recollection clean? Had she in the end accepted that the verdict which the coroner recorded was the correct one: that the hand that dropped the deadly crystals into Edmund's beer, Vera's soup and Violet's medicine was indeed that of 'some person or persons unknown'?

Or were there times in the still watches of the long dark

nights when she sat with ghosts? Times when the years between seemed to fall away, and there beside her again was Edmund, forty years dead, yet tanned, vital, lusty as of old. And there Vera, the same kind, cheery, sensible Vera, who met so cruel a death in the unfulfilled prime of life. And there, too, Violet, a strangely old-fashioned figure now, forever in mourning and agelessly old. Anguished ghosts these. Locked and frozen in their eyes a question. A question to which perhaps only she — wife, sister, daughter — knew the answer.

AFTERWORDS

By THOMAS SIDNEY

As the one surviving member of the Sidney family at Bird-hurst Rise, I am glad to see this book published. I consider it to be a fair and accurate account of what happened to us in Croydon in the late 1920s.

About eighty years ago, when I was barely six years old, I fell into a pond on my grandfather's estate at Southgate, Middlesex. My sister, Grace, three years my senior, heard my cries for help and pulled me out. Therefore, I owe my life to her.

I think, on looking back, it has been a happy life on the whole. Tragedies were few and far between, but the worst tragedy took place when I was thirty years old. This was the sudden death of my mother and sister, which, after inquests, turned out to be murders 'by person or persons unknown'.

Their deaths followed in the wake of the sudden death of my brother-in-law, Edmund Duff, a few months earlier, which was thought at the time to have been from natural causes. Subsequently, however, after a second inquest, it was discovered to be another murder.

So here we had three murders in the family, and for some time I was looked upon as the number one suspect in each case. This was chiefly due to the fact that I possessed a quantity of arsenical weed-killer, and each death was the result of poisoning by arsenic. I was soon exonerated, though, and my sister, Grace, became the number one suspect in my place.

Unfortunately, my uncle, William Sidney, accused my sister to her face. He regretted this a little later, and tried to impli-cate my mother, who was already dead. Why he did this I'm not sure. I think it was probably because he did not relish the idea of a trial at the Old Bailey, with all the unpleasant pub-licity and expense it would entail.

His theory, which would have been easily disproved in court, was that my mother killed Edmund Duff, her son-in-law, because she hated him, and hoped that, with him out of the way, Grace would be able to marry Dr Elwell, a rich man, with whom she had fallen in love. But when, after many months, my mother realized that no marriage would take place, she regretted what she had done and killed her own daughter, Vera, as a punishment to herself. Then, in remorse, took her own life.

I am one hundred per cent certain that my mother had nothing to do with the deaths of Edmund Duff, Vera or herself.

When the inquests were all over and I had been cleared of any crime, I was advised by officers of Scotland Yard to put as much distance between myself and my sister as possible, for Grace was considered dangerous to my family. I did so and settled in America.

I never saw my sister again.

The three deaths were put down as an unsolved mystery.

Now, Richard Whittington-Egan has written his book — *The Riddle of Birdhurst Rise*. I think he answers the 'riddle' very cleverly, and I recommend the book as a masterpiece of research work.

By GRACE MARY DUFF

I am Grace Duff's daughter.

By the courtesy of the author and publishers of this book, I am able to add this final chapter. There are so many points in the book with which I disagree — very many of which I regard as totally untrue — that it would take a book of equal length to refute them.

I naturally would have preferred this book never to have been published, but the law as it stands today in England, however cruelly hurtful to the offspring, relations and friends, allows any libel and lies to be printed about the dead.

I wish, as briefly as possible, to portray to the reader the kind of woman I knew my dear mother to be, and to show how utterly impossible it would have been for her to have committed these awful crimes.

Although only young at the time of the tragedies, I have very vivid recollections of certain facts, and particularly of the atmosphere of our home-life. The sad deaths of my two sisters probably caused us to be even more close and loving as a family. Mother and Father doted on one another. They were very affectionate, and flirted and fooled together like a couple of youngsters. They both had an outstanding sense of humour, and our house always had an atmosphere of love and laughter.

Father was a kind, wise man, extremely good tempered. He had a wide knowledge of Africa, and was extremely well thought of in Colonial circles.

Mother was a deeply kind person, generous to a fault. She was a complete extrovert — a gay, happy-go-lucky person with a buoyant, dominant personality, who did not give a button for conventionalism. Indeed, she was almost too open and honest for some more conventional types. She was also a great champion of the underdog.

Could such a woman creep about sneaking poison into drinks?

When they became engaged, Father asked Mother, "How do you want to live, bread and butter every day, or cake one day and dry bread the next?"

Mother settled for the cake, and that was how we always lived. We were often hard-up, but it never worried us.

After the tragedies, Mother lived a really hard-working life, making continual sacrifices for us children, but also making a very happy home for us. She was kind and generous to other people, too. Animals and small children adored her. Never, during all the many years I have known her. have I seen or heard of her doing any mean or unkind action. Cruelty and untruthfulness were the only things we were ever really punished for as children — the two vices she hated.

All through the years my father's photograph in its silver frame was always by her, and right up to the time she died Mother was constantly re-reading the many letters from Father. I have in my possession a great hamper full of them.

We discussed, conjectured and theorised about the murders through the years. Mother had her own ideas, but found it very difficult to come to a hard and fast conclusion. Sometimes she even thought it might be a series of dreadful accidents. On other occasions she did wonder about Grandmother. And she also wondered about another relation.

But when Mother knew that she had not much longer on earth, she said, "Now I shall never know who did those terrible things."

Inspector Hedges told us after the inquests were over that the police were closing the files of the case, because they considered that my grandmother was guilty of two deaths and had taken her own life.

Grandmother disliked, perhaps even hated, my father — who had been the close friend of her husband, who had deserted and humiliated her. She loved Aunt Vera devotedly, but may have thought she was going mad — owing to her very depressed state. Vera had been dreadfully hurt by the Reverend Deane's unfounded view that her friendship with his wife was unhealthy, and he had forbidden them to meet again.

What motive had my mother?

She loved my father deeply. It is suggested that she wanted to marry Dr Elwell. He did indeed ask her to marry him after Father had died. He even asked us children if we would like him as a father. But Mother could not fancy anyone after my father.

Before Aunt Vera died, she and Grandmother discussed (I was present) a settlement on us children which would give Mother the lion's share of their legacies. They knew that Tom was earning quite well, and that his in-laws were well-to-do, but they worried about Mother's finances (she did not). It would, therefore, have been greatly to her advantage had they not died when they did.

As I have said, cruelty was utterly repugnant to my mother, and I just cannot conceive of her killing three people with arsenic, and willingly causing all the consequent pain and suffering that the victims obviously endured.

And, anyway, where was the arsenic obtained from? There were two tins of weed-killer — not of the type used for the killings — purchased by my father. One remained unopened in the cellar, and was later given to the gardener. The other was used, and the tin thrown away. A cat was said to have died owing to this weed-killer. I cannot remember this, but I can remember the used tin lying in the yard-passage, and my mother telling Father to put it in the dustbin, as the cats might lick it — or something of that sort. (Hence my confused statement to Inspector Hedges.)

The type of arsenic used in the murders was in my Uncle Tom's possession. How could Mother have obtained it? Tom's doors were kept locked. It is suggested that Mother went by devious methods and obtained access to Tom's shed while he was away and helped herself to weed-killer. This to me is absurd. How did she know he had any? And his tenants would have been sure to comment on such a queer incident to Tom.

Mother was a highly intelligent woman — Head Girl at school, had passed the Senior Oxford Wrangler exam. She read detective books, knew that arsenic was very easily traced, so that had she wanted to do these dreadful deeds it is extremely unlikely that she would have used anything as ill-contrived and elementary as arsenic.

Uncle Tom's memory, which seems to play him a lot of tricks, is out of context. Mother said *during the inquests* that she wondered why the murderer had used arsenic, as even she knew there were poisons that could kill without trace.

I remember only too well the awful grief she endured when my father died, and how only her steadfast devotion and responsibility to us children kept her going. Mother was perfectly willing to have Father exhumed, even anxious to clear up any mystery as to his sudden death, in case it could have been some germ that could have affected her beloved children.

Mother had many friends, and I have countless letters in my possession written during the inquests to affirm their writers' complete belief in her innocence. These included some charming ones from old servants, some of whom had known her as a child and a young girl.

I have also letters from her solicitor, Dumville Smythe, who writes after the inquests: "As you know, my faith in your innocence never wavered".

Letters, too, perfectly friendly, from Uncle Willie (said to have accused her), and Aunt Gwen (also said to have accused her) — all signed affectionately.

There is a charming letter, too, from Fearnley-Whittingstall.

Of the people who speak against my mother, Uncle Tom, with his failing memory, states categorically that he never wrote to Mother after the inquests. Yet I have a letter from him written to her from America in 1930. It is perfectly friendly, and signed "With love from us all, Your affectionate brother, Tom."

I have shown all the letters mentioned to Mr Whittington-Egan.

Mother had certainly been very upset when Tom had tried to implicate John, and felt that she could no longer trust him. But, always charitable, she put his excitable manner, accusations and odd statements at the inquests, down to the very bad sunstroke he had contracted as a youngster.

Tom says that Mother had a "fanatical" feeling against people leading useless lives. There was no welfare state in those days and doubtless many people suffered appalling hardships, while some rich and titled people sat on their backsides doing nothing to help. Mother did indeed feel very strongly about this, and those were the useless lives she meant. I hardly think poor Vera, who did good works anyway, or my poor old grandmother could be accused of despotism.

Having the bailiffs in, or Mother's being blackmailed, are utter fabrications. However, calling the money received as legacies from Grandmother and Vera "blood money", I think Mother could well have said that, as she did consider that it had been received in horrible circumstances. When the national Sunday newspapers offered her a fortune for an "exclusive", she refused with revulsion.

I cannot conceive of anyone's taking seriously the suggestion that Mother said that she would kill the baby if someone did not give her a hundred pounds. How ridiculous! She worshipped the baby and would never hurt any of her beloved children.

Uncle Tom speaks of animosity between Father and himself. Father certainly did think him a bit of a fool, but they were perfectly friendly — although I can remember both my parents being irritated with Tom when he said he would like to live in America if he had sufficient capital. They were intensely patriotic and did not approve of this.

Something else that is sheer conjecture is Aunt Vera's threatening to stop paying John's public school fees if Mother did not stop seeing Dr Elwell. Vera would never have done such a thing. She knew Elwell was a dear friend and very helpful to Mother after Father died. Actually, Mother would have been delighted if Vera had, as Mother never wanted John to go away.

Tom said in a letter to me, "His (Richard Whittington-Egan's) book should certainly be published, chiefly to clear *me* of any involvement in the deaths."

I think that sentence shows why his attack on my poor dead parents is so vicious.

Then we come to Dr Binning. Dr Elwell always said he thought that Binning was guilty. He also said that Binning was "besotted over" Mother. Binning certainly made advances to her, but Mother laughingly rejected him. She did not take him seriously, but she was irritated by his disloyalty to his wife. When John and I heard him saying, "I'm only a man, Grace", it became an hilarious catch-phrase, and when he called we used to warn Mother, "*Cave!* 'Only a Man' is coming."

And Mother by the death-beds, quietly conceding the dignity of death, her eyes full of unshed tears, is said to be "gloating". What can I say, except that Dr Binning strikes me — and others — as a poor, unbalanced creature, more concerned with fantasy and the occult than with fact.

Who else? A handful of catty women and widows of the men who expressed their thoughts in writing, saying that Mother was innocent. I have their letters.

Inspector Hedges (dead), who perhaps could not find anyone else to blame.

The Reverend Deane (dead), who all the family detested as an unctuous hypocrite.

Another complete fabrication: Mother accused of painting the face of my poor little sister, Suzanne, when she was dead. I was there. I remember kissing her in her little white coffin. She was not painted, or dressed up.

Poor old Miss Kelvey. I do not remember her very well. She was fond of us children, and very fond of Mother. She was very queer, and I can remember her saying, "Your mother is my mother, too." I, a child, was very indignant. There was an objectionable woman who used to call and scrounge money from her. Miss Kelvey and Mother used to make plans to thwart her.

Now, finally, the author, Richard Whittington-Egan.

What exactly were these "extraordinary outbursts of passion" described on page 266? That Mother told Binning he was trying to put a rope round her neck? Was that an outburst — or just a rebuke?

Totally unexplained, too — and, again, secondhand hearsay by a widow — is an outburst in front of Fearnley-Whittingstall. What was it? Like all these statements against my mother, another uncorroborated conjecture.

What amazes me, however, is that a woman, losing a beloved husband, a mother and a sister, facing five months of inquests, worrying over a gravely ill baby and her favourite aunt (Aunt Kathleen) who was dying of cancer, did not have a dozen outbursts. Not forgetting, of course, the hounding of hordes of reporters.

Mother conducted herself during this awful period with the natural dignity of the innocent, keeping a tight rein on her suffering and looking after her children. I have letters which she wrote to John when he was at school during those dreadful times. Not a thought of self. No bemoaning of the ordeal she was enduring.

It would not be at all difficult for me to make a case against any of the main characters who gave evidence at the inquests — or, indeed, some who did not — if I were to use conjecture as the author does. My cases would be even more convincing, as I have knowledge of the family and could provide substantial motives.

I had originally intended to include my theories as to who could have been guilty, together with motives and opportunity, but by so doing I should put myself on a par with the author, condemning the dead who cannot protect themselves, or, of course, running the risk of libel if I attacked the living.

It is a pity that the author approached my mother in the manner described. Unless anyone has actually experienced the hounding of reporters during a time of grief, it is probably difficult to understand the utter revulsion of speaking to strange reporters (who anyway print things you have not said, as we found) about things that touch so deeply into private emotions. Why indeed should they intrude into one's private life *and expect to be welcomed?* Little do they care that the splash in the headlines causes bitterness between relations and ostracism by friends.

I fail to understand the author's description of Mother, who was a very pretty woman right up to the time of her death. Everyone used to say so to me. I feel she must have been unwell at the time, but I have never seen her with yellow eye-whites.

Or perhaps it was the author whose eye was jaundiced . . . as it seems to me to be throughout this prosecution witness book.

FOR THE BEST IN PAPERBACKS, LOOK FOR THE

In every corner of the world, on every subject under the sun, Penguin represents quality and variety – the very best in publishing today.

For complete information about books available from Penguin – including Pelicans, Puffins, Peregrines and Penguin Classics – and how to order them, write to us at the appropriate address below. Please note that for copyright reasons the selection of books varies from country to country.

In the United Kingdom: For a complete list of books available from Penguin in the U.K., please write to *Dept E.P., Penguin Books Ltd, Harmondsworth, Middlesex, UB7 0DA*

In the United States: For a complete list of books available from Penguin in the U.S., please write to *Dept BA, Penguin, 299 Murray Hill Parkway, East Rutherford, New Jersey 07073*

In Canada: For a complete list of books available from Penguin in Canada, please write to *Penguin Books Canada Ltd, 2801 John Street, Markham, Ontario L3R 1B4*

In Australia: For a complete list of books available from Penguin in Australia, please write to the *Marketing Department, Penguin Books Australia Ltd, P.O. Box 257, Ringwood, Victoria 3134*

In New Zealand: For a complete list of books available from Penguin in New Zealand, please write to the *Marketing Department, Penguin Books (NZ) Ltd, Private Bag, Takapuna, Auckland 9*

In India: For a complete list of books available from Penguin, please write to *Penguin Overseas Ltd, 706 Eros Apartments, 56 Nehru Place, New Delhi, 110019*

In Holland: For a complete list of books available from Penguin in Holland, please write to *Penguin Books Nederland B.V., Postbus 195, NL–1380AD Weesp, Netherlands*

In Germany: For a complete list of books available from Penguin, please write to *Penguin Books Ltd, Friedrichstrasse 10 – 12, D–6000 Frankfurt Main 1, Federal Republic of Germany*

In Spain: For a complete list of books available from Penguin in Spain, please write to *Longman Penguin España, Calle San Nicolas 15, E–28013 Madrid, Spain*

FOR THE BEST IN PAPERBACKS, LOOK FOR THE 🐧

PENGUIN OMNIBUSES

The Penguin Book of Ghost Stories

An anthology to set the spine tingling, including stories by Zola, Kleist, Sir Walter Scott, M. R. James and A. S. Byatt.

The Penguin Book of Horror Stories

Including stories by Maupassant, Poe, Gautier, Conan Doyle, L. P. Hartley and Ray Bradbury, in a selection of the most horrifying horror from the eighteenth century to the present day.

The Penguin Complete Sherlock Holmes   Sir Arthur Conan Doyle

With the fifty-six classic short stories, plays *A Study in Scarlet*, *The Sign of Four*, *The Hound of the Baskervilles* and *The Valley of Fear*, this volume is a must for any fan of Baker Street's most famous resident.

Victorian Villainies

Fraud, murder, political intrigue and horror are the ingredients of these four Victorian thrillers, selected by Hugh Greene and Graham Greene.

Maigret and the Ghost   Georges Simenon

Three stories by the writer who blends, *par excellence*, the light and the shadow, cynicism and compassion. This volume contains *Maigret and the Hotel Majestic*, *Three Beds in Manhattan* and, the title story, *Maigret and the Ghost*.

The Julian Symons Omnibus

Three novels of cynical humour and cliff-hanging suspense: *The Man Who Killed Himself*, *The Man Whose Dreams Came True* and *The Man Who Lost His Wife*. 'Exciting and compulsively readable' – *Observer*

CRIME AND MYSTERY IN PENGUINS

Deep Water Patricia Highsmith

Portrait of a psychopath, from the first faint outline to the full horrors of schizophrenia. 'If you read crime stories at all, or perhaps especially if you don't, you should read *Deep Water*' – Julian Symons in the *Sunday Times*

Farewell My Lovely Raymond Chandler

Moose Malloy was a big man but not more than six feet five inches tall and not wider than a beer truck. He looked about as inconspicuous as a tarantula on a slice of angel food. Marlowe's greatest case. Chandler's greatest book.

God Save the Child Robert B. Parker

When young Kevin Bartlett disappears, everyone assumes he's run away . . . until the comic strip ransom note arrives . . . 'In classic wisecracking and handfighting tradition, Spenser sorts out the case and wins the love of a fine-boned Jewish Lady . . . who even shares his taste for iced red wine' – Francis Goff in the *Sunday Telegraph*

The Daughter of Time Josephine Tey

Josephine Tey again delves into history to reconstruct a crime. This time it is a crime committed in the tumultuous fifteenth century. 'Most people will find *The Daughter of Time* as interesting and enjoyable a book as they will meet in a month of Sundays' – Marghanita Laski in the *Observer*

The Michael Innes Omnibus

Three tensely exhilarating novels. 'A master – he constructs a plot that twists and turns like an electric eel: it gives you shock upon shock and you cannot let go' – *The Times Literary Supplement*

Killer's Choice Ed McBain

Who killed Annie Boone? Employer, lover, ex-husband, girlfriend? This is a tense, terrifying and tautly written novel from the author of *The Mugger*, *The Pusher*, *Lady Killer* and a dozen other first class thrillers.

CRIME AND MYSTERY IN PENGUINS

Call for the Dead   John Le Carré

The classic work of espionage which introduced the world to George Smiley. 'Brilliant . . . highly intelligent, realistic. Constant suspense. Excellent writing' – *Observer*

Swag   Elmore Leonard

From the bestselling author of *Stick* and *LaBrava* comes this wallbanger of a book in which 100,000 dollars' worth of nicely spendable swag sets off a slick, fast-moving chain of events. 'Brilliant' – *The New York Times*

The Soft Talkers   Margaret Millar

The mysterious disappearance of a Toronto businessman is the start point for this spine-chilling, compulsive novel. 'This is not for the squeamish, and again the last chapter conceals a staggering surprise' – *Time and Tide*

The Julian Symons Omnibus

The Man Who Killed Himself, *The Man Whose Dreams Came True*, *The Man Who Lost His Wife*: three novels of cynical humour and cliff-hanging suspense from a master of his craft. 'Exciting and compulsively readable' – *Observer*

Love in Amsterdam   Nicolas Freeling

Inspector Van der Valk's first case involves him in an elaborate cat-and-mouse game with a very wily suspect. 'Has the sinister, spell-binding perfection of a cobra uncoiling. It is a masterpiece of the genre' – Stanley Ellis

Maigret's Pipe   Georges Simenon

Eighteen intriguing cases of mystery and murder to which the pipe-smoking Maigret applies his wit and intuition, his genius for detection and a certain *je ne sais quoi* . . .

PENGUIN CLASSIC CRIME

The Big Knockover and Other Stories Dashiell Hammett

With these sharp, spare, laconic stories, Hammett invented a new folk hero – the private eye. 'Dashiell Hammett gave murder back to the kind of people that commit it for reasons, not just to provide a corpse; and with the means at hand, not with handwrought duelling pistols, curare, and tropical fish' – Raymond Chandler

Death of a Ghost Margery Allingham

A picture painted by a dead artist leads to murder . . . and Albert Campion has to face his dearest enemy. With the skill we have come to expect from one of the great crime writers of all time, Margery Allingham weaves an enthralling web of murder, intrigue and suspense.

Fen Country Edmund Crispin

Dandelions and hearing aids, a bloodstained cat, a Leonardo drawing, a corpse with an alibi, a truly poisonous letter . . . these are just some of the unusual clues that Oxford don/detective Gervase Fen is confronted with in this sparkling collection of short mystery stories by one of the great masters of detective fiction. 'The mystery fan's ideal bedside book' – *Kirkus Reviews*

The Wisdom of Father Brown G. K. Chesterton

Twelve delightful stories featuring the world's most beloved amateur sleuth. Here Father Brown's adventures take him from London to Cornwall, from Italy to France. He becomes involved with bandits, treason, murder, curses, and an American crime-detection machine.

Five Roundabouts to Heaven John Bingham

At the heart of this novel is a conflict of human relationships ending in death. Centred around crime, the book is remarkable for its humanity, irony and insight into the motives and weaknesses of men and women, as well as for a tensely exciting plot with a surprise ending. One of the characters, considering reasons for killing, wonders whether the steps of his argument are *Five Roundabouts to Heaven*. Or did they lead to Hell? . . .'

A CHOICE OF PENGUIN FICTION

Other Women   Lisa Alther

From the bestselling author of *Kinflicks* comes this compelling novel of today's woman – and a heroine with whom millions of women will identify.

Your Lover Just Called   John Updike

Stories of Joan and Richard Maple – a couple multiplied by love and divided by lovers. Here is the portrait of a modern American marriage in all its mundane moments and highs and lows of love as only John Updike could draw it.

Mr Love and Justice   Colin MacInnes

Frankie Love took up his career as a ponce about the same time as Edward Justice became vice-squad detective. Except that neither man was particularly suited for his job, all they had in common was an interest in crime. But, as any ponce or copper will tell you, appearances are not always what they seem. Provocative and honest and acidly funny, *Mr Love and Justice* is the final volume of Colin MacInnes's famous London trilogy.

An Ice-Cream War   William Boyd

As millions are slaughtered on the Western Front, a ridiculous and little-reported campaign is being waged in East Africa – a war they continued after the Armistice because no one told them to stop. 'A towering achievement' – John Carey, Chairman of the Judges of the 1982 Booker Prize, for which this novel was shortlisted.

Every Day is Mother's Day   Hilary Mantel

An outrageous story of lust, adultery, madness, death and the social services. 'Strange . . . rather mad . . . extremely funny . . . she sometimes reminded me of the early Muriel Spark' – Auberon Waugh

1982 Janine   Alasdair Gray

Set inside the head of an ageing, divorced, alcoholic, insomniac supervisor of security installations who is tippling in the bedroom of a small Scottish hotel – this is a most brilliant and controversial novel.

FOR THE BEST IN PAPERBACKS, LOOK FOR THE ⦿

PENGUIN OMNIBUSES

Life with Jeeves   P. G. Wodehouse

Containing *Right Ho, Jeeves*, *The Inimitable Jeeves* and *Very Good, Jeeves!*, this is a delicious collection of vintage Wodehouse in which the old master lures us, once again, into the evergreen world of Bertie Wooster, his terrifying Aunt Agatha, and, of course, the inimitable Jeeves.

Perfick! Perfick!   H. E. Bates

The adventures of the irrepressible Larkin family, in four novels: *The Darling Buds of May*, *A Breath of French Air*, *When the Green Woods Laugh* and *Oh! To Be in England*.

The Best of Modern Humour   Edited by Mordecai Richler

Packed between the covers of this book is the teeming genius of modern humour's foremost exponents from both sides of the Atlantic – and for every conceivable taste. Here is everyone from Tom Wolfe, S. J. Perelman, John Mortimer, Alan Coren, Woody Allen, John Berger and Fran Lebowitz to P. G. Wodehouse, James Thurber and Evelyn Waugh.

Enderby   Anthony Burgess

'These three novels are the richest and most verbally dazzling comedies Burgess has written' – *Listener*. Containing the three volumes *Inside Enderby*, *Enderby Outside* and *The Clockwork Treatment*.

Vintage Thurber: Vol. One   James Thurber

A selection of his best writings and drawings, this *grand-cru* volume includes *Let Your Mind Alone*, *My World and Welcome to It*, *Fables for Our Time*, *Famous Poems Illustrated*, *Men, Women and Dogs*, *The Beast in Me* and *Thurber Country* – as well as much, much more.

Vintage Thurber: Vol. Two   James Thurber

'Without question America's foremost humorist' – *The Times Literary Supplement*. In this volume, where vintage piles upon vintage, are *The Middle-aged Man on the Flying Trapeze*, *The Last Flower*, *My Life and Hard Times*, *The Owl in the Attic*, *The Seal in the Bedroom* and *The Thurber Carnival*.

BIOGRAPHY AND AUTOBIOGRAPHY IN PENGUIN

Jackdaw Cake   Norman Lewis

From Carmarthen to Cuba, from Enfield to Algeria, Norman Lewis brilliantly recounts his transformation from stammering schoolboy to the man Auberon Waugh called 'the greatest travel writer alive, if not the greatest since Marco Polo'.

Catherine   Maureen Dunbar

Catherine is the tragic story of a young woman who died of anorexia nervosa. Told by her mother, it includes extracts from Catherine's diary and conveys both the physical and psychological traumas suffered by anorexics.

Isak Dinesen, the Life of Karen Blixen   Judith Thurman

Myth-spinner and storyteller famous far beyond her native Denmark, Karen Blixen lived much of the Gothic strangeness of her tales. This remarkable biography paints Karen Blixen in all her sybiline beauty and magnetism, conveying the delight and terror she inspired, and the pain she suffered.

The Silent Twins   Marjorie Wallace

June and Jennifer Gibbons are twenty-three year old identical twins, who from childhood have been locked together in a strange secret bondage which made them reject the outside world. *The Silent Twins* is a real-life psychological thriller about the most fundamental question – what makes a separate, individual human being?

Backcloth   Dirk Bogarde

The final volume of Dirk Bogarde's autobiography is not about his acting years but about Dirk Bogarde the man and the people and events that have shaped his life and character. All are remembered with affection, nostalgia and characteristic perception and eloquence.

PENGUIN TRUE CRIME

A series of brilliant investigations into some of the most mysterious and baffling crimes ever committed.

Titles published and forthcoming:

Crippen: The Mild Murderer   *Tom Cullen*
The famous story of the doctor who poisoned his wife and buried her in the cellar.

Who Killed Hanratty?   *Paul Foot*
An investigation into the notorious A6 murder.

Norman Birkett   *H. Montgomery Hyde*
The biography of one of Britain's most humane and respected judges.

The Complete Jack the Ripper   *Donald Rumbelow*
An investigation into the identity of the most elusive murderer of all time.

The Riddle of Birdhouse Rise   *R. Whittington-Egan*
The Croydon Poisoning Mystery of 1928–9.

Suddenly at the Priory   *John Williams*
Who poisoned the Victorian barrister Charles Bravo?

Stinie: Murder on the Common   *Andrew Rose*
The truth behind the Clapham Common murder.

The Poisoned Life of Mrs Maybrick   *Bernard Ryan*
Mr Maybrick died of arsenic poisoning – how?

The Gatton Mystery   *J. and D. Gibney*
The great unsolved Australia triple murder.

Earth to Earth   *John Cornwell*
Who killed the Luxtons in their remote mid-Devon farmhouse?

The Ordeal of Philip Yale Drew   *R. Whittington-Egan*
A real-life murder melodrama in three acts.